PLACE NAMES OF ALBERTA

VOLUME II

This book has been published with the help of a grant from
the Alberta Foundation for the Arts.

PLACE NAMES OF ALBERTA

VOLUME II

Southern Alberta

Edited and Introduced by
Aphrodite Karamitsanis

Alberta Culture and Multiculturalism
and
Friends of Geographical Names of Alberta Society
and
University of Calgary Press

ISBN 0-919813-91-7 (set)
ISBN 0-919813-95-X (v.2)

University of Calgary Press
2500 University Drive N.W.
Calgary, Alberta, Canada T2N 1N4

Canadian Cataloguing in Publication Data

Main entry under title:
Place names of Alberta

   Contents: v. 1. Mountains, parks and foothills
- v. 2. Southern Alberta

   ISBN 0-919813-73-9 (v. 1).
   ISBN 0-919813-95-X (v. 2)

   1. Names, Geographical-Alberta. 2. Alberta
-History, Local. I. Karamitsanis, Aphrodite,
1961-
FC3656.P62 1990   917.123'003   C90-091236-7
F1075.4.P62 1990

Cover photo: Vision Quest in Red Deer River Badlands.
Photo by Robert van Schaik

Typography by Department of Communications Media,
The University of Calgary
Printed and bound in Canada by D W Friesen.

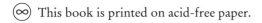 This book is printed on acid-free paper.

For my sisters
Stavroula, Ourania
and Constadina

TABLE OF CONTENTS

ACKNOWLEDGEMENTS

As with Volume I of this series, the current work is an assisted project. Grateful acknowledgement is extended to Tracey Harrison, without whom the project would not have been possible and to whom I owe the greatest debt. To Penelope White, who again spent tireless volunteer hours in the various archives searching out historic photographs for use in this volume, a very special thank you is given. And, as with the first volume, this work owes a very great debt to the pioneering efforts of Marie Dorsey, the first administrator of the Geographical Names Programme, and also to Eric and Patricia Holmgren, whose work *Over 2000 Place Names of Alberta* was the first of its kind in Alberta. The University of Calgary Press and its very capable staff, especially the Director, Linda Cameron, and the Production Coordinator, John King, provided great assistance in the transition of this work from a concept to an actual publication. I wish to thank Dr. William C. Wonders for his assistance with the photographs. To the President of the Friends of Geographical Names of Alberta Society, Mrs. Ruth Groves, I owe a huge debt of gratitude for her tireless support and her endless enthusiasm. For their support and assistance, I thank Frits Pannekoek, Les Hurt, Michael Payne, and all the "Friends."

Have you ever driven down a highway somewhere in the world and seen a particularly interesting name on a map or on a roadside sign? So often, we are confronted with the question of "What's in a name"? The answer, Shakespeare aside, is that toponymy, the study of place names, reveals a great deal about the fascinating history and unique cultural heritage of any populated region. Toponymic research is primarily concerned with the origins and meanings of place names, and as a key component of reliable maps and charts enabling smooth navigation, a geographical name unlocks a valuable store of information.

Mutual sharing of information is the focus of Alberta's Geographical Names Programme, and the purpose of this publication, the second in the series *Place Names of Alberta*, remains a twofold one. Over the course of several years, archival and field research has been conducted in this area of the province in order to provide the most accurate data for public use. This volume makes that information accessible to readers, although the refinement process is continual. Beyond presenting the most up-to date information that the Geographical Names Programme has collected, this volume also invites those with additional information on individual names to assist in this research by making their information public. Such individuals are a vital resource to whom we owe great respect and from whom co-operation and help would be very much appreciated. Information may easily be entered by contacting the Geographical Names Programme, Alberta Culture and Multiculturalism, 8820 – 112 Street, Edmonton, Alberta, Canada, T6G 2P8.

The formal process of geographical naming is a lengthy one, based on specific principles and procedures. It should be noted that the first function of geographical names is to ensure the most accurate identification of places. Recognition of the importance of rendering a correct spelling, use and translation of a geographical name, as well as providing a generic definition of the type of feature being described, led to the creation of the Geographic Board of Canada through Order-in-council in 1897. Dedicated to the standardization of principles and procedures to be followed in naming geographical features, the Board has changed its centralized approach very little over the years. A name adjustment in 1948 to the "Canadian Board on Geographical Names" left provincial representation minimal. In 1961, however, the responsibility for geographical naming was left up to the individual provinces and territories, though the necessity for coordination of activities at a national level remained. Creation of the Canadian Permanent Committee on Geographical Names provided the opportunity for continued liaison between federal officials and the naming authorities of each province and territory, but provincial agencies like Alberta's Geographical Names Programme now conduct all research and maintain all information on proposed names, name changes and names previously established. Alberta's approach has drawn increasing attention to the cultural dimensions of the province's geographical names.

Research has shown that the connection between geographical naming and the development of an area is very close: as individuals explore, develop, and survey and map a region, the need to give places specific names increases. Indeed, geographical naming both affects and reflects the culture and heritage of a place. The aboriginal peoples of Alberta, fur traders, surveyors and chartmakers, ranchers and businessmen alike required familiar and common points of reference in order to continue their work, but in the choice of names they identified the landscape with their particular culture.

The specific area that this volume addresses (outlined on page xxiv), contains the Badlands, the vast ranching areas and the mineral-rich oil and coal belts of Alberta. The map located on this page is designed to aid the reader in locating some of the features in a general way, relative to nearby populated places. The earliest place names in this region were those used by aboriginal peoples. The legacy of Alberta's First Nations is preserved and commemorated in many names that have survived over the decades. Nor is it unusual to find the names of early settlers and homesteaders on the vast expanses of coulees and plains. Similarly, the names of early ranchers can be traced in the names of localities and towns. The impact that these early arrivals had on the face and nature of the places in our study area is easily demonstrated in the names Cardston (page 23), Emerson Lake (page 41), and Galt Island (page 49)—all named for early pioneers, ranchers or entrepreneurs. Not only are early people reflected in the names in this area, but their endeavours may be charted as well. The early history of mining concerns is evident in the hamlet of Nacmine (page 85) named for the North American Collieries (NAC) and the word "mine." Irricana (page 62), a village located 42 kilometres north-east of Calgary, received its name when the newly opened post office combined the words "irrigation" and "canal" to produce the name. Like its predecessor *(Volume I: Mountains, Mountain Parks, and Foothills)*, this volume is a collection of geographical names that pay tribute to the individuals and groups who contributed so much of their lives to a variety of enterprises that have made southern Alberta what it is today.

Alberta's history is multi-faceted, both culturally and regionally. Southern Alberta has a most historically important and interesting heritage, and one which differs in important respects from other areas of the province. Long before fur traders and explorers made their first forays along the great watercourses into this vast land, it was inhabited by dynamic and vital native groups. Archaeologists have found evidence of several native groups who inhabited this area more or less continuously for over 1,500 years, and many suspect that actual occupation far preceded this date. At the time of first European contact with the native peoples of southern Alberta, the main tribal and linguistic groupings in this volume's study area were of the Blackfoot Confederacy, which was composed of the Blood (historically Kainah or "many chiefs") and the Peigan (historically the Pikuni or "scabby robes") as well as the Siksika, the Blackfoot proper, and the Sarcee. In addition, the Kootenay lived among the mountains and foothills and may have ventured out onto the plains on occasion. The Gros Ventre and other Siouan and Shoshone groups also were present on the southern plains. On the northern edges of the study area Stoney and Cree could be found, and later other groups also established some presence in the area as a result of the fur trade. Archaeologists and ethnohistorians continue to debate the exact location of these groups in the pre-contact period and their subsequent migrations. Jack Brink's succinct outline of this early history of southern Alberta gives some idea of just how complicated this history is:

> Several accounts indicate that the Snake, feuding with the Blackfoot and stricken by disease, were moving south into Montana. Plains Kutenai [sic] largely lost their small hold on the Plains in southwestern Alberta and were confined almost entirely to the foothills and mountains... Sarsi [sic] were firmly fixed on the Plains, concentrated in the Bow Valley but moving with the various Blackfoot groups. The Blackfoot moved south to fill much of the Plains proper formerly occupied by the Snake... Blackfoot were firmly in control of the Saskatchewan Basin... the Gros Ventre were likewise moving to south of their former position, still occupying some of the area near the Saskatchewan

forks but primarily situated on and below the South Saskatchewan.[1]

Almost all of these groups have at least one feature named for their tribe. Within the existing Blackfoot Indian Reserve, there exists a crossing on the Bow River known as Blackfoot Crossing (page 12) that has apparently been a good ford over the river for centuries. The Blackfoot Indian Reserve (page 12) itself takes its name from the Blackfoot, who call themselves Siksika, apparently due to the discoloration of their moccasins from the ashes of prairie fires. Blood Indian Creek (page 13), which flows south into the Red Deer River, approximately 98 kilometres north-west of Medicine Hat, bears the name of the Blood Indians who seem to have acquired this name in a bloody skirmish with the Saulteaux. Gros Ventre Creek (page 54) was named to commemorate an attempted Atsina raid in 1868 on a band of Blackfoot Indians encamped along this creek. Far more common than the names of the major Indian bands and tribes in the unfolding history of southern Alberta are the names that they themselves assigned to their lands. Most of these names were handed down from generation to generation until they were finally accepted as official. Names such as Okotoks (page 89) for the place of the "crossing by the big rock" reflect the Blackfoot presence in the area, but most bands had a name for the huge glacial erratic now known as the Big Rock (page 11). The Sarcee called this place *chachosika* or "valley of the big rock" and the Stoney name is *ipabitungaingay* or "where the big rock is." All three groups chose a descriptive name for this unusual feature and most native names in Alberta are in fact either descriptive or they commemorate some major event that may have occurred on or near the site. An interesting and apparently unique aspect of native geographical nomenclature is the refusal to name features after either living or dead persons. This is a phenomenon that is found across Canada and is a shared trait of the people of the First Nations.

The history of the southern portion of Alberta is different from the northern and central areas of the province in a number of ways. The fur trade had less impact on the south because a lack of marketable furs made trading in this area much less profitable than it had proven to be elsewhere. Because there was little profit to be made from trading in the south and the impact of missionary activity was quite limited in this area, there exists in the official record very few names for geographical features associated with the fur trade or missionary activity. There are, however, some names connected to the buffalo robe trade that had its origins in the competition between American traders on the Missouri River and Hudson's Bay Company traders on the North Saskatchewan River for the commerce of the members of the Blackfoot Confederacy.[2] Although the Plains tribes had always participated in the buffalo robe trade among themselves and as an adjunct to the provisions trade (pemmican, grease and dried meat), it was not until the 1870s that the trade emerged as the primary economic activity in this region. The traders of the Hudson's Bay Company competed for robes with traders from the United States, primarily centred at Fort Benton in Montana. This explains the name of a locality called Benton Station (page 10) located some 165 kilometres east of Drumheller, that was apparently named for the Benton Trail from Fort Benton to Fort Macleod that was commonly used by the Blackfoot and the traders when trading for buffalo robes. Although the locality is not in the immediate vicinity of the Benton Trail, its reputation

---

[1] Jack Brink. *Dog Days in Southern Alberta*. Archaeological Survey of Alberta, Occasional Paper 28, Department of Culture and Multiculturalism, 1986, p. 58.

[2] R.F. Beal, J.E. Foster, and Louise Zuk. "The Metis Hivernement Settlement at Buffalo Lake, 1872-1877." Unpublished study, 1987, p. 3.

was very popular. Very quickly the so-called whisky traders entered the buffalo robe trade and several trading posts were established with this commodity acting as the major form of payment for buffalo robes. The locality of Kipp (page 67) located seven kilometres north of the city of Lethbridge became one of these whisky trading posts. Originally located several kilometres west of the present locality at the confluence of the Oldman and Belly rivers, Fort Kipp was named for one of its founders, Joseph Kipp. The trail that connected the main trade at Fort Benton with several whisky posts in southern Alberta was known as the "Whoop-Up Trail" and generally followed the courses of the Oldman and Belly rivers.

Partly to stay the traffic in whisky in exchange for buffalo robes and in part to prevent conflicts between the Indians and whites, the Dominion Government decided to send a contingent of the North West Mounted Police to what was then called the North West Territories. Led by their Commissioner, George Arthur French and Colonel James Macleod, the force decided to build their fort on an island in the Oldman River. It was named Fort Macleod (page 47) after Colonel Macleod who succeeded French as Commissioner and who later became a judge in the Territories. And one year later, a further 50 recruits were dispatched to the junction of the Bow and Elbow rivers where they established a Mounted Police Fort which they called Fort Calgary, later to become the city of Calgary (page 21). This is the name of the ancestral estate of Macleod's cousins, the MacKenzies, on the island of Mull, Scotland, which he had visited shortly before his trek west to the North West Territories.

Much of the information about this area of the Dominion, information that was used by both the NWMP as well as the railway companies in the later period, was the result of a British North American Exploring Expedition headed by Captain John Palliser (1817–1887) between the years 1857 and 1860 and known as the Palliser Expedi-

tion. The expedition itself was initiated by Palliser, but when he applied to the Royal Geographical Society for funding, the expedition grew and Palliser was instructed by the Imperial Government to expand the project into a scientific fact-finding mission. Charged with charting the land, especially the lands under the ownership of the Hudson's Bay Company, Palliser was to conduct his explorations across the plains south of the North Saskatchewan River to and through the Rocky Mountains. The expedition collected vast amounts of data on the meteorological, geological and magnetic importance of this vast territory, and Palliser also collected information about the country's food supply, its flora, its inhabitants and its potential for settlement and routes of transportation. Palliser identified in his reports an area, now known as Palliser's Triangle, that he called "semi-arid" stretching across the American boundary into the prairies of Alberta. This loosely shaped triangle extended from what is now the Manitoba–U.S. border south of Brandon, north-west to Saskatoon, Saskatchewan. It then looped west to Calgary, before dipping south to Lethbridge and on to the American border. He believed this area to be virtually worthless for intensive cultivation, although it was surrounded by a fertile belt that he believed to be well-suited for the raising of stock and even possibly for agriculture. Palliser's published reports, and especially his comprehensive map of 1865, were for some time the main source of information about the lands in the south of what is now Alberta and they became the basis for later railway routes and surveys of land. Since the vast majority of Palliser's treks involved routes through the mountains, the expedition itself left few names in this study area.

By the late 1880s and early 1900s, ranching emerged as the main industry in southern Alberta. Supported by Palliser's reports, ranchers claimed this land was unsuitable for other forms of agriculture. Ranchers in the south became very powerful and were owners of extremely large ranching operations. In the late 1890s, about 200 cattlemen controlled almost the entire region and, because of their business and political friends, they formed a powerful economic, social and political elite. Because so many of these early ranchers were either immigrants from the United Kingdom or former members of the North West Mounted Police, they created a "transplanted British Victorian lifestyle that lasted until World War I" complete with "formal balls, formal dress dinners, fox hunts, polo, cricket and tennis."[3]

Ranching is amply represented in the names of geographical features in this area. Senator Matthew Henry Cochrane established The Cochrane Ranche Company in 1885 which was the first large-scale ranching company in the area. A few kilometres west of the ranch, a community began to emerge (originally named "Mitford") which, when the Canadian Pacific Railway line was established, was renamed Cochrane (page 29) after the Senator. Several of the larger ranches were named for places in England from whence their owners had come. Oxley Creek (page 91), located some 84 kilometres north-west of Lethbridge was named after the nearby Oxley Ranch which in turn was named for Oxley Manor in Wolverhampton, England. And many of the cowboys who worked the ranches also left legacies of their names of the land. The locality of Nier (page 87), located 43 kilometres north north-west of Calgary, was named for "Shorty" Nier, an early rancher who came from Arizona to the Calgary area in the late 1800s and who homesteaded at the turn of the century west of Crossfield. When the C.P.R. spur line to Cremona

was established, it passed through Shorty's property and the railway siding at this point became known as Nier.

Priorities set by the Dominion Government in the east set the stage for the next major development in southern Alberta: the coming of the railways. No other phenomenon in western Canadian history so affected the toponymy of western Canada as railroad development. The Dominion Government hoped that the railway would improve transportation and communication lines across the prairies and between the east and west, but, more important, they believed that the railway would open up a new economic hinterland for eastern and central Canada. The pace for settlement of the west was decided, almost exclusively, by the routes chosen for development by these various companies. As the famous prairie historian L.G. Thomas has noted: "The tide of agricultural settlement ebbed and flowed, but after 1870 it was consistently directed by the availability of railway services."[4]

The choice of names of the various stations that dotted the routes of the lines of these railways varied from the names of the nabobs of the railway industry to names that were purely descriptive. The village of Stirling (page 115), located 30 kilometres south-east of Lethbridge was named in 1901 for John A. Stirling, the Managing Director of the company that had large-scale holdings in the Alberta Railway and Coal Company. The town of Strathmore (page 116), located 45 kilometres east of Calgary was originally a Canadian Pacific Railway station that was established in 1884 and named for Claude Bowes-Lyon, the 13th Earl of Strathmore (1824–1904). The hamlet of Balzac (page 5), located approximately 18 kilometres north of Calgary, illustrates a certain whimsy or caprice in railroad naming practices. Originally a C.P.R. station that began operating in 1910, it was named by W.C. Van Horne, then the president of the railway, after one of his favourite authors, Honoré de Balzac (1799–1850), the noted French novelist. Completed through

---

[3] Howard Palmer with Tamara Palmer. *Alberta: A New History*. Edmonton: Hurtig Publishers Ltd., 1990, p. 55.

[4] L.G. Thomas. "Introduction" in *The Prairie West to 1905: A Canadian Sourcebook* by David H. Breen (ed). Toronto: Oxford University Press, 1975, p. 6.

modern Alberta in 1883, the transcontinental railway (the C.P.R.) set the stage for the coming of settlement and the further development that followed very closely the main line westward across the prairies.

By 1884, the settlement at Fort Macleod had become the largest in Alberta. The second largest town, Calgary, was well on its way to becoming a major centre as well, due almost exclusively to the push of the C.P.R. westward. Increasingly, railway movement began to give impetus to industries other than ranching. One such industry was coal mining and many of the earliest mines and mine towns still bear the names of those who founded them. The city of Lethbridge (page 70) was named for William Lethbridge (1824–1901), first President of the North Western Coal and Navigation Company, Limited, which was formed in 1882 to mine coal from the banks of the Oldman River to sell to the Canadian Pacific Railway. After the opening of the Sheran mine in 1872, the settlement there was locally called "The Coal Banks," but the name was changed to Lethbridge around 1882. There already was a Lethbridge in Ontario, and according to Post Office practice no two post offices anywhere in Canada were to have the same name. Postal authorities changed the town's name to "Coalhurst," to the irritation of town residents. Public pressure forced the Postmaster General to restore the name Lethbridge in 1885. Although the greatest volume of coal from Alberta came from the Crowsnest Pass at the foot of the Canadian Rockies, the success of coal mining in the Lethbridge area was considerable. Before 1920, 42 shafts were opened in the Lethbridge area and many of the place names around Lethbridge reflect this involvement. For example, the locality of Hardieville (page 56) was established in 1910 and named for W.D.L. Hardie, Superintendent of the Galt Coal Mine when it opened in 1909. Galt Island (page 49), located immediately west of Medicine Hat is named after the Galt family who provided the capital to develop the

valuable coal resources of southern Alberta and branched out to river shipping and railroad building. Sir Alexander Tilloch Galt (1817–1893) served as Canada's first high commissioner to Great Britain from 1880 to 1883 and organized the North Western Coal and Navigation Company, Limited with British capital, to develop and market the coal of this area. Along with his son, Elliott Torrance Galt, he developed coal mines in Alberta with a daily capacity of over 2,000 tonnes. Other pioneer businessmen also left their names on southern Alberta's settlements. The town of Magrath (page 75) was named in 1899 for Charles A. Magrath (1860–1949), who was a Dominion Topographical Surveyor and later became one of the managers of the locally prominent Alberta Railway and Irrigation Company from 1885 to 1906.

While many of the geographical names reflect the names of the various people involved in mining ventures, others are more original. The hamlet of Diamond City (page 37) was named for the mine located in the area and was descriptive of the vast quantities of coal located in the mine. The town of Black Diamond (page 12) likewise received its name from the fanciful nickname for coal in these areas. And many of the most interesting geographical features, the long rugged coulees, also reflect names indicative of mining activity. Coal Coulee (page 28), located 58 kilometres south of Calgary and Miner's Coulee (page 83), located 120 kilometres south south-west of Medicine Hat both received names that reflect the early coal extraction industries of southern Alberta.

Attempting to flee the repressive anti-polygamy laws in the United States, a group of Mormons migrated from Utah to Alberta in 1885. The small group of colonizers chose southwestern Alberta because of the good land, accessible timber and coal, and most important, water for irrigation. Several geographical names owe their origins to the members of this church. The town of Cardston (page 23), located approximately 65 kilometres south south-west of Lethbridge, was named for Charles Ora Card (1839–1906), who came to the present site of the town in order to establish a new home for members of the Church of Jesus Christ of Latter Day Saints (the Mormons). A post office was established in 1892 and Cardston was incorporated as a town in 1901 with Charles Card as its first mayor. In 1901, Jesse Knight, a prominent Mormon southern Alberta rancher originally from Utah, contracted with the Alberta Railway and Irrigation Company for 10,522 hectares (26,000 acres) of land to grow sugar beet and to build Canada's first sugar factory. A townsite was selected, located 25 kilometres south of Lethbridge, and the majority of the land was donated by Knight. The gift carried the provision that no liquor outlet could ever be established in the town or the land would revert to the Knight family and its heirs. Knight named the town Raymond (page 101), after his eldest son, and mainly because of the sugar beet factory, the town attracted over 1,500 people within two years. Many companies became convinced that in irrigation lay the key to continuing economic success in the region since it would provide a means of settling the vast dryland.

Between 1891 and 1911 large-scale cattle and beef production was giving way to farming. While ranching was never totally abandoned, World War I and the increased accessibility of settlement due to the railways, caused many small-scale ranchers to abandon their holdings and many of the large-scale ranchers lost the sense of destiny they had felt for over thirty years. Wheat suddenly became Canada's great commodity and western lands attracted many thousands of farmers. Many communities in southern Alberta bear the names of those who helped establish them as important grain-growing districts. The village of Nobleford (page 87), located 22 kilometres north-west of Lethbridge was named in 1913 after Charles S. Noble (1873–1957), a farmer and organizer of this community, which was known as "Noble" until 1918.

Noble originally homesteaded near Claresholm in 1902, but a few years later he bought 2,023 hectares (5,000 acres) near Lethbridge and began what was to become a huge farming operation. The Noble Foundation was established and by World War I, 14,164 hectares (35,000 acres) were under cultivation, making his the largest and highest-yielding farmland in the British Empire.

In 1928, a post office was established approximately 55 kilometres south-west of Medicine Hat and was given the name Granlea (page 52). The word is a combination of the words "grain" and "lea" and was suggested due to the rich agricultural value of the land which combined high grain production and valuable tracts of pasture lands or leas. The post office closed in 1962, although the name remains in the official record. The amount of wheat that emerged from southern Alberta during these boom years was phenomenal and many localities were named in honour of this agricultural bonanza. The village of Champion (page 25), located 65 kilometres north-west of Lethbridge was created when the Canadian Pacific Railway established a station in 1909 and a post office followed in 1910. By 1915, Champion became known as the "million bushel town" when over one million bushels of wheat were shipped from this community that year. Irrigation in southern Alberta had important economic and social effects and assisted many farmers with the dry conditions of Palliser's Triangle.

Of all the economic activities in which Albertans have engaged, perhaps the most famous is the oil and gas industry. And like the coal mining that preceded it, this energy industry has seen its share of boom-bust conditions that helped create the names that dot the landscape. The first oil well to actually produce oil was located in what has since become Waterton Lakes National Park, named after Charles Waterton (1782–1865), a famous English naturalist. The townsite that grew up around the Rocky Mountain Development Company's oil strike was appropriately named "Oil City." But when it was discovered that geological reports indicated that further drilling would be unsuccessful, the townsite was abandoned.[5] Aside from the hamlet of Naphtha (page 86) which was named for the light gas taken from oil wells there, the vast majority of geographical names, both for features as well as localities, mainly commemorate the pioneer developers of the oil and gas industry. The Keystone Hills (page 66), located approximately 64 kilometres west north-west of Calgary were named after an American oil company that drilled in the area around the 1930s. Baymar Creek (page 7), located 58 kilometres west north-west of Calgary was also named for the oil well that was located near the mouth of the creek.

Prior to the establishment of official policies for geographical naming, features were often named for individuals or for companies or organizations that assisted in the development of industries in the various areas of the province. This practice has, however, been largely discontinued and geographical names are now chosen according to very stringent principles that govern the adoption of commemorative names.

With the development of official naming procedures came the opportunity to accumulate extensive records on existing and proposed or local names. What follows is the geographical names history of the southern Alberta prairies and badlands. The volumes in this series treat their respective study areas with a similar approach (see map on page xxiv), heralding the uniqueness of each territory. The intent of these maps is to provide a reference guide for the reader to accurately find locations using individual topographical map sheets as orientative tools.

The brief summaries are intended to give readers information on the origin and significance of the place names of Alberta and to suggest the close connection between culture and heritage of the province and its citizens, and the geographical names that describe and define the landscape.

---

[5] Palmer, *Alberta: A New History*, p. 162.

EXPLANATORY NOTES

Individual place name entries in this volume may best be understood by considering the following example:

1. **Excoffin Bottom (bottom)**

2. **82 H/10 - Lethbridge**
3. **W-16-8-22-W4**
4. **49°38′50″N 112°55′50″W**
5. **Approximately 9 km south-west of Lethbridge.**

6. **Named for John Excoffin, a bachelor who came to the Lethbridge area from France, prior to the 1902 flood, and...**

1. Specialists in geographical nomenclature prefer to think of most place names as being comprised of two parts (both exemplified in the first line of this example): one part is called the *specific* (here "Excoffin"), whereas the other is referred to as the *generic* (here "Bottom"). The generic identifies the *type* of feature, while the specific identifies the name of the feature of that type. Although generics very often form parts of place names (as in "Excoffin Bottom"), many place names lack them. In this volume, the appropriate generics are always provided in parentheses at the end of the first line. The generics used here are consistent with those found in *Generic Terms in Canada's Geographical Names; Terminology Bulletin 176*, Minister of Supply and Services Canada, 1987; Catalogue No. S52-2/176-1987. An asterisk (*) preceding a place name indicates that the name has been rescinded or designates a former locality. A square box (■) at the beginning of an entry indicates that a colour photograph of the feature is to be found at the end of this volume.

2. The National Topographic System Grid Reference is a system that "blocks out" the country using map sheets of increasing scales. The second line of each entry identifies the map sheet corresponding to the described feature—in this case "82 H/10 - Lethbridge." Maps may be obtained from any Maps Alberta outlet in the province.

3. Where available, a legal description (here "W-16-8-22-W4") is given in the line that follows. It specifies the section, range, township, and meridian.

4. Next is the latitude and longitude location description, e.g. "49°38′50″N 112°55′50″W."

5. As a further aid to locating the described feature, the approximate distance to the nearest populated community (as the crow flies) is also provided.

6. The concluding sentence or paragraph of most entries summarizes any available descriptive or historical information concerning the feature or its name. Where a geographical name shares a specific with a number of entries, to avoid duplication the origin information for the common name is usually located under only one of the entries. Since the surrounding features are often named as a result of their proximity to the originally named feature, it seems appropriate to present the origin information under the feature that was named first. Wherever this is the case, the other entries conclude with a cross-reference.

PHOTO CREDITS

Feature Name	Number of Photograph	Location	Page
Bassano, 1911	A5141	P.A.A.	7
Big Rock	RG 86-1-1	Geog Names	147
Bow Island, ca. 1909	A7146	P.A.A.	15
Bow River, 1907	B9666	P.A.A.	15
Calgary, 1912	P4103	P.A.A.	21
Cardston, n.d.	P4028	P.A.A.	23
Chin Coulee	RG 85-7-17	Geog Names	147
Cochrane Lake, n.d.	P228	P.A.A.	29
Cypress Hills	RG 85 7 3,4,5	Geog Names	148
Drumheller, 1918	P833	P.A.A.	38
Eagle Butte	RG 85-6-5	Geog Names	148
East Fort Macleod Wheatfields, 1965	1500, 21 July/65 Pearce, Alberta	Wonders	149
Etzicom Coulee	RG 85-7-14	Geog Names	149
Foremost, 1966	1630, 15 Sept/66	Wonders	150
Head-Smashed-In Buffalo Jump	RG 81-6-1	Geog Names	150
Lost River	RG 85-6-30,31	Geog Names	151
Maher Coulee	RG 85-7-2	Geog Names	151
Manyberries Creek	RG 85-6-36	Geog Names	152
Medicine Hat, 1885	B10102	P.A.A.	80
Milk River, 1912	A10366	P.A.A.	82
Oldman River, 1911	A1752	P.A.A.	90
Red Rock Coulee	RG 85-7-25	Geog Names	152
Reesor Lake	RG 85-6-12	Geog Names	152
Writing-on-Stone, 1897	A1607	P.A.A.	133

Maps

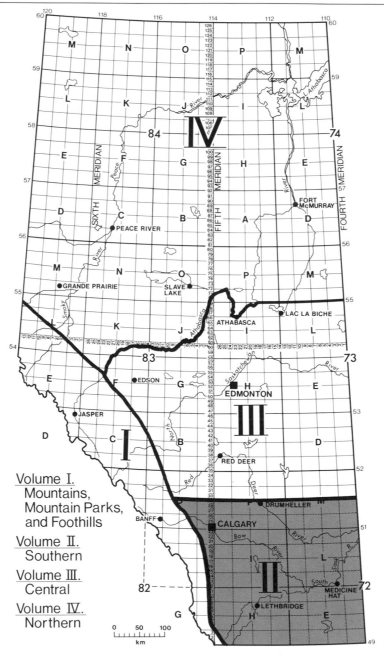

Volume I.
Mountains,
Mountain Parks,
and Foothills

Volume II.
Southern

Volume III.
Central

Volume IV.
Northern

Map showing study areas in the *Place Names of Alberta* series

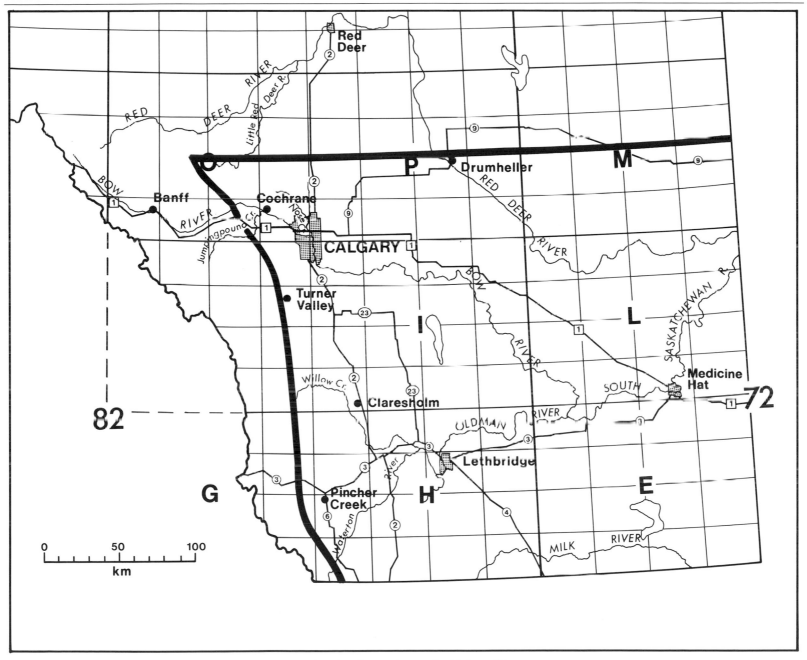

Map showing study area for Volume II

A~B

*Academy (former locality)

82 J/16 - Priddis
10-22-1-W5
50°51′N 114°03′W
Approximately 5 km south of Calgary.

This former locality was named some time after 1914. The station began handling grain in 1928, and continued to do so until the United Grain Growers elevator was demolished in 1971.

Acadia Valley (hamlet)

72 M/1   Acadia Valley
27-25-2-W4
51°08′N 110°13′W
Approximately 125 km north north-east of Medicine Hat.

The post office established here in 1911 was named by the area's settlers who had come from Nova Scotia. Acadia, or *Acadie* in French, was the name given by France to all New World Atlantic Seaboard possessions, that included Nova Scotia, New Brunswick, and parts of Quebec and Maine from the early 17th century to the mid-18th century. The name is possibly derived from the Abnaki, Malecite or Micmac language, and is translated as "nothing here."

Acme (village)

82 P/5 - Drumheller
19-29-25-W4
51°30′N 113°30′W
Approximately 63 km north north-east of Calgary.

This settlement bears a name derived from the Greek word, *acme*, meaning "summit." When it was named, it was the most northerly point on the Canadian Pacific Railway branch. Many of the street names in the village take their names from early C.P.R. surveyors. The post office was

known as "Tapscott" from 1905 through 1909.

Aden (locality)

72 E/3 - Aden
8-1-10-W4
49°02′N 111°19′W
Approximately 115 km south south-west of Medicine Hat.

The first postmaster, H.E. Anderson, requested that the area be called Aden, after a seaport located at the southern end of the Red Sea, in Arabia, now South Yemen. Anderson had been a sailor in the Middle East prior to emigrating to Canada to homestead. Some area residents suggested that the Grassy Butte Hills may have reminded Anderson of the coastal regions of South Yemen.

Aerial (locality)

82 P/7 - Drumheller
28-28-19-W4
51°25′N 112°38′W
Across the Red Deer River from the Rosedale Railway Station, approximately 2 km south-east of Drumheller.

A post office was established here 15 August 1916. An aerial tramway conveyed coal from the Star Mine across the Red Deer River to Rosedale Railway Station.

Aetna (hamlet)

82 H/3 - Cardston
23-2-25-W4
49°08′N 113°15′W
Approximately 68 km south-west of Lethbridge.

Named in 1893 by John W. Taylor, a Mormon general authority from Salt Lake City, Utah, because one of the surrounding hills looked like Mount Etna, a volcanic mountain in Sicily for which a district in Italy is named. The spelling of Aetna is a modification of the original, and the hill to

which Taylor was referring is now locally known as "Buffalo Hill." C.O. Card noted a store, school, etc., at Aetna, the centre of the district in 1898. The Aetna post office was established on this site 1 November 1900.

Aetna Creek (creek)

82 H/3 - Cardston
31-2-24-W4
49°10′N 113°12′W
Flows north-east into St. Mary River, approximately 63 km south-west of Lethbridge.

(see Aetna)

Agatha (locality)

72 L/3 - Suffield
4-14-10-W4
50°08′N 111°17′W
Approximately 46 km west north-west of Medicine Hat.

A Canadian Pacific Railway station was established here in 1914 and was named after Agatha, Lady Hindlip, a major shareholder in the railway company.

Airdrie (city)

82 O/8 - Crossfield
12-27-1-W5
51°18′N 114°02′W
Approximately 25 km north of Calgary.

According to the official Tourist Guide of Airdrie, Scotland, the Alberta city got its name as follows: "There is an Airdrie in Canada founded in 1889 between Edmonton and Calgary, and we have it on good authority that this settlement was named by

---

*denotes rescinded name or former locality.

William Mackenzie, a Scot by birth and a contracting engineer by profession—after one situated a few miles north-east of Glasgow, in a quarry and mining section." The precise origin of the name Airdrie is lost in history but many possibilities have been the subject of considerable discussion. One theory suggests that the name comes from the atmospheric condition "air-dry." This is suggested by Mr. James Knox who wrote a history of Airdrie, Scotland. He further dismisses another theory that the origin of the name is Celtic and means "high level" for although Airdrie may "stand high" it has no level part. A third interpretation of the name suggests that it means "high pasture run."

Historians of the town are now satisfied that the true meaning of the name is "The King's Height." A British historian, Chalmars, accepts this view and considers that the rising ground upon which the modern Scottish town now stands was the scene of the Battle of Arderytn fought in 577 between Aeddan, King of Kintire and Rydderich the Bountiful, King of Strathclwyd.

Albert Park (locality)

82 P/4 - Dalroy
24-29-W4
51°02′N 114°00′W
Within the city limits of Calgary.

The precise origin is unknown for the name of this locality.

* Albion Ridge (former locality)

82 H/15 - Picture Butte
35-11-22-W4
49°57′N 112°55′W
Approximately 26 km north north-west of Lethbridge.

This ridge was named by English settlers who were reminded of their homeland,

particularly the White Cliffs of Dover. The Romans named England Albion, derived from the Latin word *albus*, which means "white" and possibly refers to the cliffs at Dover.

Alderson (locality)

72 L/6 - Alderson
20-15-10-W4
50°17′N 111°20′W
Approximately 53 km north-west of Medicine Hat.

This locality was named in 1915 for Lieutenant-General Sir Edwin Alfred Harvey Alderson, K.C.B. (1859-1927). Alderson served the British Army through-out the Empire and from 1914 to 1918 he commanded the First Canadian Division in Europe. The community first came into being with the coming of the railway in 1883. Its original name was "Langevin," but this was changed to "Carlstadt" in 1900. This name was maintained until 1915, when for patriotic reasons, like so many other Canadian communities, the German name was changed to honour the celebrated British General.

Aldersyde (hamlet)

82 I/12 - High River
7-20-28-W4
50°41′N 113°52′W
Approximately 40 km south south-east of Calgary.

The name was suggested by a Scottish settler after *Aldersyde*, the story of Annie S. Swan, who writes under date 18 March 1927: "Nearly fifty years ago when I was a girl in my father's house in Midlothian, I wrote a story of the border country dealing with Scottish life and character and named in Aldersyde, a purely fictitious name, a combination of typical Border syllables. There are many 'sydes' in the Borders, notably Bermersyde, the heritage of the Haigs and where Earl Haig now lives. We

are just building a modest house at Gullane, East Lothian, which will bear the name Aldersyde engraved on its stone gateway."

Alkali Creek (creek)

72 L/15 - Buffalo
16-22-4-W4
50°52′N 110°30′W
Approximately 90 km north of Medicine Hat.

The name is likely descriptive of the soluble mineral salts present in the water. Alkali water is not potable and is detrimental to the growing of most crops.

Alkali Lake (lake)

82 P/1 - Finnegan
4-24-16-W4
51°01′N 112°11′W
Approximately 63 km south south-east of Drumheller.

(see Alkali Creek)

* Allerston (former locality)

72 E/4 - Coutts
34-2-14-W4
49°10′N 111°48′W
Approximately 108 km south south-west of Medicine Hat.

Named in 1914 for Jake Allers who settled in the district with his family. The post office was opened in July 1911 and was originally called "Doran," after Mrs. Vedee Hierath's (postmistress) son. In January 1914, the post office was moved to a new site and the name was changed to Allerston.

* Alyth (former railway point)

82 O/1 - Calgary
24-1-W5
51°02′N 114°02′W
Within the city limits of Calgary.

This former Canadian Pacific Railway station now located within the city limits of

---

*denotes rescinded name or former locality.

Calgary, was named after Alyth, a village in Perthshire (now Tayside), Scotland.

Anastasia (locality)

82 I/11 - Arrowwood
30-20-22-W4
50°44′N 113°02′W
Approximately 78 km east south-east of Calgary.

Located near Arrowwood, this locality was apparently named in honour of a Doukhobor queen.

Antelope Lakes (lake)

82 P/8 - Dorothy
7-27-16-W4
51°17′N 112°14′W
Approximately 40 km south-east of Drumheller.

The precise origin for the name of these lakes is unknown.

Antonio (locality)

72 E/13 - Grassy Lake
14-10-14-W4
49°49′N 111°48′W
Approximately 75 km east of Lethbridge.

Named for a Mr. Antonio, one of a number of Italians who settled in the general vicinity. The name was not recorded in the earlier period, however, because Mr. Antonio was unable to prove-up his homestead, and moved on.

Appleyard Coulee (coulee)

82 P/6 - Carbon
13-10-29-22-W4
51°28′20″N 113°01′40″W
Approximately 20 km west of Drumheller.

Named for the George William Appleyard family. He and his parents arrived in Alberta in 1904 from Leeds, England, and homesteaded at the entrance to this coulee in 1905. The first school and teacherage of the Lenox School District were on the Appleyard homestead.

Ardenode (hamlet)

82 P/3 - Strathmore
21-25-25-W4
51°08′N 113°26′W
Approximately 42 km east of Calgary.

Ardenode was originally a siding along the Canadian National Railway line from Calgary to Drumheller circa 1911. The first name given to this community was "Hawick," but this name was a duplicate of another settlement in northern Alberta. An alternate name was selected by Major George Davis, after a beautiful village in Ireland. The post office operated from 15 May 1915 through 28 November 1959.

Ardenville (locality)

82 H/11 - Fort Macleod
10-7-26-W4
49°33′N 113°27′W
Approximately 49 km west of Lethbridge.

Named after Arden Simpson, an early homesteader to the district, originally from Ontario. The post office operated at this site from 1910 through 1948.

Armada (locality)

82 I/7 - McGregor Lake
12-17-21-W4
50°25′N 112°46′W
Approximately 80 km north of Lethbridge.

Armada is the Spanish word for "fleet" or "squadron." It is not clear, however, why this particular name was chosen for the post office which opened 1 January 1915 and closed 1 July 1959.

*Armelgra (former station)

72 L/4 - Hays
29-13-13-W4
50°07′N 111°43′W
Approximately 73 km west of Medicine Hat.

A Canadian Pacific Railway station operated here beginning in 1917 and was named after Arthur Melville Grace, C.E., an Engineer with the C.P.R., using the beginning letters from each of his names.

Armstrong Coulee (coulee)

72 E/9 - Elkwater Lake
1-18-8-1-W4
44°38′25″N 110°07′25″W
Approximately 60 km south-east of Medicine Hat.

This coulee was used by the Armstrong family, who arrived in the Cypress Hills in 1897, as a hay and calf camp, a practice that was common to all the ranchers in the area. Most of the coulees leading off the beach were appointed to ranchers for similar uses.

Arneson (locality)

72 M/1 - Acadia Valley
4-26-1-W4
51°12′N 110°04′W
Approximately 130 km north-east of Medicine Hat.

Named for C.B. Arneson, the original owner of the land where the locality is now located. A post office was established on this site 16 December 1928 and operated until 2 April 1957.

Arrowsmith Coulee (creek)

82 H/15 - Picture Butte
27-11-19-W4
49°56′N 112°30′W
Flows east into Little Bow River, approximately 30 km north-east of Lethbridge.

Named for George Arrowsmith (b. Hereford, England 1865 - d. Turin, Alberta, 1935) who was a homesteader, rancher and a member of the North West Mounted Police. Arrowsmith spent five years in the force, leaving to become manager of the Cameron Ranch until he homesteaded his own quarter section with his wife. In addition to this, they leased land for their own ranching activities. Arrowsmith served as postmaster of Turin from 1920 until his death.

Arrowwood (village)
82 I/11 - Arrowwood
32-20-23-W4
50°44′N 113°09′W
Approximately 68 km east south-east of Calgary.

The name came from the two creeks, the East and West Arrowwood that traversed the Blackfoot Reserve lands south of the Bow River. The creeks had received their names from the short willow bush "Salix" that grew in abundance on their banks. During the period 1905 to 1909, the Southern Alberta Land Co. had used the name Arrowwood in its correspondence with the Department of the Interior to describe that section of their irrigation works between the two creeks. Not surprisingly, in 1909, the Federal Post Office Department named the post office located on East Arrowwood Creek, Arrowwood.

Atkinson Creek (creek)
82 O/7 - Wildcat Hills
30-28-6-W5
51°25′N 114°50′W
Flows east into Little Red Deer River, approximately 70 km north-west of Calgary.

This creek is named after John Atkinson (1874-1950) who came to Canada from England in 1904 to work for a horse breeder. He homesteaded in the Horse Creek area for several years until he became a Dominion Forest Ranger in 1915. He retired in 1935 and moved to Calgary.

Atlee (locality)
72 L/15 - Buffalo
5-22-7-W4
50°50′N 110°57′W
Approximately 90 km north of Medicine Hat.

Named for W. Atlee James, Assistant Chief Engineer of the Canadian Pacific Railway.

***Avalon** (former locality)
72 E/3 - Aden
23-3-9-4
49°13′N 111°07′W
Approximately 100 km south-west of Medicine Hat.

A post office operated here from 1 August 1911 through 25 April 1956 and was named after a peninsula in Somerset, England, where it is reputed that King Arthur was buried.

Azure (locality)
82 I/12 - Gleichen
12-18-29-W4
50°30′N 113°52′W
Approximately 40 km south south-east of Calgary.

It is assumed that Azure was given a descriptive name, for its surrounding blue skies.

Badger Lake (lake)
82 I/8 - Gleichen
30-16-18-W4
50°23′N 112°28′W

Approximately 78 km north-east of Lethbridge.

(see Badger Lake)

***Badger Lake** (former locality)
82 I/8 - Scandia
19-16-18-W4
50°22′N 112°27′W
Approximately 77 km north-east of Lethbridge.

A significant number of badgers inhabited the area around the nearby lake when this post office opened 1 February 1913 and the name was used as a result. The post office closed 28 February 1946.

Bad Land Hills (hill)
72 L/4 - Hays
13-13-W4
50°05′N 111°45′W
Approximately 70 km east of Medicine Hat.

The precise origin for the name of this feature is unknown.

Badland Hills (hills)
82 I/10 - Queenstown
20-19-W4
50°40′N 112°35′W
Approximately 110 km east south-east of Calgary.

The name for these hills is probably descriptive.

Bailey's Bottom (bottom)
82 H/10 - Lethbridge
E1/2-9-8-22-W4
49°37′45″N 112°55′15″W
Approximately 8 km south-west of Lethbridge.

This floodplain derives its name from Jim Bailey who homesteaded the land around the turn of the century. The Baileys, Jim and Mabel, were Irish and Scottish, respectively. In 1902, they lost all their belongings when the Oldman River flooded, and in 1904, Bailey filed on SE-34-8-22. Mrs. Bailey taught school in the area. Both Baileys were well-liked and had a reputation for being very sociable. The name was officially approved 5 May 1987.

Bain (locality)
72 E/8 - Thelma Creek
6-4-3-W4
49°17′N 110°24′W
Approximately 83 km south of Medicine Hat.

Established in 1922 by the Canadian Pacific Railway, the locality of Bain was named for James Bain, a section foreman. Bain was decorated twice during World War I with the Distinguished Conduct Medal and the Military Medal.

Baintree (locality)
82 P/3 - Strathmore
35-25-24-W4
51°10′N 113°15′W
Approximately 55 km east north-east of Calgary.

A Canadian National Railway station was established here in 1917 and a post office operated here from 1 March 1917 through 30 May 1957. The precise origin for the name of the feature is unknown; however, one source states that once a certain man was travelling along the Serviceberry Creek when a tree broke onto his wagon. The man then cut this tree down from along the banks of the creek. Shortly after this, the man bought a Bain wagon. It is rumoured that the site was originally called "Wagontree," but the name was later altered to Baintree. The location of this

community, on the banks of Serviceberry Creek, led to its demise. Apparently, whenever the creek flooded from rain or snow, so too did the townsite.

Ballina (station)
82 I/14 - Gleichen
6-23-24-W4
50°55′N 113°12′W
Approximately 60 km east of Calgary.

This Canadian Pacific Railway station opened circa 1912-15, and was named after a village in County Mayo, in Ireland.

Balzac (hamlet)
82 O/1 - Calgary
13-26-1-W5
51°13′N 114°01′W
Approximately 18 km north of Calgary.

A Canadian Pacific Railway station began operating at this site in 1910. It was named by W.C. Van Horne, then president of the railway, after one of his favourite authors, Honoré de Balzac (1799-1850) a noted French novelist. The post office here was opened 1 April 1912 under the name "Beddington," after the town near Croydon, England. The name was changed on 1 July 1925.

Bantry (locality)
72 L/5 - Tilley
5-18-13-W4
50°29′N 111°45′W
Approximately 90 km north-west of Medicine Hat.

Named in 1884 after Bantry Bay in Ireland, a long inlet of the Atlantic Ocean in the south-west of County Cork, Ireland. The bay is 48 km long and 16 km wide at its widest point and separates the Caha and the Sheep's Head peninsulas. The town of Bantry is near the head of the bay. The French entered Bantry Bay in 1689 and 1796 during attempted invasions of Ireland.

Bantry Reservoir (Timko Lake)
(reservoir and lake)
72 L/5 - Tilley
33-17-13-W4
50°29′N 111°45′W
Approximately 90 km north-west of Medicine Hat.

(see Timko Lake)

*****Baraca** (former locality)
72 M/5 - Sunnybrook
4-27-11-W4
51°17′N 111°30′W
Approximately 86 km east south-east of Drumheller.

The name was suggested by Mrs. E.E. Boggess, a Lutheran preacher, and is derived from the Biblical word *Berachah* (Barach) meaning "blessing" or "the blessed." The post office was located at 36-26-12 and was known as "Wharranton," after postmaster Forest Wharran. It was renamed in 1913 when it was moved to its present location.

Bare Creek (creek)
72 E/1 - Cripple Creek
25-3-1-W4
49°14′N 110°00′W
Flows south-east into Lodge Creek, approximately 95 km south-east of Medicine Hat.

This feature derives its name from an alleged humorous incident which took place some time prior to 1891. Travelling by means of a democrat wagon, a Mountie and his wife came upon a group of cowhands having dinner. While stepping down from the wagon, the woman's dress became tangled on the foot brake. The camp cook cut her dress to free her, but in the process, her "hindmost extremities" were exposed. The creek has since been known as Bare Creek.

---

*denotes rescinded name or former locality.

Barkenhouse Lake (lake)

82 I/16 - Gleichen
30-17-22-W4
50°54′N 112°22′W
Approximately 132 km east of Calgary.

The precise origin for the name of this feature is unknown.

Barlow (railway point)

82 P/4 - Dalroy
23-29-W4
51°00′N 113°58′W
Within the city limits of Calgary.

The Canadian National Railway established a station here. The precise origin for the name is not known.

*Barlow Junction (former station)

82 P/4 - Dalroy
23-1-W5
51°00′N 114°00′W
Within the city limits of Calgary.

(see Sarcee Junction)

Barnett Lake (lake)

82 P/3 - Strathmore
25-24-24-W4
51°04′N 113°14′W
Approximately 50 km east of Calgary.

This spring-fed lake was apparently named after a Mr. Thomas Barnett, one of the first settlers in the area. He arrived in 1909, followed by his wife and two children two years later. Despite the fact that the family owned land close to the lake, they never actually owned any land right on the lake until circa 1950 when Thomas' son, James Thomas Barnett, bought one half section on its north-west end.

* Barney (former post office)

82 I/1 - Vauxhall
34-12-17-W4
50°04′N 112°16′W
Approximately 55 km north-east of Lethbridge.

It is not known after whom the original post office was named when it opened 15 October 1910, but the name was changed to Retlaw in 1913. (see Retlaw)

Barnwell (village)

82 H/16 - Taber
28-9-17-W4
49°46′N 112°15′W
Approximately 40 km east of Lethbridge.

Named in 1909 for Richard Barnwell, a purchasing agent for the Canadian Pacific Railway in Winnipeg. The original C.P.R. station, located on the site of the present village, was once named "Woodpecker," after Woodpecker Island in the Oldman River located to the north. Woodpecker Island is a translation of the Blackfoot name *akka-kima-toskway* , translating to "many woodpeckers." The village was founded in 1902 by four pioneering Mormon families. In 1908, the name of the community was changed to "Bountiful," which likely described the high hopes of the early settlers for their future harvests. By 1909, it received its current name.

Barons (village)

82 H/14 - Monarch
16-12-23-W4
50°00′N 113°05′W
Approximately 35 km north-west of Lethbridge.

The Canadian Pacific Railway purchased the land upon which the village now sits in the spring of 1909, and the name "Baron" was chosen for a high ranking railway official. The first bank on the townsite, the Union Bank, called itself Baron's Bank, and

other firms soon added the possessive term to their business names. Through local usage, the "s" became part of the name, and the C.P.R. changed the name officially within a few years' time. A store and a post office owned by Jack Warnock was opened nearby in 1907, on 16-12-23, but across the tracks from the future site of Barons. Mr. Warnock chose the name "Blayney," after Blayney Castle in Ireland for his settlement which was later replaced by the name Barons.

Bartman Reservoir (reservoir)

72 M/3 - Big Stone
25-11-W4
51°07′N 111°27′W
Approximately 96 km south-east of Drumheller.

Named for Russell Secord Bartman, the owner of the land upon which this body of water is located. The reservoir was created when the Bartman Dam was built in 1936. The dam was washed out in 1937, but was subsequently rebuilt.

Bartstow (locality)

82 I/14 - Gleichen
20-22-23-W4
50°53′N 113°09′W
Approximately 55 km east of Calgary.

A Canadian Pacific Railway station was established here circa 1917 and was named after a renowned Winnipeg merchant, F.W. Stobart. His name has been transposed to avoid confusion with the other locality nearby named Stobart.

Bassano (town)

82 I/16 - Gleichen
17-21-18-W4
50°47′N 112°28′W
Approximately 125 km east south-east of Calgary.

This community was named by the Canadian Pacific Railway in 1884 for one of

---

their major shareholders, the Marquis de Bassano, a native of Italy. His wife, Lady Bassano, née Marie-Anne-Claire Symes, was a native of the province of Quebec. Bassano was the site of a major dam, as part of the C.P.R.'s irrigation scheme, and led to the slogan "the best in the west by a dam site." It is the second largest dam of its kind in the world, exceeded in size only by the one at Assuan or Aswan, Egypt, which holds back the waters of the Nile.

Bassano, 1911

Bateman Creek (creek)

82 O/2 - Jumpingpound Creek
8-24-5-W5
51°03′N 114°48′W
Flows south-east into Jumpingpound Creek, approximately 40 km west of Calgary.

Tom Bateman (postmaster and rancher) and his family were early pioneers of the Jumpingpound district. The name was officially approved 12 December 1939.

Bateman Ridge (ridge)

82 O/2 - Jumpingpound Creek
25-5-W5
51°05′N 114°35′W
Approximately 25 km west of Calgary.

(see Bateman Creek)

Battle Creek (creek)

72 E/9 - Elkwater Lake
13-8-1-W4
49°38′N 110°00′W
Flows east, crossing the Alberta-Saskatchewan boundary, approximately 60 km south-east of Medicine Hat.

Named after an armed engagement in the Cypress Hills region in May 1873, between American wolf hunters and a small group of Assiniboine Indians, led by Chief Little Soldier. The Americans were "hot-tempered" about a number of missing horses, and they believed that Indians were to blame. Encamped by the creek, a number of Chief Little Soldier's band were drinking cheap, "rot gut" whisky which they had obtained from a nearby trading post. When the American wolfers came upon Little Soldier's group, they accused the Indians of horse theft, an argument ensued and gunfire soon followed. Although they were outnumbered, the Americans killed 36 Indians, gaining the upper hand with their superior position and repeating Henry rifles. This incident became known as the "Cypress Hills Massacre" and provided Prime Minister John A. Macdonald with a strong case to have the necessary legislation passed through the House of Commons to establish the North West Mounted Police.

Baymar Creek (creek)

82 O/7 - Wildcat Hills
4-27-6-W5
51°16′N 114°48′W
Flows north into Ghost River, approximately 58 km west north-west of Calgary.

The locally well-established name for this creek was submitted by D.A. Nichols in 1950 and officially approved in the same year, from the name of the oil well near the mouth of the creek.

Bear Creek (creek)

72 E/3 - Aden
30-2-9-W4
49°09′N 111°14′W
Approximately 116 km south south-west of Medicine Hat.

The precise origin for the name of this feature is unknown.

Bearspaw (locality)

82 O/1 - Calgary
14-25-3-W5
51°08′N 114°18′W
Approximately 20 km west north-west of Calgary.

A Canadian Pacific Railway station was established here in 1879 and was named after Chief Masgwaahsid, or Bear's Paw, who signed the treaty at Blackfoot Crossing 22 September 1877.

Beaupre Creek (creek)

82 O/2 - Jumpingpound Creek
15-26-5-W5
51°13′N 114°37′W
Flows south-east into Bow River, approximately 30 km north-east of Calgary.

Named after Louis Beaupré, an early settler who bought squatter's rights there. The Beaupre School District (without the accent) No. 4182 was established in 1925. In the 1880s, Louis Beaupré, a French-Canadian settler and his Métis wife settled on this creek. Beaupré was a rancher who also cut and sold logs to the Cochrane Ranche Company. Other features in this district are also named for members of this family. The name was officially approved 12 December 1939.

Beaupre Hill (hill)

82 O/7 - Wildcat Hills
4-27-5-W5
51°17′N 114°41′W

Approximately 19 km north-west of Cochrane.

Originally approved 11 June 1930. (see Beaupre Creek)

Beaupre Lake (lake)

82 O/2 - Jumpingpound Creek
20-26-5-W5
51°14′N 114°40′W
Approximately 35 km north-west of Calgary.

(see Beaupre Creek)

Beaver Creek (creek)

82 H/12 - Lethbridge
11-8-28-W4
49°39′N 113°42′W
Flows south-east into Oldman River, approximately 64 km west of Lethbridge.

This creek was named *kakghikstakiskway* by the Blackfoot which translates to "where the beaver cuts wood." It was likely descriptively named early in the century.

Beaverdam Lake (lake)

82 H/4 - Waterton Lakes
31-1-27-W4
49°05′N 113°36′W
Approximately 50 km south-east of Pincher Creek.

This lake was officially named 3 November 1942. There is no other origin information available for this locally well-established name.

Beazer (hamlet)

82 H/3 - Cardston
13-2-27-W4
49°07′N 113°29′W
Approximately 80 km south-west of Lethbridge.

Named for Mark Beazer (?-1937), the area's first homesteader, postmaster and Mormon Bishop. Beazer and his wife Ellen Burton (1859-1956) married in 1880 and farmed in Utah until 1889 when they came to the Cardston area. They bought a homestead on this site in 1890, and eventually set up a post office from which a hamlet grew.

Beazer Ridge (ridge)

82 H/3 - Cardston
13-2-27-W4
49°07′N 113°30′W
Approximately 79 km south-west of Lethbridge.

(see Beazer)

Becker Coulee (creek)

72 E/6 - Foremost
28-6-11-W4
49°29′N 111°26′W
Approximately 80 km south-west of Medicine Hat.

This coulee was named for the Beckers, early settlers in the vicinity.

* **Beddington** (former locality)

82 O/1 - Calgary
23-25-1-W5
51°09′N 114°03′W
Within the city limits of Calgary.

A Canadian Pacific Railway station was established here sometime before July 1893 and was named after Beddington, Croydon, England. The post office, later named Balzac (see Balzac) operated under this name from 1 April 1912 through 1 July 1925.

Beddington Creek (creek)

82 O/1 - Calgary
23-25-1-W5
51°08′30″N 114°02′30″W

Flows south-east into Nose Creek, approximately 1 km north of Calgary.

(see Beddington)

Beebe Flats (flat)

82 H/4 - Waterton Lakes
16-1-27-W4
49°02′00″N 113°41′00″W
Approximately 55 km south-east of Pincher Creek.

Chauncy "Chance" Beebe was a son of "Old Man" Beebe. Chance was one of the first of the Glacier National Park Rangers (Lockwood-G.N.P., personal communication). He later left the Canadian Parks Service and went to work for the Department of the Interior as a Predator Control Officer, and was said to have shot and killed more than 300 bears, both Black and Grizzly. It was he who killed the famous "Medicine Grizzly" of Blackfoot lore. In 1910 Chance Beebe and Charlie Wise homesteaded on the north Fork of the Flathead River in British Columbia. Charlie's homestead was the land where the Flathead Canadian Customs Office now stands. After the sad death of his wife, Nettie Closinsky, Charlie gave his homestead to the government. Chance Beebe was with Charlie when the two of them gathered up and buried the few remaining bones of Dave "Slim" Link after Slim was killed and eaten by a Grizzly on the Lower Kishinena in the spring of 1912. Chance had been a partner of Slim's on their trapline, but had been at Whitefish when Slim accidentally shot himself in the stomach, and was subsequently dragged alive from the cabin and met his horrible death in the jaws of the Grizzly. There are Beebes living on the Blood Reserve north of Cardston who are apparently descendants of "Old Man Beebe."

---

*denotes rescinded name or former locality.

Behanhouse Creek (creek)

82 O/7 - Wildcat Hills
36-26-6-W5
51°15′N 114°43′W
Flows south-east into Ranche Creek,
approximately 40 km west north-west of
Calgary.

The name for this creek was officially
approved 23 April 1940. Mr. Behan was a
cook on a survey party in 1912.

Beiseker (village)

82 P/5 - Irricana
12-28-26-W4
51°23′N 113°32′W
Approximately 50 km north-east of
Calgary.

In the early part of the century, the Dominion Government gave the Canadian Pacific
Railway 25 million acres of land. Some was
sold to settlers, but 250,000 acres were sold
to the Calgary Colonization Company.
This was owned by two young Dakota
businessmen. One was a Mr. Davidson, and
the other was Thomas Beiseker, from
Gressenden, North Dakota. The price paid
by Beiseker was reported to be $1.00 per
acre, with ten cents down. Beginning in
1907, Mr. Sawyer, a land agent, was sent
down to the United States to recruit people
who wanted to homestead in the area, then
known as the "Rosebud Tract." The first
family to live in the area were the Ludwig
Schmaltz family. They spent the winter
here, and it is reported that Mrs. Schmaltz
never saw another woman until the
following March, when more pioneers from
North Dakota began moving in. The first
settlers were German Catholics, and bought
land west and around Beiseker. The
Seventh Day Adventists settled about 16
km east of Beiseker, and the Baptists settled
about half way between Beiseker and
Drumheller. In 1910, T.L. Beiseker donated
land for a townsite, so the village was
named after him and the C.P.R. line came

through that same year. Mr. Beiseker was
reputed to be the wealthiest man in North
Dakota at one time. Accounts say he owned
anywhere from 28 to 40 banks. Unfortunately, Mr. Beiseker apparently lost his
money in the 1920s. According to James
Schleppe, a local resident, T.L. Beiseker
never actually lived at the townsite named
for him, although he did reside in Canada,
even in Calgary for a few years.

Bellcott (station)

72 E/15 - Seven Persons
6-12-5-W4
49°57′N 110°39′W
Approximately 5 km south of Medicine
Hat.

Named for Belle Cotterell, wife of the
Assistant General Superintendent, British
Columbia district, Canadian Pacific
Railway. Prior to 1914, Bellcott was known
as "Anstead."

Belly River (river)

82 H/14 - Monarch
27-9-23-W4
49°46′N 113°02′W
Flows north-east into Oldman River,
approximately 16 km north-west of
Lethbridge.

Named for the Atsina Indians, a detached
tribe of the Arapaho and known to the
other Arapaho Indians as *hitunena*, which
means "beggars" or "spongers." This was
often incorrectly interpreted to mean "big
bellies" or "belly people." This same tribe
of Indians were known as the Gros Ventres
by the French, a name that has since
become their popular one. These people
often travelled through this region to hunt
buffalo in the summer. The Blackfoot called
this river *mokowanis*, the Siksika word for
"belly." A second theory suggests that the
Indian term *mokowanis* is descriptive and

refers to the large bend or belly in the river
as it makes a loop to the south near
Lethbridge.

Benaman Slough (marsh)

82 P/4 - Dalroy
20-25-28-W4
51°10′N 113°52′W
Approximately 5 km north-east of Calgary.

The origin for the name of this feature is
unknown.

Bennett (locality)

82 I/13 - Dalemead
13-23-28-W4
50°58′N 113°47′W
West of Langdon.

This locality was named for the Right
Honourable Richard Bedford Bennett
(1870-1947), Prime Minister of Canada
from 1930 to 1935. Originally from New
Brunswick, Bennett headed west to Calgary
in the mid-1890s after a period of teaching,
the completion of his Law degree at
Dalhousie, and several years' practice in the
town of Chatham, New Brunswick. In
Calgary, with the help of Senator
Lougheed, he became the Canadian Pacific
Railway's chief solicitor. He began his
political career in 1898, elected as a Conservative member of the Legislature of the
Northwest Territories, and remained a
member of the territorial house until
Alberta attained provincial status in 1905.
Bennett attempted provincial politics, but
was not successful until 1909, where he
remained until he resigned his seat in 1911
(the same year this town was named). At
that time, he decided to run for the federal
Conservative party. Bennett remained in
the House of Commons from 1911 to 1917
and 1925 to 1938, serving in two of Arthur
Meighan's short-lived cabinets in 1921 and
1926 as Minister of Justice and Finance
respectively. In 1927, he attained the
leadership of the party by way of the

Conservative's first leadership convention, and led the Tories to a majority victory over Mackenzie King in the 1930 election. Bennett and the Tories were badly beaten by the Liberals in the 1935 election, but he remained leader of the party for another three years. He resigned in 1938, and left Canada for good, retiring to England where he was created a Viscount in 1941, with the help of his close friend, Max Aitken, Lord Beaverbrook.

Benton (locality)
72 M/8 - Sibbald
34-27-3-W4
51°21'N 110°22'W
Approximately 165 km east of Drumheller.

(see Benton Station)

Benton Station (locality)
72 M/8 - Sibbald
34-27-3-W4
51°21'N 110°22'W
Approximately 165 km east of Drumheller.

One source suggests that Benton was named to commemorate the Benton Trail from Fort Benton, Montana to Fort Macleod, Alberta. Another suggests that the Fort, originally founded in 1846 as Fort Lewis, an American Fur Company Post, was renamed in 1850 after Senator Thomas Hart Benton (1782-1858) of Missouri. A local history implies the first store in Benton was established in the early 1900s. Still another origin for the name Benton involves a combination of the names Bentley and Denton. Mr. Bentley and Allen Denton were both prominent farmers in the area, and both were eager to have the town located on their land. A Mrs. Sigman, the locality's storekeeper, was responsible for having the townsite located on Denton's land. She travelled to Saskatoon and convinced the Canadian Pacific Railway to locate loading platforms, sidings, etc., where the locality is presently situated.

Benton was the name of the group of stores, etc. at the railway facilities, and the post office (1912-68) was named Benton Station.

Berry Creek (creek)
72 L/13 - Wardlow
4-22-13-W4
50°50'N 111°37'W
Flows south into Red Deer River, approximately 109 km north-west of Medicine Hat

(see Berry Lakes)

Berry Creek (locality)
72 M/5 - Sunnynook
36-28-12-W4
51°27'N 111°35'W
Approximately 79 km east of Drumheller.

The post office operated from 1910 to 1953 and the Municipal District was established in 1912. The precise origin for the name of this feature is unknown.

Berry Creek Reservoir (reservoir)
72 M/5 - Sunnynook
10-26-12-W4
51°17'N 111°36'W
Approximately 80 km south-east of Drumheller.

This reservoir was named for its proximity to Berry Creek.

Berry Lakes (lakes)
72 M/3 - Big Stone
32-24-11-W4
51°05'N 111°30'W
Approximately 92 km south-east of Drumheller.

The precise origin for the name of this feature is unknown.

Berrywater Lake (lake)
82 I/11 - Arrowwood
12-18-23-W4
50°30'N 113°03'W

Approximately 90 km south-east of Calgary.

The Blackfoot name for this body of water is *mene oke*, translating to "sweet water." A war party drank at this location when they were suffering from thirst. It is unclear how the name was actually derived.

Beveridge Lake (lake)
82 P/7 - Drumheller
13-29-21,22-W4
51°29'N 112°57'W
Approximately 20 km west of Drumheller.

This lake was named after a Mr. Beveridge. In 1887, he and his partner, Mr. Ingles, brought up 3,500 sheep from Montana because of the range wars between cattlemen and sheepmen over grazing land in the United States. Both individuals were held in high personal regard, hence the naming of the lake which is now dry for most of the year.

Beynon (locality)
82 P/7 - Drumheller
29-27-20-W4
51°20'N 112°47'W
Approximately 15 km south-west of Drumheller.

Originally the name of the post office named after the first postmaster, Hugh Beynon Biggs. He was born in India, received his education in England, and came to Canada in 1892. Biggs, together with some friends, took up squatters' rights to some land of which he later assumed ownership on Rosebud Creek. He called his holding *Springfield Ranch* and it became the scene of many social events of the area. When the railroad came through, the siding was named Beynon. He died in 1914. (from *The Rosebud Trail*, J.J. Martin, 1963)

Big Coulee Creek (creek)

82 O/7 - Wildcat Hills
28-28-6-W5
51°25'N 114°47'W
Flows north into Little Red Deer River, approximately 65 km north-west of Calgary.

The name for this creek is locally well-established although the precise origin is unknown.

Big Hill (hill)

82 O/1 - Calgary
25,26-3-W5
51°12'N 114°20'W
Approximately 20 km north-west of Calgary.

The name for this hill, located along the banks of the Bow River, is descriptive. Its Blackfoot name is *manachaban*. This term, when literally translated, is "the place from which bows are taken," which refers to the nearby Bow River.

Big Hill Springs Provincial Park

(provincial park)
82 O/1 - Calgary
29-26-3-W5
51°15'N 114°23'W
Approximately 30 km north-west of Calgary.

This 25.47 hectare (62.94 acre) park was created by Order-in-council 568/79, and derives its name from the prominent hill in the area (see Big Hill). The First Nations people drove bison over a jump located on Big Hill and they camped at a spring of fresh water where ample wood and shelter were found in the coulee that eventually became part of the park.

Big Jim Creek (creek)

82 J/1 - Langford Creek
29-14-1-W5
50°12'N 114°7'W

Flows south into Willow Creek, approximately 45 km north-west of Claresholm.

This creek, officially named 3 December 1941, carries the name of a notorious character who arrived in the area in 1884. "Big Jim" McDonagh was a burly blacksmith. His first job was working for the Quorn Ranch, then the Keystone on High River, but he then sold out, moved, and started the Cottonwood Ranch with some horses and three hundred head of cattle. During the course of his ownership, three men who had previously been in his employ mysteriously disappeared. In 1898, "Big Jim" met his death when his horse fell on him. H.N. Sheppard bought the Cottonwood Ranch in 1899, and when he was looking around, he found a strange box in the attic. It was large, about six feet long, and was half filled with quicklime. Lime was a substance which was used sparingly around the ranch for chinking up log buildings, but the quantity found in that attic could not possibly have been all used for that purpose. The interesting point about this fact is that quicklime is rumoured to have the potency to eat up a body. Nothing was ever proved against "Big Jim."

■ **Big Rock** (glacial erratic)

82 J/9 - Turner Valley
1-21-20-1-W5
50°42'N 114°04'W
Approximately 35 km south of Calgary.

The Big Rock is the largest member of the Foothills Erratics Train, and its name is most likely descriptive. The name of the nearby town of Okotoks is derived from the Blackfoot word *okatok* meaning "big rock."

Big Stone (locality)

72 M/3 - Big Stone
10-26-9-W4
51°12'N 111°12'W

Approximately 107 km east south-east of Drumheller.

Named after a nearby creek that is descriptively named for the big rocks in it. The post office was opened in 1911 and was closed in 1986.

Bighill Creek (creek)

82 O/1 - Calgary
34-25,26-4-W5
51°11'N 114°29'W
Flows south-west into Bow River, approximately 25 km north-west of Calgary.

This creek takes its name from its position below Big Hill, where it flows into the Bow River. (see Big Hill)

Bigspring Creek (creek)

82 O/1 - Calgary
21-26-2-W5
51°14'N 114°13'W
Flows east into West Nose Creek, approximately 21 km north-west of Calgary.

This name for this creek is descriptive and is taken from a big spring which was found at the site of the Jack Baldock ranch.

Bindloss (hamlet)

72 L/16 - Bindloss
19-22-2-W4
50°52'N 110°16'W
Approximately 95 km north of Medicine Hat.

This hamlet was surveyed by the Canadian Pacific Railway 4 January 1915 and both it and the nearby station were named after Harold Bindloss (1866-1945), British author of "western" novels including *The Protector*, *Fireside Folks*, and *Right of Way*. He spent some time in western Canada but returned to England in 1896 where he remained the rest of his life. The post office was established 15 March 1916.

Bingen (post office)
72 E/6 - Foremost
16-6-10-W4
49°29'N 111°16'W
Approximately 75 km south-west of
Medicine Hat.

The post office opened 1 February 1913
and operated until 1 January 1916 and was
named after a town in Germany possibly
due to the number of German settlers in the
area. The name of the town was changed to
Nemiskam in 1916. (see Nemiskam)

*Bingville (former locality)
72 L/7 - Watching Hill
17-7-W4
50°28'N 110°52'W
Approximately 50 km north of Medicine
Hat.

The name for this former locality was
derived from the comic strip *Bingville
Bugle*. When, in 1912, residents decided to
pick a name for their community, two
pretty names were suggested, and the
names were put into a hat. Two newcomers
from Spokane, Washington wanted a say in
the matter, but the only name they could
come up with on the spur of the moment
was Bingville, from the comic strip running
in their hometown paper. The name
Bingville was drawn out of the hat and was
thus accepted as the community name.

Bircham (hamlet)
82 P/6 - Carbon
3-29-25-W4
51°27'N 113°25'W
Approximately 60 km north-east of
Calgary.

Bircham was a siding and flag station on the
Grand Trunk Pacific Line which came

through in 1913-14. It was likely named
after Bircham, King's Lynn, England. The
name first appears as Brecham in 1174, and
means "newly cultivated land" (Ekwall).
Another version for the origin of the name
refers to the grove of birch trees located
north of here. A post office operated at this
site from 1 April 1925 through 12 October
1966.

Birdseye Butte (hill)
82 H/4 - Waterton Lakes
1-2-29-W4
49°05'N 113°45'W
Approximately 45 km south south-east of
Pincher Creek.
The name was officially applied to this
feature 8 June 1971. It may be because there
is a "bird's eye view" from its summit. No
other origin information is available for this
locally well-established name.

Black Coulee (coulee)
72 E/3 - Aden
1,2-11-W4
49°05'N 111°28'W
Flows north into Milk River, approximately 120 km south south-east of Medicine Hat.

The precise origin for the name of this
feature is unknown. It is also known locally
as "Dead Horse Coulee."

Black Diamond (town)
82 J/9 - Turner Valley
8-20-2-W5
50°42'N 114°14'W
Approximately 3 km east south-east of
Turner Valley.

The post office opened on this site in 1907,
but needed a name. The town got its
current name literally drawn out of a hat.
The General Store, which was to become
the post office, was run by the Arnold
brothers who suggested the name

"Arnoldville." Addison McPherson opened
a coal mine on the west bank of Sheep
River called the *Black Diamond Coal Mine*
and he thought the post office should be
called "Black Diamond," after the coal beds
in the vicinity. Both names were put into a
hat, and one was drawn by an old Indian in
the area. The town, when incorporated
1 January 1956, became Black Diamond.

Blackfoot Crossing (crossing)
82 I/15 - Cluny
9-21-21-W4
50°46'N 112°50'W
Approximately 85 km east south-east of
Calgary, in Blackfoot Indian Reserve #146.
This crossing on the Bow River is known as
soi-a-pohk-we by the Blackfoot which
translates "ridge under water." Apparently
this crossing has always had a good ford.
Many Indian tribes including the Blackfoot,
Blood, Peigan, Sarcee, and Stoney among
others, made a treaty with the Dominion
Government, 22 September, 1877. Sandford
Fleming (1827-1915), the Canadian Pacific
Survey's chief engineer, noted in his 1880
report, the excellent soil quality at this
crossing, continuing on to Fort Calgary.
(see Blackfoot Indian Reserve #146)

Blackfoot Indian Reserve #146
(Indian reserve)
82 I/15 - Picture Butte
21-22-W4
50°45'N 112°55'W
Approximately 75 km east south-east of
Calgary.

Named after the Blackfoot Indians, the
Peigan, Blood and Blackfoot proper, which
when combined, make up the Blackfoot
confederacy. It is commonly believed that
they derived their name from the discoloration of their moccasins from the ashes of
prairie fires. One interesting legend
regarding the origin of the Blackfoot tribe
is as follows: three sons were born to a

mighty chief. One he named Kainah, or "the blood," the second he named Peaginour, or "the wealth" and the third he left nameless. This third lad was scorned by all because of his lack of skill in the buffalo hunt, and came to his father asking for help. Touched by his son's predicament, the old man blacked the young man's feet with a charred stick from the fire and stated: "My son, you have suffered long; today I will make you a mighty hunter." As such, Sastquia (or Siksika), the Blackfoot became a successful hunter and mighty leader. His descendents formed the Blackfoot tribe, while the descendents of his two brothers established the Blood and Peigan tribes.

Blackie (village)

82 I/12 - Gleichen
13-19-27-W4
50°36′N 113°37′W
Approximately 50 km south south-east of Calgary.

This village was named by an admirer of John Stuart Blackie (1809-1895), a Scottish professor, novelist and founder of the publishing firm, Blackie and Sons. Educated at Marischal College, Aberdeen, and Edinburgh, Göttingen and Berlin universities, Blackie taught at Aberdeen and Edinburgh. The post office here opened 1 May 1911 and was named after this well-liked savant. Several of the village's street names reflect the extent of Blackie's popularity. There are, for example, Stuart, Aberdeen, Edinburgh and Marischal streets. The community also had strong Scottish origins which are commemorated in street names such as Glasgow and Burns streets.

Blackspring Ridge (ridge)

82 I/2 - Gleichen
12,13-22-W4
50°04′N 112°57′W

---

*denotes rescinded name or former locality.

Approximately 35 km north of Lethbridge.

The descriptive term for this ridge in Blackfoot is *sicehkiscon*, translating to "black springwater" because the ground was black where the water emerged. The ridge, which extends in a north-south direction, was surveyed in 1883 by Magrath (see Magrath), and commands a fine view of the surrounding countryside.

* Blacktail (former locality)

82 I/4 - Claresholm
26-13-29-W4
50°07′N 113°51′W
Approximately 87 km north-west of Lethbridge.

Named for the one-time abundance of Blacktail deer in the area. Some local residents, however, feel that the name was derived from the very dark, black forest in the area. Prior to the post office opening 1 July 1913 under the name Blacktail, this community was known as "Willows."

Blacktail Coulee (coulee)

82 I/4 - Claresholm
27-13-29-W4
50°07′00″N 113°53′30″W
Runs north into Willow Creek, approximately 90 km north-west of Lethbridge.

Named by rancher and first postmaster Tom Boulton, about 1907, for his Blacktail Ranch. Many mule deer were found in the coulee. In 1914 the Boultons moved to the south side of Willow Creek where they continued to operate the Blacktail Post Office from their ranch house. (see Blacktail)

*Blayney (former post office)

82 H/14 - Monarch
16-12-23-W4
50°00′N 113°05′W
Approximately 35 km north-west of Lethbridge.

(see Barons)

Blizzard Lake (lake)

82 I/13 - Dalemead
12-21-28-W4
50°46′N 113°46′W
Approximately 20 km south-east of Calgary.

This lake was named during the mid-1880s by Fred and Will James, the original homesteaders on the land next to it. They endured a severe blizzard on their first night, in a tent, on Fred's land. This inspired them to name the lake. The name first appeared on the Dominion Lands Office map dated April 1885.

Blood Indian Creek (creek)

72 L/14 - Halsbury
33-22-8-W4
50°55′N 111°03′W
Flows south into Red Deer River, approximately 98 km north north-west of Medicine Hat.

At the turn of the century, a 75-year-old woman passed on a story which may give the origin of the name. This "Old Woman" was of the Salteaux tribe, whose band had come west from the Lake of the Woods. The following incident occurred circa 1840: a raiding party of Blackfoot, plundering horse herds, attacked their camp and many of the Salteaux were killed. Three of her sons were among the victims and in her sorrow and anger, she organized a party of vengeance. The "Old Woman" and her war party caught up to the raiders at the mouth of the present Blood Indian Creek at an encampment where the Vee Bar Vee buildings now stand. The enemy were overwhelmed by a surprise attack and also outnumbered. The pursuing Salteaux fell upon the camp with a fierce, bloody attack. The routed remnants tried to escape across the Red Deer River, but the pursuers followed them into the river where all but a handful were killed or drowned in a ferocious hand battle. The creek literally ran red with the blood of the slain Blackfoot. Thus Blood Indian Creek received its name.

Blood Indian Creek Reservoir (reservoir)

72 M/3 - Big Stone
21-26-9-W4
51°15′N 111°13′W
Approximately 105 km south-east of Drumheller.

Named after the Blood Indians. (see Blood Indian Creek)

Blood Indian Reserve #148

(Indian reserve)
82 H/6 - Raley
6-5-24-W4
49°25′N 113°10′W
Approximately 40 km south-east of Pincher Creek.

Appointed in 1883, this is the largest reserve in Canada. It is named after the Blood Indians; the derivation of the name is in doubt, though several explanations have been recorded. (see Blood Indian Creek)

Blood Indian Reserve #148 A

(Indian reserve)
82 H/4 - Waterton Lakes
17-1-28-W4
49°03′N 113°42′W
Approximately 50 km south-east of Pincher Creek.

(see Blood Indian Reserve #148)

Bond Coulee (coulee)

72 E/2 - Comrey
34-3-7-W4
49°16′N 110°52′W
Runs north-east into Coal Creek, approximately 90 km south of Medicine Hat.

This coulee contains a creek which joins Coal Creek. It was named for Adam Bond who settled in close proximity to the coulee in the Pendant d'Oreille area circa 1909. Adam Bond applied for the water rights to the creek.

Boneyard Coulee (coulee)

82 I/4 - Claresholm
8-14-28-W4
50°07′40″N 113°47′00″W
A north-south trending coulee, approximately 85 km north-west of Lethbridge. The name for this coulee is descriptive, and reflects the accumulation of bones in the coulee at the base of an old buffalo jump on the north-west side of Table Butte. The native Indians killed the animals en masse by herding and driving them over the steep cliff.

Bonn Hill (hill)

82 J/16 - Priddis
21-23-2-W5
50°59′N 114°13′W
Approximately 4 km west of Calgary, in the Camp Sarcee Military Reserve.

The precise origin for the name of this feature is unknown.

Bottrel (hamlet)

82 O/8 - Crossfield
21-28-4-W5
51°25′N 114°30′W
Approximately 50 km north-west of Calgary.

Edward Botterel was an early settler who arrived in the area circa 1888. The post office here operated from 1 December 1909 through 31 March 1969, and was named after Mr. Botterel despite the erroneous spelling at its adoption. The error was never corrected and the current spelling is locally used.

Boundary Creek (creek)

82 H/3 - Cardston
1-1-26-W4
49°00′00″N 113°22′00″W
Flows into the U.S.A., approximately 87 km south-west of Lethbridge.

The descriptive name for this feature refers to the fact that it crosses the international border between Canada and the United States. The name has been in use since at least 1898.

* Boundary Creek (former locality)

82 H/3 - Cardston
30-1-26-W4
49°04′N 113°28′W
Approximately 83 km south-west of Lethbridge.

(see Boundary Creek)

Bow City (hamlet)

82 I/8 - Scandia
14-17-17-W4
50°26′N 112°14′W
Approximately 92 km north-east of Lethbridge.

This locality was originally known as "Eyremore" (the combination of the names of the first postmaster, W.T.P. Eyres and his wife, whose maiden name was Moore). This post office was in operation from 15 December 1908 through 23 August 1958. The locality derived its present name from its location on the banks of the Bow River (see Bow River). Frank and Ed Herrick knew of the large coal deposits along the banks of the Bow since the turn of the century. They mined it on a small scale and sold the coal for a dollar per ton to the local squatters. When the area was opened up for settlement in 1907, knowledge of the large seam of coal spread rapidly. Speculators flocked to the area, and from 1909 to 1914, lots in the locality were selling for $1,000. Shares were being sold by several large

---

*denotes rescinded name or former locality.

companies all over Canada, in the United States and in Britain. Plans for the construction of railroad lines leading to Hudson Bay and into the United States were drafted, as were grandiose plans for the "city." It appeared as if Albertans were on the verge of witnessing the rapid evolution of another major city like Edmonton or Calgary. With the onset of World War I, capital dried up. The area was briefly revitalized in 1932 by the Montreal-based Charles Westgate Company, and again with the onset of World War II. Massive quantities of coal were needed for the production of war materials, but after the war, natural gas and fuel oil became the main fuels. As the use of coal phased out, so too did the aspirations of many business people and Bow City residents. The post office here closed 4 November 1966.

Bow Island (island)

72 E/13 - Grassy Lake
22-11-13-W4
49°56'N 111°41'W
Approximately 85 km east of Lethbridge.

Bow Island, ca. 1909

This island was named for its location at the end of the Bow River, at the confluence of the Bow and Oldman rivers, which collectively become the South Saskatchewan River. This same feature is known

locally as "Spook Island" for several reasons. One story has it that Indians killed two prospectors encamped on the island. Another story posits that the North West Mounted Police hung several horse thieves on the island, due to a lack of suitable trees elsewhere. Yet another possible origin of the local name is that it was a sacred place to the Indians since a large number of Indian graves can be found throughout the valley.

(see Bow River)

Bow Island (town)

72 E/14 - Bow Island
36-10-11-W4
49°52'N 111°22'W
Approximately 54 km south-west of Medicine Hat.

This island was named after the Bow River, and according to old-timers a mistake was made in the naming of the town. The Bow and Belly rivers joined north of the village of Grassy Lake and the town of Bow Island was originally planned where the village of Grassy Lake now stands. Local tradition posits that two women in imminent danger of spinsterhood put a concerted effort into winning the hearts of two men. At their arrival into the town one said that she was "out to win a Fred." The other retorted, in an equally determined manner, "before you do a beau I'll land."

Bow River (river)

72 E/13 - Grassy Lake
22-11-13-W4
49°57'N 111°41'W
Flows south-west into South Saskatchewan River, approximately 86 km east of Lethbridge.

This feature was known to the Cree Indians as *ma-na-cha-ban sipi* , meaning Bow River. They called it this due to the growth of Douglas Fir along its banks, which they used for making bows. The French called

this feature "Rivière des Arcs," referring to the crescent course which the Bow and South Saskatchewan rivers follow. This name also applied to the frequent curves found throughout the upper regions of this river's course. The first French explorers to travel this system of rivers did so in 1752, and built Fort la Jonquière, not far from the modern town of Calgary. David Thompson dispatched four men from Rocky Mountain House in 1800 to ascend the river. North West, Hudson's Bay and XY Fur Company officials soon followed suit in order to secure trade with the Blackfoot. The Bow River appeared on the 1801 Arrowsmith map as "Askow" or "Bad River," but by the time the 1822 edition was published, this feature was cited as the Bow or "Askow River."

Bow River, 1907

Bowell (hamlet)

72 L/2 - Medicine Hat
6-14-7-W4
50°08'N 110°57'W
Approximately 21 km north-west of Medicine Hat.

This Canadian Pacific Railway station took its name after Sir Mackenzie Bowell (1823-1917), Federal Minister of Customs, when this community was named in 1884. He was born at Rickinghall, Suffolk, England on 27

December 1823. Bowell came to Canada with his parents in 1833 and began working in a printing office at an early age, eventually becoming a newspaper editor and proprietor. In 1867 he was elected to the House of Commons as a Conservative for the riding of North Hastings, Ontario. He was appointed to the Cabinet in 1878 as Minister of Customs as well as being responsible for the overall coordination and implementation of the National Policy. In the government of Sir John Abbott, Bowell served as Minister of Militia, and in the government of Sir John Thompson, he was appointed Minister of Trade and Commerce. Following the death of Prime Minister Sir John Thompson in 1894, Bowell was chosen as his successor. Serious dissatisfaction with Bowell's leadership came to a head in January 1896 when a number of Cabinet Ministers resigned. He resigned as Prime Minister in April of that same year. Bowell was appointed to the Senate in 1892 where he remained until 1906.

Bowmanton (locality)

72 L/1 - Many Island Lake
4-15-14-W4
50°13′N 110°29′W
Approximately 28 km north-east of Medicine Hat.

The post office here was opened 13 October 1913 and closed 6 January 1958. It was named after Mrs. Whitson, nee Bowman, the wife of a local farmer.

Bowness (locality)

82 O/1 - Calgary
35-24-2-W5
51°05′N 114°10′W
Within the city limits of Calgary.

The name for this place, now incorporated into the city of Calgary, may have been taken after Mr. E.W. Bowness, of Canadian Utilities. A post office operated from

2 January 1942 through 24 April 1961 under this name. Another theory for the origin of the name is that the Hon. William Beresford, the individual who bought land in the valley in 1903, was the first to apply the name, after one of his estates in England which was called the "Crag, Bowness." Others insist that the name Bowness was in use before 1903. Still others maintain that the area was named after the "Bowness Ranch," a name used at least as far back as 1896. The land was described as being "south of Bow Island," referring to the large island in the river which is now Bowness Park. Prior to 1942, the post office at the site was called "Critchley."

Boxelder Creek (creek)

72 L/1 - Many Island Lake
1-13-1-W4
50°05′N 110°02′W
Flows north into Island Lake, approximately 45 km east of Medicine Hat.

Named for the Boxelder Maple Trees that grow in the vicinity and along the banks of this creek. Boxelder Maple is also called Manitoba Maple which is a type of North American maple tree found west of the Canadian Shield, in southern Ontario, and east of the Rocky Mountains.

Bradshaw (locality)

82 H/7 - Raymond
6-5-22-W4
49°22′N 112°56′W
Approximately 50 km south south-west of Lethbridge.

Named for Richard William Bradshaw and his brother John Franklin Bradshaw who arrived in the Magrath area in 1901 and were early ranchers and homesteaders. The Bradshaw brothers were instrumental in persuading the Canadian Pacific Railway to establish a siding at this point which was later named for them.

Brant (hamlet)

82 I/12 - Gleichen
16-18-26-W4
50°31′N 113°30′W
Approximately 63 km south-east of Calgary.

Named in 1905 by its founder, E. E. Thomson of High River, this community takes its name from the Brant geese, large numbers of which were found in the vicinity that year. The Brant goose (genus *Branta*) is one of two main groups of geese, the other of which is known as the true goose (genus *Anser*). The taxonomy at the specific and subspecific level is very complicated: there are seven species of geese in North America, most of which breed in the boreal forest and tundra. Brant geese are divided into four populations, one of which inhabits the lower British Columbia mainland and the Queen Elizabeth Islands. The other three reside in Baja California, the coastal tundra of the Northwest Territories, and the Fox Basin off the coast of New Jersey.

Bratton Coulee (creek)

82 H/12 - Brocket
10-9-29-W4
49°43′N 113°51′W
Runs south-west into Beaver Creek, approximately 73 km west of Lethbridge.

Named for T.G. Bratton, who in the early 1900s owned the land through which this creek flows. At one time, this early homesteader applied for the water rights for this feature.

Bratton Spring (spring)

82 H/12 - Brocket
15-9-29-W4
49°44′N 113°51′W
Approximately 75 km west of Lethbridge.

(see Bratton Coulee)

Breast Work Hill (hill)

82 H/3 - Cardston
20,21-3-26-W4
49°14′N 113°27′W
Approximately 69 km south-west of Lethbridge.

A breast work is a hastily constructed wall of stones or other materials that is usually about chest high. This hill may be named descriptively, referring to either a natural aspect of this feature which resembles a breast work, or to an actual breast work which may have been located nearby at some point in the past.

Breed Creek (creek)

72 E/3 - Aden
28-2-10-W4
49°09′N 111°17′W
Flows north across the U.S. border, approximately 105 km south-west of Medicine Hat.

This feature was originally known as Halfbreed Creek, but the name was officially changed in March 1964 to avoid the discriminatory nature of the term.

Brickburn (railway point)

82 O/1 - Calgary
24-24-2-W5
51°04′N 114°10′W
Within the city limits of Calgary.

A Canadian Pacific Railway station was established here in 1914, and was descriptively named after the brick kilns located in the vicinity. The post office was opened 15 August 1910 and operated until 31 October 1914.

Brocket (hamlet)

82 H/12 - Brocket
8-7-28-W4
49°34′N 113°44′W
Approximately 15 km north-east of Pincher Creek.

A Canadian Pacific Railway station was established here in 1897-98 and was named after Brocket Hall, seat of Lord Mount Stephens, Hatfield, Herts, England. Stephens was a former Director of the railway company.

Brooks (town)

72 L/12 - Brooks
32-18-14-W4
50°35′N 111°53′W
Approximately 100 km north-west of Medicine Hat.

The townsite belonged to the Canadian Pacific Railway and in 1904 consisted of the stockyards, a boxcar that had been moved in for a station and Cooker's store. This cowtown had no name but when the Department of Postal Affairs decided to open a post office, a name had to be chosen. The name Brooks was chosen from a list of suggestions sent in by the department. So it was under the name of Brooks that the first post office was opened on 1 December 1904. The town was named after Noel Edgall Brooks, who was a Divisional Engineer in the C.P.R. at Calgary from 1903 to 1913. He had been asked to send his name in as suitable for the name of the town.

Brooks Hill (hill)

82 O/7 - Wildcat Hills
10-27-6-W5
51°19′N 114°43′W
Approximately 57 km west north-west of Calgary.

Frank Brooks was born in 1882 in Devon, England. He came to this district in 1902 and opened a local mill. The name was proposed for this feature 20 March 1931 and subsequently was adopted.

Brosten Reservoir (reservoir)

72 M/6 - Plover Lake
4-28-8-W4
51°22′N 111°04′W
Approximately 113 km east of Drumheller.

The precise origin for the name of this feature is unknown.

Broxburn (locality)

82 H/10 - Lethbridge
6-9-20-W4
49°43′N 112°42′W
Approximately 5 km east of Lethbridge.

This locality was named circa 1910 for either Broxburn, West Lothian Scotland, or Broxburn, East Lothian (now all Lothian) Scotland.

Brush Coulee (coulee)

72 L/10 - Easy Coulee
10-19-5-W4
50°36′N 110°37′W
Approximately 60 km north of Medicine Hat.

The name is likely descriptive of the brush that was at one time found in the area.

Brush Flats (flat)

72 L/7 - Watching Hill
13-3-W4
50°15′N 110°37′W
Approximately 30 km north of Medicine Hat.

The name for these flats is likely descriptive of the surrounding area.

Brutus (post office)

72 L/6 - Alderson
14-17-8-W4
50°25′N 111°08′W
Approximately 45 km north-west of Medicine Hat.

This former post office was named after the home town of the first postmaster, Jonas Brubacher, who hailed from Brutus, Michigan.

Bryant Coulee (creek)

72 E/3 - Aden
12-3-9-W4
49°12'N 111°05'W
Runs north-west into Pakowki Lake, approximately 93 km south south-west of Medicine Hat.

This feature was named for A.G. Bryant and family, early homesteaders who came to this region in 1909-10 from North Dakota. The coulee runs through the land they once owned. Mr. Bryant had applied for the water rights to this land.

Buffalo (hamlet)

72 L/15 - Buffalo
30-21-5-W4
50°48'N 110°40'W
Approximately 85 km north of Medicine Hat.

The hamlet was established when the Canadian Pacific Railway built a station here in 1914. It took the name suggested by Mr. Pauling, a resident living just east of the townsite who hailed from Buffalo, New York. A post office was established here 1 February 1920, which was believed to be named for the animal.

Buffalo Bird Hill (hill)

72 M/2 - Cappon
13-11-26-5-W4
51°12'45"N 110°36'10"W
Approximately 136 km north of Medicine Hat.

Named for "Buffalo Bird" Joe LeHure, who lived directly north of this hill. This man was locally well-known and owned land in the immediate vicinity from 1919. It is rumoured that this hill is where the last buffalo was killed within the region.

Buffalo Hill (hill)

82 I/11 - Arrowwood
8-19-23-W4
50°37'N 113°08'W

Approximately 75 km south-east of Calgary.

Local folklore has it that the herds of buffalo used to come to these hills to take shelter from the winter wind. The area is commonly referred to as the Buffalo Hills rather than the official singular version. A number of local histories of the area including *Gleichen Call*, *Arrowwood, A Dunkard Community*, *Furrows of Time*, and *Round up the Fun in the Foothills*, use the plural form. Alberta Sectional Maps #115, (1915) as well as the 1921 edition show it as Buffalo Hill, although these appear to be three distinct hills or high points. There is some local usage for the name "Wyatt Hill" apparently after Frank Wyatt, an early resident of the area. According to the history of the Eastway district, *Trails to Highways*, the Medicine Ring and Signal Ground on Buffalo Hill is now known as "Wyatt Hill." This medicine ring is 120 feet in diameter and apparently was used by Plains Indians and is believed to be the largest medicine ring in America.

Buffalo Lake (lake)

72 E/10 - Bulls Head
2-8-5-W4
49°37'N 110°35'W
Approximately 42 km south of Medicine Hat.

This lake is likely named for the large herds of bison that were once found in the area. Based on the large number of bones found, it is likely that this was once a favourite hunting ground of the Plains Indians.

Bull Springs Coulee (coulee)

72 L/8 - Hilda
12-17-3,4-W4
50°25'N 110°25'W
Runs north into South Saskatchewan River, approximately 45 km north of Medicine Hat.

Named because ranchers in the area used the spring that flows year-round through the coulee, to water their bulls.

Bullhead Hill (hill)

82 J/16 - Priddis
30-23-2-W5
51°0'N 114°16'W
Approximately 20 km west of Calgary.

This hill is located within the Sarcee Indian Reserve #145, and its name is likely descriptive.

Bullhorn Coulee (coulee)

82 H/6 - Raley
12-4-26-W4
49°18'N 113°22'W
Flows north-east into Layton Creek, approximately 60 km south-west of Lethbridge.

The Blackfoot name for this feature is *pomepisan*, which translates to "Grease Pound Creek." This creek received this name because a buffalo pound was built here and the meat of buffalo killed here was boiled for grease.

Bullpound (locality)

72 M/4 - Pollockville
35-24-15-W4
51°05'N 111°59'W
Approximately 60 km south-east of Drumheller.

A large corral was built on the Parker Ranch for the boarding of bulls after the breeding season. Jim and Ed Parker, with the help of one Mr. Burkell, constructed it on a suitable spot close to an unnamed creek. The creek eventually came to take on the name Bullpound Creek, and when a Canadian Pacific Railway station was constructed in the area, the name was officially adopted for it.

Bullpound Creek (creek)

72 M/4 - Pollockville
25-24-15-W5
51°04′N 111°58′W
Flows south into Red Deer River, approximately 65 km south-east of Drumheller.

(see Bullpound)

Bulls Head (butte)

72 E/10 - Bulls Head
11-8-7-W4
49°38′N 110°52′W
Approximately 45 km south-west of Medicine Hat.

The Blackfoot Indians called this feature *in-e-oto-ka*, translating literally as "buffalo head." It is shaped like the head of a large animal, either a bull or a buffalo.

Bullshead (locality)

72 E/15 - Seven Persons
22-11-6-W4
49°55′N 110°45′W
Approximately 10 km south of Medicine Hat.

Named after the prominent butte in the vicinity. (see Bulls Head)

Bullshead Creek (creek)

72 L/2 - Medicine Hat
2-12-5-W4
50°00′N 110°37′W
Flows north into Ross Creek, at the south-west city limits of Medicine Hat.

(see Bulls Head)

Bullshead Hill (hill)

72 E/10 - Bullshead
8-6-W4
49°48′N 110°55′W
Approximately 45 km south of Medicine Hat.

(see Bulls Head)

Bunn's Ford (ford)

82 H/15 - Picture Butte
NE1/4-9-12-19-W4
49°59′10″N 112°32′00″W
Approximately 35 km north-east of Lethbridge.

This ford was frequently used as a river crossing before the Turin bridge was built. The ford was conveniently named after John Bunn, who owned the homestead near this ford.

Burdett (village)

72 E/13 - Grassy Lake
23-10-12-W4
49°50′N 111°32′W
Approximately 63 km west south-west of Medicine Hat.

Named after Georgina Baroness Burdett-Coutts, who was one of the principal shareholders in a narrow-gauge railway operating throughout southern Alberta. The Baroness was born in 1814 and inherited a vast fortune from her step-grandmother, the Duchess of St. Albans, making her the "richest heiress in England," enjoying fame second only to Queen Victoria. She received a peerage from the Queen in 1871, and eventually married a young American who was an Oxford graduate and thirty-seven years younger than herself. By royal licence he assumed her name. Her wealth assisted in the development of coal mining in southern Alberta where she was a major shareholder in the North Western Coal and Navigation Company. The baroness died in 1906.

* **Burfield** (former locality)

72 M/4 - Pollockville
12-26-15-W4
51°12′N 111°59′W
Approximately 55 km south-east of Drumheller.

Named after the locality's first postmaster, H.E. Burfield.

Burke Creek (creek)

82 H/13 - Granum
7-12-29-W4
49°58′N 113°57′W
Flows north-east into Trout Creek, approximately 85 km north-west of Lethbridge.

This creek was officially named 8 July 1954 after Dennis Charles Burke, a rancher and forest ranger of the area. He was a member of the North West Mounted Police from 1896 to 1901.

Cabin Lake (lake)

72 M/3 - Big Stone
10-24-9-W4
51°02′N 111°10′W
Approximately 115 km south-east of
Drumheller.

One story suggests that Sam Mackay, an
old buffalo hunter, built a cabin near the
lake in the early 1900s for Lord Benesford
of the Old Mexico Ranch located nearby.
Another version of this story posits that a
cabin was built near the lake in 1896 to
serve as a line camp for Gordon, Ironside
and Fare, who had an 18,000 head ranch in
the area. Because of the nearby cabin, the
lake became known to ranchers, cowboys
and local residents as Cabin Lake.

Cabin Lake (locality)

72 M/3 - Big Stone
20-24-9-W4
51°04′N 111°13′W
Approximately 112 km south-east of
Drumheller.

This locality takes its name from the nearby
lake which had an old log cabin on its
shore. (see Cabin Lake)

Cairn Hill (hill)

72 E/13 - Grassy Lake
6-11-12-W4
49°53′N 111°37′W
Approximately 87 km east of Lethbridge.

Maps dated as early as 1885 indicate the
existence of an Indian cairn atop this hill.

Cairn Hill (hill)

82 O/1 - Calgary
24-2-W5
51°01′N 114°10′W
Within the city limits of Calgary.

The precise origin for the name of this
feature is unknown.

* **Caldbeck** (former locality)

82 O/7 - Wildcat Hills
14-27-5-W5
51°19′N 114°36′W
Approximately 48 km north-west of
Calgary.

A post office was established here 1 June
1913 and was named after the town of
Caldbeck in Cumberland (now Cumbria),
England. It is suggested that it is the home
of John Peel of hunting song fame. The
song was written circa 1820 by one of Peel's
friends, as they sat chatting before the fire
at Caldbeck one winter evening. The name
is first reported in 1060 as *Caldebek*
(Ekwall) and means "cold brook."

* **Caldwell** (former locality)

82 H/4 - Waterton Lakes
35-2-28-W4
49°10′N 113°38′W
Approximately 80 km south-west of
Lethbridge.

Named after the first postmaster, D.H.
Caldwell who was one of a number of the
Mormon Caldwells who came to this area
from Utah in the 1880s and 1890s. The post
office was in operation from 1900 through
1968, even though the hopes of the village
had died when the railway bypassed the
settlement in favour of Hillspring to where
a number of the original inhabitants of
Caldwell moved.

Calendula (post office)

72 M/8 - Sibbald
17-29-2-W4
51°29′N 110°10′W
Approximately 160 km north north-east of
Medicine Hat.

Named after the marigold, or other plant of
genus *Calendula*, with large yellow or
orange flowers. Perhaps these flowers were
found in abundance in this area at the time
of its naming. The post office was opened
in 1913.

Calgary (city)

82 O/1 - Calgary
24-1-W5
51°03′N 114°05′W
Approximately 297 km south of Edmonton.

Calgary, 1912

This city was so named in 1876 by Lieutenant-Colonel James Farquharson Macleod of
the North West Mounted Police. It is the
name of the ancestral estate of his cousins,
the MacKenzies, on the Isle of Mull,
Scotland, which he had visited shortly
before. In the fall of 1875, there was trouble
with the Métis and Indians in the Prince
Albert region, and Major-General E. Selby,
commanding the Canadian Militia, was sent

---

*denotes rescinded name or former locality.

from the east to investigate. He travelled across the prairie northwesterly from Winnipeg. Colonel Macleod, as he was known informally, was then in command of the Mounted Police and his headquarters were at Fort Macleod which he had built the previous year (1874). He was advised by telegraph to meet General Selby at Red Deer with fifty men. At this conference, one of the matters agreed upon was that a police post should be established on the Bow River. On his return south, Colonel Macleod sent E Troop under Inspector E.A. Brisebois to erect a barracks on the west side of the Bow River, in the angle between the two rivers, a site evidently selected by Colonel Macleod before he travelled north. The buildings were erected by the I.G. Baker Company, a fur-trading concern which had a trading post of its own in the vicinity but on the east side of the Elbow River. It is said that Inspector Brisebois wished to name the establishment after himself but Colonel Macleod who was then Assistant Commissioner of the Force decided it should be called Calgary. This suggestion was contained in a letter which was transmitted to Ottawa in February 1876 and was approved by the then Minister of Justice, the Honourable Edward Blake. By the end of 1876 there were stationed at Fort Calgary some thirty-seven men. In that year the Hudson's Bay Company opened a trading station close to the site of the Fort with Angus Fraser in charge. By 1 October 1883, a post office had been opened.

It is interesting to note that the Blackfoot name for Calgary was *moll-inistsis-in-aka-apewis*, translating to "elbow many houses," and the Cree name is *O-toos-kwa-nik*, translating to "elbow house." Both obviously refer to the Elbow River. The name Calgary is variously spelled as it appears on the Mackenzie estate on the Isle of Mull. In one account it is spelled *Calgarry* but on a recent map of the Isle of Mull the spelling as used in the Alberta city

is evident. The translation of the Gaelic word is "Clear Running Water."

A Mounted Police report dated 30 December 1876, states that there were stationed at Fort Calgary at that time, one Inspector, one Sub-inspector and thirty-five constables and sub-constables. At this time, there were three structures: a store, a residence for the manager and an interpreter's cabin-which were made of logs floated down the river from the west.

Calib Coulee (creek)

72 E/2 - Comrey
25-3-7-W4
49°14′N 110°50′W
Runs north into Coal Creek, approximately 90 km south of Medicine Hat.

The precise origin for the name of this feature is unknown.

Callum Creek (creek)

82 G/16 - Maycroft
6-10-1-W5
49°48′N 114°07′W
Flows south into Oldman Creek, approximately 95 km west of Lethbridge.

The name for this creek was officially approved 17 December 1941. Its precise origin is unknown.

Campbell Siding (railway siding)

72 L/5 - Tilley
24-26-17-13-W4
50°28′30″N 111°40′25″W
Approximately 84 km north-west of Medicine Hat.

Named 22 November 1979 for Sir Keith Campbell, a former senior executive officer with the Canadian Pacific Railway. Born in Toronto in 1916, Campbell first started with the C.P.R. in 1935, when he had summer jobs with the company, and gradually worked his way up.

Cambria (hamlet)

82 P/7 - Drumheller
15-28-19-W4
51°24′N 112°36′W
Approximately 10 km south-east of Drumheller.

The Cambria mine opened here in 1935. It was owned by Mr. Ned Howle and a Mr. McKonkey. Howle had arrived from Wales, and named the mine after a town there. The Latin name for Wales is *Cambria*, and is used by poets. The post office here operated from 1 September 1942 through 29 November 1969.

Canal Creek (creek)

72 E/7 - Manyberries
3-4-7-W4
49°17′N 110°54′W
Flows north-west into Pakowki Lake, approximately 84 km south of Medicine Hat.

The precise origin for the name of this feature is unknown.

Canalta Slough (marsh)

82 P/1 - Finnegan
15-24-16-W4
51°02′N 112°09′W
Approximately 55 km south-east of Drumheller.

The name for this feature is a combination of the abbreviated forms of the words Canada and Alberta. It was officially approved in 1955.

Canyon Lake (lake)

82 I/4 - Claresholm
13-31-12-28-W4
50°03′00″N 113°49′15″W
Approximately 81 km north-west of Lethbridge.

South-west of Willow Creek Campgrounds, in the north-east corner of the old 44 Ranch there is a basin-like valley which local people call "The Canyon." A steep treed slope can be seen from the main Willow Creek road. At one time this whole area was owned by J.J. Bowlen (one of Alberta's early lieutenant-governors) and was used as a horse ranch. It was originally part of Leed & Elbot Holdings, then Leeds, then sold to a Peter Robins.

Some maps call the area "Cañon Lakes" but local people always refer to it as "The Canyon."

Cappon (locality)
72 M/2 - Cappon
2 25 5 W4
51°06'N 110°36'W
Approximately 123 km north of Medicine Hat.

This locality probably takes its name from the original post office, named by J.W. Jake for Professor Cappon (1854-1924) of Queen's University. Jake himself was a B.A. graduate of Queen's, and was the first in a line of family postmasters who ran the post office from 1 November 1912 through 12 June 1968.

Carbon (village)
82 P/6 - Carbon
15-29-23-W4
51°29'N 113°09'W
Approximately 75 km north-east of Calgary.

Ranchers settled in the area as early as the 1880s and the first settlers were likely Captain William Thorburn and his brother Dave, and the Wyndhams, who arrived circa 1882. The first coal mines also had their beginnings around this time. Carbon remained primarily a ranching and coal mining area (hence the name) until 1904, when homesteaders began arriving. Farm-ing then began to take the place of ranch-ing. 1 October 1904 saw the opening of the post office, operated by Mr. E. J. C. Davey. On 18 August 1905, a townsite was surveyed on the Kneehill Coal Company property, and development began. The name for the community was "Kneehill" for a span, but the descriptive name, Carbon, suggested by a local farmer, John M. Bogart, replaced it. The Canadian Pacific Railway line arrived in 1920.

Carcass Hill (hill)
82 I/13 - Dalemead
23-26-W4
50°57'N 113°31'W
Approximately 25 km east of Calgary.

The precise origin for the name of this feature, in use since at least 1928, is un-known. It may possibly be descriptive of buffalo carcasses strewn nearby.

Cardston (town)
82 H/3 - Cardston
9-3-25-W4
49°12'N 113°18'W
Approximately 65 km south south-west of Lethbridge.

Named for Charles Ora Card (1839-1906), son-in-law of Brigham Young, who came to the present site of Cardston, on Lees Creek in 1886 from Utah, to establish a new home for members of the Church of Jesus Christ of Latter day Saints (the Mormons). "Ton" in Old English means "town." Card came to Canada a talented and ambitious leader, and also as a fugitive, having escaped custody while awaiting trial on charges of polygamy. The following year, the main colony, consisting of ten families, arrived and took up squatter's rights since the official Dominion Land Survey had not yet been completed. A crude survey was done by the Mormons and J.S. Dennis, D.L.S., resurveyed the land in the fall of 1887. Cardston was granted a post office in 1892, became a village in 1898 and a town in 1901. Ora Card was the town's first mayor.

Cardston, n.d.

* Carlstadt (former post office)
72 L/6 - Alderson
20-15-10-W4
50°17'N 111°20'W
Approximately 53 km north-west of Medicine Hat.

(see Alderson)

Carmangay (village)
82 I/3 - Carmangay
32-13-23-W4
50°08'N 113°07'W
Approximately 50 km north north-west of Lethbridge.

The post office opened at this location 1 March 1907, and was named for Charles Whitney Carman, his wife Gertrude nee Gay, and their son, Gay. In 1904, Mr. Carman purchased 1,500 acres of land to establish the Carmangay Farm Company and later built a home and the Little Bow Inn on it. The property became valuable when the Canadian Pacific Railway decided in 1907 to cross the Little Bow at that location. When the railway reached the surveyed townsite in 1909, townsite lots were auctioned off with Carman and the C.P.R. splitting the proceeds.

Carolside (hamlet)
72 M/4 - Pollockville
16-26-12-W4
51°13′N 111°38′W
Approximately 78 km south south-east of Drumheller.

Named after a nearby ranch owned by George and Harry Purvis in 1910 who called it Carolside, after their home in Scotland. The name was adopted from the ranch for the post office in 1920 following the relocation of the post office from 34-26-12-W4, where it had the name "Jethson," to this site, near the Purvis ranch. George was killed in France in World War I, while Harry remained in Canada and operated the ranch for several more years before leaving the area.

Carseland (hamlet)
82 I/14 - Gleichen
7-22-25-W4
50°51′N 113°28′W
Approximately 35 km south-east of Calgary.

The name is descriptive and refers to the rich soil of "river valley land." The word carse is Scottish in origin and means fertile alluvial land or bottomland. The post office here was originally known as "Griesbach," after Emil Griesbach, the first postmaster. The name was changed 1 December 1914, although Griesbach continued his role as postmaster after this time.

Carstairs Creek (creek)
82 P/5 - Irricana
28-28-27-W4
51°25′N 113°45′W
Flows east into Rosebud River, approximately 45 km north north-east of Calgary.

This creek takes its name from the town of Carstairs, located 3 km from its headwaters. The town was named after Carstairs, Lanarkshire (now Strathclyde) in Scotland. Many of the first settlers were of Scottish descent. The derivation of the name is from the Old English, castel tarres, meaning "castle of Turres." Terras or Turres is still a Scandinavian name.

Caruso (locality)
82 P/3 - Strathmore
17-24-25-W4
51°03′N 113°28′W
Approximately 35 km east of Calgary.

A Canadian Pacific Railway station was established here circa 1884, and was named "Cheadle." The name was changed in 1917 to Caruso, after the famous Italian tenor, Enrico Caruso (1873-1921).

Carway (hamlet)
82 H/3 - Cardston
2-1-26-W4
49°00′N 113°23′W
Approximately 86 km south-west of Lethbridge.

Named in 1926 by William Roberts, the first officer posted to this port of entry, when it was classified as a preventative station. Roberts claims that the route from Babb, Montana, to Cardston, Alberta, was originally known as the "Cardston Highway." Roberts combined the two words, "car" from Cardston and "way" from Highway to create the name Carway.

Cassils (hamlet)
82 I/9 - Cassils
5-19-15-W4
50°35′N 112°02′W
Approximately 112 km north-east of Lethbridge.

Named for Charles Cassils of Cassils, Cochrane & Co. of Montreal. Cassils was a

rancher during the early settlement years in the west, and was widely known by colleagues and friends as a gentleman. A post office opened here 15 May 1921 and closed 5 August 1954.

Castle River (river)
82 H/12 - Brocket
27-7-30-W4
49°36′N 113°59′W
Flows north-east into Oldman River, approximately 86 km west of Lethbridge.

The source of this river is the runoff from Castle Peak, located on Windsor Mountain which has a descriptive name. F.W. Godsal, a prominent land owner in the district, suggested the name for this river in 1914.

Cavan Lake (lake)
72 E/16 - Irvine
19-11-3-W4
49°56′N 110°24′W
Approximately 18 km south-east of Medicine Hat.

Named after Henry Cavan (died ca. 1965). He was a long time resident, pioneer and rancher and partly responsible for the organization of the Ross Creek Irrigation District which formed this lake circa 1950. Henry Cavan was born at Dunmore Junction on 21 April 1887, the first white child born in Southeastern Alberta.

Cavendish (hamlet)
72 L/16 - Bindloss
26-21-4-W4
50°49′N 110°27′W
Approximately 88 km north of Medicine Hat.

Originally known as "Pancras," the village was renamed in 1917 after Victor Christian William Cavendish, Duke of Devonshire (1869-1938), governor-general of Canada from 1916 to 1921. Homesteaders first arrived in the area in 1910, and a railroad linc was laid in 1914. The townsite of Pancras was surveyed at this time and was named after St. Pancras, a borough in London, England.

Cayley (village)

82 I/5 - Nanton
19-17-28-W4
50°27′N 113°51′W
Approximately 55 km south of Calgary.

Named after Hugh St. Quentin Cayley (1857-1934) who moved to Calgary in 1882 after studying law at the University of Toronto. Cayley was owner/editor of the *Calgary Herald* in 1884-85 and was appointed to the Council of the Northwest Territories in 1886. Following the Council's dissolution in 1888, Cayley was elected to the Assembly of the Northwest Territories. In 1897, he moved to Vancouver and was appointed to the Bench in 1917.

Cecil (locality)

72 L/4 - Hays
29-13-12-W4
50°07′N 111°36′W
Approximately 70 km west of Medicine Hat.

The locality is named after Mrs. J.M. Cameron, wife of General Superintendent of the Canadian Pacific Railway centred in Calgary, formerly called Terrace. A C.P.R. station was established here some time after 1924.

Cemetery Hill (hill)

82 J/16 - Priddis
11-23-2-W5
50°57′N 114°09′W
Approximately 1 km south of Calgary within the Sarcee Indian Reserve #145.

This hill was named by the Canadian Permanent Committee on Geographical Names 29 March 1971. The precise origin for the name of this feature is unknown although this may have been the site of a cemetery at one time.

Cereal (village)

72 M/7 - Cereal
28-28-6-W4
51°25′N 110°48′W
Approximately 138 km east of Drumheller.

The name was suggested by Reverend R.J. McMillan in 1910 and later adopted by the post office. Reverend McMillan, a retired Presbyterian minister, was impressed by the large volumes of grain produced in the area and believed the region was destined to become the "Bread Basket of the West." When local storekeeper J.A. Sully was gathering signatures on a petition to get a post office built in the area, he also gathered suggestions for the name, including McMillan's. The post office was established under the name Cereal 1 June 1911.

Cessford (hamlet)

72 M/4 - Pollockville
36-23-12-W4
51°01′N 111°33′W
Approximately 94 km south-east of Drumheller.

This is a simplified version of *Cess Fiord*, the name of the nearby homestead from which the post office operated before being moved to its present location. Axel Anderson and his wife hailed from Sweden, and they chose the name *Cess Fiord* for their homestead to commemorate their ancestral home. The post office was previously called "Shandleigh," after its first postmaster.

Cessford Reservoir (reservoir)

72 M/3 - Big Stone
24-11-W4
51°02′N 111°27′W
Approximately 101 km south-east of Drumheller.

(see Cessford)

Champion (village)

82 I/3 - Carmangay
7-15-23-W4
50°14′N 113°09′W
Approximately 65 km north north-west of Lethbridge.

A settlement located very close by was called Cleverville after one Martin G. Clever form Iowa, an early settler in the district. His offer of free land to anyone who wished to start a business on his land virtually created the village overnight. The railway arrived in 1909, and the Canadian Pacific Railway began its own station, calling it Champion, after H.T. Champion, of the Winnipeg bankers, Alloway & Champion. Residents of Cleverville had little choice but to relocate to Champion, and the new post office opened here 30 September 1910. In 1915, Champion became known as the "million bushel town," as one million bushels of wheat were shipped from this community that year.

Chancellor (hamlet)

82 P/2 - Hussar
35-24-21-W4
51°05′N 112°50′W
Approximately 85 km east of Calgary.

The community here consisted predominantly of settlers of German descent, and the hamlet was named for Germany's political leader, the Chancellor, in 1913. The post office opened 1 October 1918, and commemorated Theobald von Bethman-Hollweg (then Chancellor of Germany). A devastating fire in the 1930s demolished most of the buildings in the settlement. The structures were never rebuilt because Chancellor was too close to both Hussar and Standard. Today it is largely known as a grain shipping point.

Chandler Coulee (coulee)

82 J/1 - Langford Creek
11-13-30-W4
50°04′N 113°59′W
Runs east into Lyndon Creek, approximately 92 km north-west of Lethbridge.

The precise origin for the name of this feature is unknown.

Chappice Lake (lake)

72 L/1 - Many Island Lake
16-14-3-W4
50°10′N 110°22′W
Approximately 28 km north-east of Medicine Hat, west of Many Island Lake.

The precise origin for the name of this feature is unknown.

Cheadle (hamlet)

82 P/4 - Dalroy
2-24-26-W4
51°01′N 113°32′W
Approximately 40 km east of Calgary.

Cheadle was a Canadian Pacific Railway siding named in 1884 after Dr. Walter Butler Cheadle (1835-1910), who was an explorer and co-author with William Fitzwilliam Viscount Milton (1839-1877) of *The North-West Passage By Land* (London: 1865). Their journey of 1862-63 took them across the Canadian Prairies, the Rocky Mountains through Yellowhead Pass and to the Pacific Coast. The post office operated here from 1 May 1902 through 26 October 1970.

Cherry Coulee (coulee)

72 E/14 - Bow Island
9-11-11-W4
49°53′N 111°27′W
Runs north-west into South Saskatchewan River, approximately 57 km west of Medicine Hat.

Originating out of the Blackfoot name, *ami-onaskway*, the name refers to the chokecherries that grow along the coulee. Cherry Coulee acts as the drainage ditch running from the eastern edge of the town of Bow Island, north-west into the South Saskatchewan River.

* Chestermere Lake (former post office)

82 P/4 - Dalroy
23-24-28-W4
51°05′N 113°40′W
Approximately 15 km east of Calgary.

Chestermere Lake was locally known as "Kinniburgh Slough" until 1906, when an intermittent lake was dammed to create the reservoir for the Canadian Pacific Railway irrigation project. There are varied accounts for the origin of the name. Some say it was named for a Lord Chester, a director of the C.P.R. Others say it was named for Lord Chestermere. Another version suggests that some of the early settlers came from Chesterville, Ontario and Nova Scotia, and decided on the present name in preference to "Kinniburgh Slough." Chester comes from the Latin, *castra* and means "camp," while *mere* is from the Old English word *meer* for lake. The C.P.R. built a railroad station here in 1914, but it was never used. In 1959, the land was bought from the Western Irrigation District to build a provincial campsite near the bridge that crosses the north end of the lake.

Chestermere Lake (lake)

82 P/4 - Dalroy
11-24-28-W4
51°02′N 113°49′W
Approximately 15 km east of Calgary.

(see Chestermere Lake - former post office)

Chestermere Lake (summer village)

82 P/4 - Dalroy
3-24-28-W4
51°02′N 113°49′W
Approximately 15 km east of Calgary.

This summer village was formed 22 March 1977, effective 1 April 1977, according to Order-in-council 298/77. (see Chestermere Lake - former post office)

Chief Mountain (port of entry)

82 H/4 - Waterton Lakes
3-1-28-W4
49°00′N 113°40′W
Approximately 60 km south-east of Pincher Creek, on the Canada-U.S. border.

The location of the port of entry is in the vicinity of Chief Mountain, itself a landmark and a very prominent feature of northern Montana. The customs port was opened to traffic on 15 June 1936. This area was very important to the Indians and is known to them as *ninais-toko*. A legend states that after a Blackfoot Indian chief was killed in battle, his wife, crazed with grief, threw herself and her baby over the precipice. The bodies were gathered and buried at the foot of the mountain. The Indians believe Chief Mountain to be the home of the Thunderbird, the cause of thunder and lightning, and a stopping place for Nappeo, the Old Man. The name was officially approved 8 June 1971.

* Chilmark (former locality)

72 M/2 - Cappon
21-24-7-W4
51°03′N 110°54′W
Approximately 135 km east south-east of Drumheller.

Likely named after the village of the same name located in Wiltshire, England. The post office was opened here 1 January 1915 and closed 1 June 1928.

Chimney Hill (hill)

82 P/3 - Strathmore
26-25-23-W4
51°09′30″N 113°06′15″W
Approximately 50 km east of Calgary. Erosion has created chimney-like features

along the summit of this hill. The descriptive name was officially applied to this feature 6 March 1986.

Chin (hamlet)

82 H/16 - Taber
25-9-19-W4
49°46'N 112°27'W
Approximately 25 km east of Lethbridge.

The locality derived its name from a nearby butte that was given its descriptive name because from a distance, it looked like a chin. The Blackfoot Indians call the butte *mistoamo*, which translates as "beard," also a descriptive name.

Chin Butte (butte)

82 H/9 - Chin Coulee
35-8-18-W4
49°41'N 112°20'W
Approximately 32 km east of Lethbridge.

(see Chin)

■ Chin Coulee (coulee)

82 H/9 - Chin Coulee
8-17-W4
49°38'N 112°15'W
A north-west, south-east trending coulee, approximately 25 km east of Lethbridge.

(see Chin)

Chin Lakes (lake)

82 H/9 - Chin Coulee
7,8,9-16,17-W4
49°37'N 112°13'W
Approximately 25 km east of Lethbridge.

(see Chin)

Chinook (hamlet)

72 M/7 - Cereal
4-29-7-W4
51°27'N 110°56'W
Approximately 150 km north of Medicine Hat.

The post office was opened here in 1910, six years after the official naming on 28 July 1904. This locality is named after the meteorological term for the warm, dry westerly wind emerging from the Rocky Mountains. Chinook's incorporation as a village took place 21 October 1913 and was dissolved 1 April 1977.

A chinook begins out over the Pacific Ocean as a low pressure area and begins to move eastward gathering warmth and moisture. When this air reaches the Rocky Mountains, it rises, cools, and releases its moisture. As it crosses the mountains and drops down their eastern slopes, the atmospheric pressure as well as the temperature increases. One of the most dramatic chinooks occurred in 1930 when a southern Albertan set out to ski on one of the local foothills. He trudged up the incline in heavy snow, only to be faced with bare land just as he reached the top of the hill. The chinook had sublimated the snow during his ascent. In meteorology, the term "sublimation" is applied with respect to water as direct evaporation from an ice surface as well as direct disposition of ice from water vapour. During a chinook, the snow is directly converted to a vapour without the intermediate stage of melting.

Chokio (locality)

82 H/12 - Brocket
24-7-28-W4
49°36'N 113°39'W
Approximately 62 km west of Lethbridge.

The name is native in origin and descriptive in nature, referring to the abundance of chokecherries that grow in the area. The word "chokio," like the more commonly known chokecherries, is a corruption of the Indian word *chok-ieo* for the berry. During the construction of the Canadian Pacific Railway, the Indians sold quantities of these berries to the railroad construction crews.

Circus Coulee (coulee)

82 P/8 - Dorothy
4-27-17-W4
51°17'N 112°19'W
Runs south-west into Red Deer River, approximately 30 km south-east of Drumheller.

The descriptive name for this feature was officially applied in 1955 to represent its resemblance to an old theatre or amphitheatre. The natives used to refer to it as "The Store."

Claresholm (town)

82 I/4 - Claresholm
26-12-27-W4
50°02'N 113°35'W
Approximately 64 km north-west of Lethbridge.

Named in 1891 by John Niblick, a Canadian Pacific Railway superintendent, for the name of his home in Medicine Hat. His wife's name was Clare, and they referred to their house as "Clare's Home." The first buildings established on the townsite were the water tower for the trains, and a section house for supplies needed to build the railroad which came through what is now Claresholm in 1891. Claresholm was incorporated as a village 15 June 1903. The town of Claresholm was incorporated 31 August 1905, and this was the last official act carried out by the Northwest Territorial Administration. The following day, Alberta became a province.

* Clarinda (former locality)

72 E/4 - Coutts
17-1-13-W4
49°03'N 111°43'W

---

*denotes rescinded name or former locality.

Approximately 120 km south south-west of Medicine Hat.

Named in 1911 for Mrs. F. Clarinda Clark, mother of Miss F. Clark who operated the first post office and served as its first postmistress. The name was rescinded 28 May 1970 but continues to be kept in the historical record.

Clear Brook (brook)
82 I/3 - Carmangay
12-14-26-W4
50°09'N 113°25'W
Flows south-east into Clear Lake, approximately 65 km north-west of Lethbridge.

(see Clear Lake)

Clear Lake (lake)
82 I/3 - Carmangay
6-13-25-W4
50°09'N 113°25'W
Approximately 63 km north-west of Lethbridge.

The name is probably descriptive of the clean, clear water contained within the lake. The feature is also locally known as "Three Mile Lake," describing its length.

Clear Water Lake (lake)
72 L/1 - Many Island Lake
36-12-3,4-W4
50°03'N 110°25'W
Approximately 28 km east of Medicine Hat.

The name is likely descriptive of the water's clarity.

Clivale (locality)
82 P/8 - Dorothy
26-16-W4
51°16'N 112°09'W
Approximately 42 km south-east of Drumheller.

A post office operated here from 1 September 1916 through 31 January 1932 and was named after a town in either England or Ireland.

Cluny (village)
82 I/15 - Cluny
5-22-21-W4
50°50'N 112°52'W
Approximately 75 km east of Calgary.

A Canadian Pacific Railway station was established here in 1884, and was named after Cluny Parish in Aberdeenshire, Scotland. The owner and operator of the local trading post was named "Cluny" McPherson Stades. There is a branch of the MacPherson clan called MacPherson of Cluny, from Cluny Castle near Newtonmore, and Cluny is strongly associated with this name. As this Cluny dates back to the 14th century, it predates the parish in Aberdeen—which city has little or no connection with the MacPherson clan. It is possible that Mr. Stades got his nickname from that.

Coal Coulee (coulee)
82 J/9 - Turner Valley
9-18-2-W5
50°30'15"N 114°13'40"W
Approximately 58 km south of Calgary.

During the late 1800s, local ranchers were able to obtain coal from open seams exposed along the coulee. A number of mines were located in the coulee later on. The "coal trail" ran from this coulee, through Longview, to High River. The locally well-established name was officially approved 29 July 1986.

Coal Creek (creek)
72 E/2 - Comrey
30-3-6-W4
49°16'11"N 110°51'00"W
Flows north-west into Pakowki Lake, approximately 93 km south of Medicine Hat.

This creek was likely named by early settlers who discovered coal along its banks. Surveyor's notes make numerous references to the abundance of coal in the vicinity, and its use by homesteaders.

Coal Creek (creek)
82 J/9 - Turner Valley
9-18-2-W5
From 50°30'15"N 114°13'40"W
to 50°27'00"N 114°24'10"W
Flows east into Highwood River, approximately 55 km south of Calgary.

In the late 1800s early ranchers obtained coal from exposed seams in the coulee through which the creek runs (known as Coal Coulee). A number of mines were also situated along the creek. The "Coal Trail" originated here and went through Longview to High River. At one point, the creek had been misdesignated "Bull Creek." That error has since been corrected.

Coal Mine Coulee (coulee)
82 H/3 - Cardston
SE-22-1-25-W4
49°03'N 113°15'10"W
Approximately 70 km south south-west of Lethbridge.

There was a small coal mine which operated for a short time that was located along the coulee in the early 1900s. The feature was known previously as "Coal Canyon."

Coaldale (town)
82 H/10 - Lethbridge
11-9-20-W4
49°43'N 112°37'W
Approximately 10 km east of Lethbridge.

This town grew around a railroad siding, which was named after the nearby residence of Elliott T. Galt. This residence had been named "Coaldale" to distinguish it from the nearby "Coalbanks" (now Lethbridge).

Elliott Galt was the son of Sir Alexander T. Galt (1817-1893), one of the Fathers of Confederation, and the founder and manager of the North Western Coal and Navigation Co. Ltd., later called the Alberta Railway and Coal Company, which provided the economic base for Lethbridge's creation and continued survival.

Coalhurst (village)

82 H/10 - Lethbridge
21-9-22-W4
49°45′N 112°56′W
Approximately 7 km west of Lethbridge.

The name which came into use in the mid-1870s was derived from a combination of the word "coal," which is abundant in the Lethbridge area, and an early settler by the name of Hurst. Until 1885, Coalhurst was the official name of what is now Lethbridge, although this settlement was also known to locals as "Coalbanks." In 1885, the name Lethbridge was adopted to replace both names. The village of Coalhurst was reincorporated at this site in 1979, under the Municipal Government Act, O.C. 32/79.

Cochrane (town)

82 O/1 - Calgary
2,3-26-4-W5
51°11′N 114°28′W
Approximately 25 km west north-west of Calgary.

The Cochrane Ranche Company (Limited) was established in 1881 and was owned by Senator Matthew Henry Cochrane as the first big ranching company in the west. Colonel James Walker, a veteran from the North West Mounted Police, was the local manager of the ranch. A few miles west of the settlement of Cochrane, a small com-

munity sprang up. It was named "Mitford" in honour of a close friend of Lady Adela Cochrane, daughter of the Earl of Stadbroke, and wife of T.B.H. Cochrane, founder of the settlement in 1885. When the Canadian Pacific Railway line went through the mountains, the company named the new station on their line after Senator M.H. Cochrane. The first building in the new town of Cochrane was the C.P.R. station.

Cochrane Lake (lake)

82 H/5 - Pincher Creek
30-4-27-W4
49°20′N 113°37′W
Approximately 69 km south-west of Lethbridge.

This 1.1 km by 1.2 km lake was named 9 July 1942 after W.F. Cochrane, proprietor of the Waterton Lake operation of the Cochrane Ranche Company (Limited). W.F. Cochrane bought this operation from his father, Senator M.H. Cochrane (1823-1903), after whom the town of Cochrane is named.

(see Cochrane).

Cochrane Lake, n.d.

Cochrane Lake (lake)

82 O/8 - Crossfield
27,34-26-4-W5
51°15′N 114°29′W
Approximately 38 km north-west of Calgary.

(see Cochrane)

Coleman Lake (lake)

72 M/5 - Sunnynook
28,29-14-W4
51°26′N 111°52′W
Approximately 57 km east of Drumheller.

The precise origin for the name of this feature is unknown.

Coleridge (post office)

72 E/15 - Seven Persons
12-5-W4
49°58′N 110°36′W
Approximately 5 km south-east of Medicine Hat.

The precise origin for the name of this feature is unknown. (see Dunmore)

* Colles (former post office)

82 H/3 - Cardston
20-2-24-W4
49°05′N 113°12′W
Approximately 71 km south-west of Lethbridge.

The post office was opened at this site in 1893 and was named after its first postmaster, J.C. Colles. The name was changed to Kimball in 1903. (see Kimball)

Collicutt (locality)

82 O/8 - Crossfield
26 28 1 W5
51°25′N 114°02′W
Approximately 45 km north of Calgary.

Originally a Canadian Pacific Railway siding, it was named for Frank Collicutt, a

---

*denotes rescinded name or former locality.

pioneer rancher. He was born in New Brunswick in 1876, educated in Calgary and went to work as a cowboy for Pat Burns. In 1898 he was freighting from Edmonton to Athabasca Landing for the Klondike. He then went into business as a cattle buyer on his own and later for Pat Burns. In 1912 he started his own herd—the Willow Spring herd—which achieved fame winning many awards between 1922 and 1940. He was president of a number of cattle breeders' associations and in 1955 received an honorary Doctor of Laws degree from the University of Alberta.

* Commerce (former locality)

82 H/15 - Picture Butte
12-10-22-W4
49°48′N 112°52′W
Approximately 12 km north of Lethbridge.

Early settlers hoped that the name chosen for this settlement would foretell growth. This was not the case, however, and the post office was closed in 1931.

* Comrey (former locality)

72 E/2 - Comrey
12-2-6-W4
49°09′N 110°44′W
Approximately 98 km south of Medicine Hat.

In 1906, Columbus Larson, Comrey's first postmaster and one of six residents of the community, suggested a scheme for deriving a name for the new post office. The first letter of the six settlers' Christian names were to be used. Because of incompatibility, two used the initial letter of their last names. The six letters were re-arranged until the name "Comrey" was derived. The six individuals were Columbus Larson (C), Ole Roen (O), Mons Roen (M), R. Rolfson

(R), J.J. Evanson (E), and Ed Yager (Y). The Comrey post office was closed in June 1968.

Connemara (locality)

82 I/5 - Nanton
32-16-28-W4
50°24′N 113°49′W
Approximately 59 km south of Calgary.

Likely named by the Canadian Pacific Railway, after Connemara, Ireland, a region in County Galway. The name is an altered form of Conmacne, which means seaside. Some local residents refer to this locality as "Silver City." A homesteader by the name of Newell settled on the west side of the lake north of where the Connemara grain elevators once stood. Newell promoted the area and the sale of lots on his land to people in Toronto and England with the idea of founding "Silver City." Although Newell sold some lots, his dream never materialized.

Conrad (locality)

72 E/12 - Skiff
32-6-15-W4
49°31′N 111°58′W
Approximately 60 km south-east of Lethbridge.

The precise origin for the name of this locality is not known. It may be named for Charles Conrad, an early trader in the region and manager of I.G. Baker and Company, or it may also be named for the Polish-born British author, Joseph Conrad.

Conrich (hamlet)

82 P/4 - Dalroy
5-25-28-W4
51°06′N 113°52′W
Approximately 10 km east of Calgary.

This small hamlet got its start as a flag station on the Grand Trunk Pacific Railway. A flag station was exactly that:

passengers wanting to board had to flag the train down. The land for the site was obtained from W.F. Birch. The railroad reached here in 1913, and the name comes from the surnames of two real estate developers, Connacher and Richardson. The Canadian National Railway took over the line in 1918. A post office operated at this site from 15 August 1925 through 12 December 1960.

Control (railway point)

72 M/4 - Pollockville
6-24-14-W4
51°01′N 111°57′W
Approximately 73 km south-east of Drumheller.

The name is possibly descriptive because this station was a control point on the Canadian Pacific Railway line.

Cope Creek (creek)

82 O/2 - Jumpingpound Creek
14-25-5-W5
51°08′N 114°36′W
Flows south-east into Pile of Bones Creek, approximately 30 km west north-west of Calgary.

This creek was named after Thomas "Stanley" Cope and his family, early ranchers in the area. The name was made official 12 December 1939.

Cope Ridge (ridge)

82 O/2 - Jumpingpound Creek
25-5-W5
51°08′N 114°37′W
Approximately 30 km west north-west of Calgary.

(see Cope Creek)

Copithorne Ridge (ridge)

82 O/2 - Jumpingpound Creek
25-4,5-W5
51°07′N 114°33′W

---

*denotes rescinded name or former locality.

Approximately 25 km west north-west of Calgary.

The Copithorne family were early home-steaders (as early as 1883) in the Jumpingpound district. It is after them that this ridge is named. It was officially approved 12 December 1929.

Cottonwood Creek (creek)

82 H/4 - Waterton Lakes
20-2-29-W4
49°08′N 113°51′W
Flows south into Galwey Brook, approximately 40 km south south-east of Pincher Creek.

This feature was officially named 19 May 1946, for the abundance of cottonwood trees along the banks of the creek.

Cottonwood Grove (grove)

72 L/7 - Watching Hill
16-6-W4
50°20′N 110°41′W
Approximately 32 km north of Medicine Hat.

The precise origin for the name of this feature is unknown.

Countess (locality)

82 I/16 - Bassano
15-21-17-W4
50°47′N 112°17′W
Approximately 139 km south-east of Calgary.

This locality was named in 1914, after Countess Bassano. The post office was established 1 August 1924, and was closed 15 April 1969. Bassano and Countess are adjacent railway stations.

(see Bassano)

Cousins (locality)

72 L/2 - Medicine Hat
2-13-6-W4
50°04′N 110°43′W
Within the city limits of Medicine Hat.

Named for William Cousins, one of Alberta's earliest settlers, a businessman and former mayor of Medicine Hat. Born in London, Ontario in 1856, Cousins headed west in 1883. Reaching the end of steel west of Swift Current, William continued to Medicine Hat on horseback, and in conjunction with a partner, established a merchant business. He went on to expand throughout the 1880s and 1890s with a new partner, establishing Cousins and Scatcherd. In 1900, William sold his business interests to become the first clerk of the Supreme Court of the Northwest Territories, Bow Island district. He also served as Justice of the Peace, Registrar for Bills of Sale and Chattel Mortgages, Founder and President of the Agricultural Society, Chairman of the School Board, and eventually became the Mayor of Medicine Hat in 1906. As mayor, he pushed for the development of the city as a manufacturing and industrial centre.

Coutts (village)

72 E/4 - Coutts
4-1-15-W4
49°00′N 111°57′W
Approximately 95 km south-east of Lethbridge.

One source suggests that Coutts was named for Sir William Lehman Ashead Bartlett-Coutts, a banker and member of the British Parliament in the 1880s. He was also Director of the Alberta Railways and Irrigation Company (see Galt Island). Another source argues that the name was chosen in honour of Georgina Baroness Burdett-Coutts, Sir William's daughter. The locality of Burdett was named for the Baroness. She was a large stockholder in the

A.R.& I.Co. The A.R.& I.Co. built a narrow gauge line in 1890 from Lethbridge south to the Coutts region for the purpose of hauling coal. The village of Coutts became the southern terminus of the line.

Cowoki (lake)

72 L/12 - Brooks
2-18,19-13-W4
50°35′N 111°42′W
Approximately 92 km north-west of Medicine Hat.

The precise origin for the name of this feature is unknown.

Coyote Lake (lake)

82 P/8 - Dorothy
7-28-15-W4
51°22′N 112°06′W
Approximately 43 km east of Drumheller.

This lake is likely named after the coyote, the New World member of the dog family whose name is derived from the Aztec *coyotl*. It is also known as a Prairie Wolf, Brush Wolf, or Little Wolf.

Craddock (locality)

82 H/8 - Warner
11-6-19-W4
49°28′N 112°27′W
Approximately 33 km south-east of Lethbridge.

Named after Rear Admiral Sir Christopher Cradock (1862-1914) who was commander of a British squadron which engaged a superior German squadron under Admiral Graf von Spee 1 November 1914, at Coronel off the Chilean coast. Cradock perished in the naval battle. Three British ships were sunk and the German squadron was later destroyed at the Battle of the Falkland Islands 8 December 1914. The locality had grown around a Canadian Pacific Railway station which was originally spelled with one "d." The spelling has been altered over the years.

Craig Creek (creek)
82 H/13 - Granum
2-11-29-W4
49°53'N 113°52'W
Flows north into Muddypound Creek, approximately 75 km north-west of Lethbridge.

This creek was officially named 8 July 1954 after John R. Craig, original promoter and first manager of the Oxley Ranch, the oldest and most historic ranch of the area. Oxley was the country residence of Mr. Staveley Hill, in Wolverhampton, England. Mr. Craig came to this area in 1882 as a permanent resident. He had grazing rights on 100,000 acres of land, obtained from the Dominion Government (*The Butte Stands Guard: Stavely and District*, 1976, p. 15). A few years after Mr. Craig became manager, some disagreement arose, and he left the company. Later, the New Oxley Ranch was formed. John R. Craig is the author of *Ranching With Lords and Commons*.

Craigdhu (locality)
82 P/5 - Irricana
12-27-26-W4
51°17'N 113°31'W
Approximately 50 km north-east of Calgary.

Craigdhu is a gaelic expression meaning "black rock," perhaps referring to the coal deposits so commonly found in southern Alberta. Denny Howle was the manager of the Craigdhu ranch, and it is believed he named the Canadian Pacific Railway siding in 1912 and later the school.

* Craigower (former station)
72 E/7 - Manyberries
32-4-4-W4
49°20'N 110°31'W

Approximately 77 km south of Medicine Hat.

The precise origin for the name of this feature is unknown.

Cranford (locality)
82 H/16 - Taber
27-9-18-W4
49°46'N 112°21'W
Approximately 33 km east of Lethbridge.

Possibly named for Cransford, Suffolk, England, which means "ford of the cranes or herons." This area of southern Alberta is a popular breeding and nesting area for these kinds of birds. Cranford was originally established as a Canadian Pacific Railway station and was formerly known as "Jamieson."

Crawford Plateau (plateau)
82 O/2 - Jumpingpound Creek
36-25-4,5-W5
51°10'N 114°34'W
Approximately 30 km north-west of Calgary.

Arthur Crawford was an early rancher and homesteader who moved to Cochrane from Hand Hills and previously Three Hills, in 1918. Arthur and his wife, Ethel eventually made their way to a ranch on the junction of the Bow River and Jumpingpound Creek. The name Crawford Plateau was officially approved 12 December 1939.

Crawling Creek (creek)
82 P/1 - Finnegan
4-24-26-17-W4
51°13'N 112°15'W
Flows north into Red Deer River, approximately 40 km south-east of Drumheller.

The precise origin for the name of this feature is unknown; however, it may describe the speed of the stream's course. The name was officially applied in 1955.

Crawling Valley (valley)
82 P/1 - Finnegan
24,25-17-W4
51°05'N 112°18'W
Approximately 53 km south-east of Drumheller.

(see Crawling Creek)

Crescent Lake (lake)
82 I/4 - Claresholm
16,17-14-28-W4
50°10'15"N 113°46'25"W
Approximately 87 km north-west of Lethbridge.

The name is descriptive of the lake's crescent shape although the lake is often dry, particularly in years of limited precipitation.

Cressday (locality)
72 E/1 - Cripple Creek
31-3-2-W4
49°15'N 110°16'W
Approximately 88 km south-east of Medicine Hat.

This railway station was named for W. Cresswell and Tony Day. They were ranching and business partners in North Dakota prior to moving to Alberta between 1901 and 1903. Together, they operated twolarge ranches and a freighting business in this vicinity for six years. The railway point was officially named after them in 1922.

Cripple Creek (creek)
82 H/13 - Granum
1-12-29-W4
49°58'N 113°50'W
Flows north-east into Trout Creek, approximately 78 km north-west of Lethbridge.

The precise origin for the name of this creek is unknown. The name was officially approved 8 July 1954.

Cripple Creek (creek)

72 E/1 - Cripple Creek
9-3-3-W4
49°12′N 110°22′W
Flows east into Sage Creek, approximately 90 km south-east of Medicine Hat.

This tributary of Sage Creek derived its name from an Indian legend, according to which an injured elk was found on the banks of the creek.

Crocodile Lake (lake)

82 I/4 - Claresholm
7-13-28-W4
50°04′N 113°48′W
Approximately 82 km north-west of Lethbridge.

The precise origin for the name of this feature is unknown; however, the name may describe the shape of the lake.

Cronkhite Coulee (coulee)

72 E/7   Manyberries
15-6-7-W4
49°28′N 110°53′W
Runs south-west into Fourways Creek, approximately 70 km south of Medicine Hat.

Named for G.H. Cronkhite, who lived along this coulee, and was one of the region's earliest settlers.

Crooked Creek (creek)

82 H/4 - Waterton Lakes
8-2-29-W4
49°07′N 113°50′W
Flows west into Waterton River, approximately 40 km south south-east of Pincher Creek.

The name of this stream is a translation of a Cree Indian name, *wawa-katinau*, translating to "crooked." The name is descriptive

of its winding trail, and was officially approved 19 May 1943.

Cross Creek (creek)

82 J/8 - Stimson Creek
15-16-1-W5
50°21′N 114°03′W
Flows north into Mosquito Creek, approximately 40 km south-east of Turner Valley.

This creek was officially named 12 December 1939 after Alfred Ernest Cross (1861-1932). Mr. Cross came west in 1884 as a bookkeeper and veterinarian for Senator Cochrane. This job was unsatisfactory and he decided to move further south to take up ranching. He remained a rancher until the early 1890s, when he established the Calgary Brewing and Malting Company and became involved in several developments in and around Calgary. In 1912, as one of the "Big Four" cattlemen, he helped finance the first Calgary Stampede.

Crossfield (town)

82 O/8 - Crossfield
26-28-1-W5
51°26′N 114°02′W
Approximately 45 km north of Calgary.

The name of this town commemorates a railway engineer employed by the Calgary and Edmonton Railway Company. The post office opened 1 August 1902.

Crossfield Creek (creek)

82 P/5 - Irricana
27-27-26-W4
51°20′N 113°34′W
Flows east into Rosebud River, approximately 45 km north-east of Calgary.

(see Crossfield)

Crow Indian Lake (lake)

72 E/5 - Legend
11-5-13,14-W4
49°22′N 111°48′W

Approximately 70 km south-east of Lethbridge.

Named after the Crow Indians, a Siouan tribe forming part of the Hidatsa group.

Crowchild (locality)

82 J/16 - Priddis
1/-23-2-W5
50°57′N 114°14′W
Approximately 7 km south-west of Calgary.

This Indian village, found within the Sarcee Indian Reserve was given this name 29 March 1971, by the Canadian Permanent Committee on Geographical Names. Its precise origin is unknown.

* Crowfoot (former locality)

82 I/15 - Cluny
25-21-20-W4
50°49′N 112°39′W
Approximately 111 km south-east of Calgary.

Named for the head-chief of the Blackfoot confederacy, Crowfoot (ca. 1836-1890). His native name was *Saho-Muxika-Sapo-Mukikow*. Crowfoot was a shrewd negotiator, not a warrior, keeping his people at peace with the whites even during the 1885 North West Rebellion. He secured excellent tracts of land for their reserves during the signing of Treaty Number 7 in 1877. Crowfoot stood in good stead with the Canadian Pacific Railway, from which he received a lifetime pass on the railway. He was buried beside the Bow River overlooking the locally named "Treaty Flats."

Crowfoot Creek (creek)

82 I/15 - Cluny
22-21-20-W4
50°48′N 112°39′W
Flows south-west into Bow River, approximately 110 km south-east of Calgary.

(see Crowfoot)

Crowlodge Creek (creek)

82 H/12 - Brocket
8-8-27-W4
49°38′N 113°38′W
Flows north into Oldman River, approximately 59 km west of Lethbridge.

The name is translated from the Blackfoot words *ataw-is-toik-akwapi* or *mastowistooek-akapi*, translating to "the lodges with crows painted," according to J.C. Nelson, of the Dominion Land Survey who compiled a *Report of the Geological Survey for 1882-4* with A.P. Patrick. It is also referred to by the Blackfoot as *ahkisikaseme*, which translates to "Medicine Root Creek," because the Indians used to dig roots here for medical and spiritual purposes, according to Major General Sir Sam Steele, author of *Forty Years in Canada* and, throughout many years, collected much information regarding Indian place names in the province.

Cullen Creek (creek)

82 O/1 - Calgary
7-24-2-W5
51°02′N 114°17′W
Flows south into Elbow River, approximately 15 km west of Calgary.

This creek flows through land owned by the Cullen family, the first of which, William Cullen, arrived in the Calgary area with his wife, Annie (née Hamilton) in 1887. One of their sons, Keys, started the Pure Milk Company which he later sold to the Carlyle Dairy.

Cutbank Creek (creek)

72 E/1 - Cripple Creek
4-1-1-W4
49°00′N 110°04′W
Flows south, crossing the U.S. border, approximately 118 km south-east of Medicine Hat.

This name is descriptive of the extensive number of cutbanks found along the channel through which this creek flows. Cutbanks are usually the steeper of the two riverbanks, located at the point where a river bends. The river is usually deeper, and the current swifter along this bank, and the shoreline tends to drop off steeply. A greater amount of erosion will occur along this riverbank, often creating overhangs. The creek was originally called "Cutbank Coulee" because during the 1920s and 1930s the only time that water flowed through the channel was during the spring run-off or very infrequent heavy rains.

Cutting Lake (lake)

72 L/12 - Brooks
24-19-15-W4
50°37′N 111°57′W
Approximately 110 km north-west of Medicine Hat.

The precise origin for the name of this feature is unknown.

■ **Cypress Hills** (hills)

72 E/9 - Elkwater Lake
7,8-1,2-W4
49°34′N 110°08′W
Approximately 45 km south-east of Medicine Hat.

The name is the English translation of the French name "Les Montanes des Cyprès." This name was given to this region by the Red River Métis who travelled west to hunt bison and trade with the Indians. The Métis incorrectly identified jack pines, native to Manitoba, as *le cypre*. When they travelled west, they mistook the lodgepole pine, native to the Cypress Hills region, for jack pines. As a result, they called this area "Les Montagnes des Cyprès" which was later anglicized by English settlers. Cypress, or *cyprès* in French, refers to several species of coniferous trees of the genus *Cupressus*, having dark green, scalelike, overlapping leaves.

The natives have their own names for these hills: In Cree, *mi-na-ti-kak* or *ne-a-ti-kak*, translating to "the beautiful highlands;" in Stoney, *pa-ha-toonga*, which translates to "thunder building hills;" in Blackfoot, *aiekunekwe*, or "the hills of whispering pines."

Cypress Hills Provincial Park

(provincial park)
72 E/9 - Elkwater Lake
15-8-2-W4
49°38′N 110°12′W
Approximately 45 km south-east of Medicine Hat.

In 1886 a major fire destroyed most of the Cypress Hills forest, and much of the unburned forest was cut for lumber and firewood over the next two decades. This rapid depletion of animal and plant habitat, coupled with increased interest in the conservation movement, led to the passing of the Forest Reserve Act in 1906, establishing a 47-square-kilometre section of protected land. In 1911, the Forest Reserves and Parks Act superceded the 1906 Act, and the section of protected land was enlarged to 490 square km, 207 square km of which were in Alberta, and the area was called the "Elkwater Block." Excluding some minor boundary changes, the 1911 "Elkwater Block" coincides with the Cypress Hills Provincial Park. From 1911 to 1930, this area was under the jurisdiction of the Federal Department of the Interior. In 1930, with the Transfer of Resources Act of 1930, control was passed to the province. This caused little change, and reforestation, regulated timber harvesting and fire protection continued. There was no interest in recreational development at this time. In 1929, the area around the south shore of Elkwater Lake was recommended for designation as a park. Administration of the townsite, however, was not transferred to the Provincial Parks Board until 1947. In 1951, the provincial park was extended to include all lands held in the forestry reserve within Alberta. (see Cypress Hills)

Daigle Lake (lake)

82 G/8 - Beaver Mines
14,23-5-1-W5
49°23′N 114°02′W
Approximately 12 km south-west of
Pincher Creek.

The precise origin for the name of this
feature is unknown.

Dalemead (hamlet)

82 I/13 - Dalemead
14-22-27-W4
50°52′N 113°38′W
Approximately 22 km south-east of
Calgary.

The name for this hamlet is a combination
of its location, and the name of a prominent
citizen. Dalemead is located in a valley,
hence "dale," and Dr. Ellwood Mead was
an irrigation specialist in the area, hence
"mead." The community was originally
called "Needmore," although a local school
had the name "Strathmead" which was
passed on to a Canadian Pacific Railway
station in 1914, when it was established
nearby. In 1915 the local United Farmers of
Alberta group gathered petitions to change
the first part of the name to Dale. They
wanted to change the name to avoid
confusion with Strathmore and to establish
a greater sense of individual identity for
their community. As a result, the first part
of the name was changed by February 1916
when the U.F.A. group sent a delegate to a
provincial meeting under the name
"Dalemead U.F.A."

Dalemead Lake (lake)

82 I/13 - Dalemead
35,36-22-27-W4
50°55′N 113°37′W
Approximately 11 km east of Calgary.

(see Dalemead)

_____

*denotes rescinded name or former locality.

Dalroy (hamlet)

82 P/4 - Dalroy
14-25-27-W4
51°08′N 113°40′W
Approximately 25 km east of Calgary.

There are two differing opinions regarding
the name Dalroy. One maintains that it was
named after Mr. G.M. McElroy, an early
settler who ran cattle through the area. *Dal*
is a Scottish prefix, and means "dale" or
"valley." The second story states that a
member of the construction crew for the
Canadian Pacific Railway (1910) came from
a place with a similar name in Scotland. The
post office operated at the site from 15
January 1913 through 30 April 1968.

Dalum (locality)

82 P/7 - Drumheller
1/-27-19-W4
51°18′N 112°38′W
Approximately 15 km south of Drumheller.

"Dansk Folksamfund" had been organized
under the leadership of F.L. Grundtvif, by
men and women from various Danish
communities with the aim of strengthening
the cultural heritage of Danish-American
immigrants on the North American
continent. In 1916, representatives for this
group made contact with the Canadian
Pacific Railway Company, and soon
negotiations were underway for a tract of
land for a colony in Alberta. Mr. J.
Gregersen and Mr. Jens Hvass, both of
Chicago, were sent on a trip to Alberta,
and, in 1917, reserved a settlement for
Danish people. The area was settled in
1917-18 and named Dalum after Mr. Hvass'
home town, and a well-known agriculture
school in Denmark.

* Dauntless (former station)

72 E/15 - Seven Persons
35-11-6-W4
49°57′N 110°43′W

Approximately 10 km south of Medicine
Hat.

This former railway station was named by
the Canadian Cement Company in 1913.
The post office was in operation from 1
January 1914 through 1 December 1917.
The name's precise origin is unknown.

Davis Bottom (bottom)

82 H/10 - Lethbridge
SW-24-9-22-W4
49°44′50"N 112°51′20"W
Approximately 4 km north of Lethbridge.

Named for John Rogers and Samuel Davis
who came to the Lethbridge area in 1884
from the United States, and homesteaded
some of the land along this river bottom.
John was a freighter and Samuel was an
entrepreneur who promoted development
as he moved about. They spent time in
Boulder, Colorado and in northwestern
Montana. In 1882, they obtained jobs
freighting supplies from Fort Benton to
Fort Macleod, and eventually moved to
"Coalhurst" (now Lethbridge).

Davy Coulee (creek)

82 H/15 - Picture Butte
6-11-21-W4
49°52′N 112°51′W
Flows east into Piyami Coulee, approximately 15 km north of Lethbridge.

Named for the first applicant of water
rights to this feature.

Dawson Lake (lake)

82 P/3 - Strathmore
14-25-25-W4
51°08′N 113°23′W
Approximately 45 km east of Calgary.

The name for this lake, officially approved 12 March 1976, was likely after Charles O. Dawson (1876-1956), an early homesteader who located on the north side of this feature. He and his wife, Emily and son, Clifford, arrived from England in July of 1910.

De Winton (hamlet)

82 J/16 - Priddis
36-21-1-W5
50°49′N 114°01′W
Approximately 10 km south of Calgary.

This hamlet was named in 1892 after Major-General Sir Francis De Winton, G.C.M.G., C.B. (1835-1901). He was the Military Secretary to the Marquis of Lorne, the Governor-General of Canada. He organized the De Winton Ranch Co., also known as Brecon Ranch.

Deadfish Creek (creek)

72 L/13 - Wardlow
21-23-13-W4
50°58′N 111°45′W
Flows south-east into Berry Creek, approximately 128 km north-west of Medicine Hat.

The precise origin for the name of this feature is unknown.

Deadhorse Creek (creek)

82 P/2 - Hussar
30-24-19-W4
51°05′N 112°39′W
Flows south into Deadhorse Lake, approximately 38 km south of Drumheller.

Named for its proximity to Deadhorse Lake.

(see Deadhorse Lake)

Deadhorse Lake (lake)

82 P/2 - Hussar
24-24-19,20-W4
51°05′N 112°40′W
Approximately 40 km south of Drumheller.

An Indian legend, dating back to the 1880s, states that there was a Pinto stallion that led a herd of mares and foals. The stallion was sly and would often lead away the Indian horses and no one was able to catch him. The natives, determined to stop the stallion, chased him in relays, around and around the lake, until he got away into the night. The next morning, he was found dead beside the lake, having drunk the water, which is full of alkali. The Indian who found him yelled *spatsa-da-otas*, translating from Blackfoot as "deadhorse."

Deadlodge Canyon (canyon)

72 L/14 - Halsbury
8-10-21-11-W4
50°46′N 111°30′W
Approximately 94 km north north-west of Medicine Hat.

The name is a translation of a Blackfoot term, *eh-taka-skeeneema* translating to "where there are many of our dead lodges." Apparently, a smallpox epidemic destroyed the lives of many natives in this area.

Deadman Gulch (coulee)

72 L/7 - Watching Hill
17-5-W4
50°29′N 110°41′W
Approximately 54 km north of Medicine Hat.

The precise origin for the name of this feature is unknown.

Deer Creek (creek)

72 E/4 - Coutts
2-2-12-W4
49°06′N 111°23′W

Flows north-east into Milk River, approximately 115 km south-east of Lethbridge.

The precise origin for the name of this feature is unknown.

Del Bonita (hamlet)

82 H/2 - Shanks Lake
18-1-21-W4
49°02′N 112°48′W
Approximately 70 km south of Lethbridge.

This point near the Canada–U.S. border has served as a port of entry. *Del Bonita* is the Spanish name meaning "of the pretty," or "beautiful valley," both descriptive names. This port of southern Alberta was once claimed by Spain as part of its American Possession, as the Milk River which flows nearby drains into the Mississippi River, eventually emptying into the Gulf of Mexico. The region was given to France as part of the Mississippi Purchase before being claimed by Britain. This locality has another possible origin: local residents say that the "del" is for "dell" and Bonita for St. Bonita, a tenth-century French saint who was a goose-girl. The native name used for this area is *dai-kim-i-kay*, translating as "opening through the ridge."

Delacour (hamlet)

82 P/4 - Dalroy
24-25-28-W4
51°09′N 113°46′W
Approximately 20 km north-east of Calgary.

This station was named after a foreman on the Grand Trunk Pacific Railway construction crew. The line became part of the Canadian National Railway line in 1914. It was previously believed that Delacour was a French name meaning "of the heart;" however, it has since been revealed that Mr. DeLacour was from Denmark. The first passenger train went through here 28 February 1914. The post office has been in operation since 15 November 1915.

Delmas Coulee (creek)

72 E/9 - Elkwater Lake
36-6-3-W4
49°31'N 110°17'W
Flows south-west into Thelma Creek, approximately 58 km south-west of Medicine Hat.

This coulee, a tributary of Thelma Creek, was named for Henry Delmas and his wife, who lived in Thelma for 35 years. Henry operated the Thelma post office for a short time. They eventually moved to Saskatchewan in 1947.

Dempster Coulee (creek)

72 E/9 - Elkwater Lake
22-8-4-W4
49°40'N 110°28'W
Runs north into Bullshead Creek, approximately 40 km south-east of Medicine Hat.

Named for Mr. John Dempster, originally of Belfast, Northern Ireland, who established a horse ranch in the Eagle Butte district in 1905. John expanded his ranching operation and his son Jack eventually took over. Jack operated it as a mixed farming operation before selling out and moving to Medicine Hat where he opened a car dealership. The coulee is found on what was once the original Dempster ranching land.

Denhart (locality)

72 I/11 - Jenner
2-20-11-W4
50°40'N 111°25'W
Approximately 87 km north-west of Medicine Hat.

Formerly called "Rainy Hills" (see Rainy Hills), the post office here opened 1 November 1916 and was named after a local farmer. The post office closed 31 July 1918, but it served as a Canadian Pacific Railway station for some years afterward.

---

*denotes rescinded name or former locality.

* Dennis (former locality)

72 L/3 - Suffield
17-14-9-W4
50°11'N 111°03'W
Approximately 38 km west north-west of Medicine Hat.

This former Canadian Pacific Railway station opened circa 1910 and was named after Col. J.S. Dennis, of the Department of Colonization and Development associated with the railway.

* Dewdney (former post office)

82 I/12 - High River
28-20-29-W4
50°44'N 113°59'W
Approximately 33 km south of Calgary.

The post office which operated here between 1 August 1891 and 1 March 1897 was named after the Lieutenant-Governor of the Northwest Territories from 1881 to 1888, Sir Edgar Dewdney (1835-1916). He was also Indian Commissioner for the Northwest Territories from 1879 to 1888. The community was known as Okotoks before the post office was called Dewdney. The name was changed back to Okotoks in March 1897.

(see Okotoks)

Diamond City (hamlet)

82 H/15 - Picture Butte
6-10-21-W4
49°48'N 112°51'W
Approximately 6 km north of Lethbridge.

Originally, the community was to be named "Black Diamond Mine," after the mine located here, and was probably descriptive of the vast quantities of coal situated in the area. Much prosperity had been derived from this valuable resource. As this name had already been used for another post office, the alternative name, Diamond City was chosen.

Dickinson Creek (creek)

72 E/3 - Aden
25-1-12-W4
49°03'N 111°29'W
Flows north-east into Macdonald Creek, approximately 120 km south south-west of Medicine Hat.

Named for Norman and Robert Dickinson, immigrants from England, who were early homesteaders in the region. This creek runs through their original homestead.

Dinosaur Park (provincial park)

72 L/13 - Wardlow
9-21-11,12-W4
50°47'N 111°30'W
Approximately 97 km north-west of Medicine Hat.

This provincial park, 5945.92 hectares in size, was created in 1955 by Order-in-council 569/79. The park encloses one of the most extensive and productive sources of Cretaceous dinosaur fossils in the world. Over seventy million years ago, this area provided a fertile habitat for dinosaurs. The park and the prairie located along the Red Deer River has been declared a United Nations Educational, Scientific, and Cultural Organization World Heritage Site.

* Dinton (former locality)

82 I/12 - High River
28-20-26-W4
50°43'N 113°35'W
Approximately 50 km south-east of Calgary.

This former locality takes its name from a place in England with the same name. The post office operated from 1 August 1904 to 31 August 1924.

Dip Creek (creek)

82 P/1 - Finnegan
18-25-16-W4
51°08'N 112°05'W

Flows south-west into Red Deer River, approximately 55 km south-east of Drumheller.

The precise origin for the name of this feature is unknown.

Dipping Vat Lake (lake)

82 H/5 - Pincher Creek
7-4-27-W4
49°17′N 113°37′W
Approximately 72 km south-west of Lethbridge.

The precise origin for the name of this lake is unknown. The name was made official 9 July 1942.

Dishpan Lake (lake)

72 L/10 - Easy Coulee
7-19-4,5-W4
50°36′N 110°33′W
Approximately 60 km north of Medicine Hat.

The precise origin for the name of this feature is unknown.

Dogpound (locality)

82 O/8 - Crossfield
5-29-3-W5
51°28′N 114°24′W
Approximately 52 km north north-west of Calgary.

The name for this locality was first used in 1883 by a surveyor named Fawcett. The post office opened 1 January 1900 and closed 1 March 1900 at which time the name "Bradbourne" was used. It reopened under the name Dogpound 1 March 1905 and remained open until 10 March 1970. The Cree name, *mizekampehpoocahan* means, "wolf caught in Buffalo Pound." Joseph Burr Tyrrell, a geologist and historian on the staff of the Geological Survey of Canada from 1881 until 1898 suggested the Cree name *ko-ma-tas-ta-*

moin, meaning "stolen horse (or dog)" creek as another interpretation. The Stoney Indian name, *so-mun-ib-wapta*, which translates, "Edge Creek," is yet another possibility. The Palliser Expedition map of 1865 shows this particular feature as "Edge Creek."
   Of these several versions of the origin, perhaps the most likely is its derivation from the translation given by the Cree. It refers to the dogs pounding on the banks of the creek as the Indian braves returned to winter camp after hunting food. During the winter, it is said that some tribes settled along the banks of the creek, as it provided a natural roadway to the game area.

Dorothy (hamlet)

82 P/8 - Dorothy
4-27-17-W4
51°18′N 112°19′W
Approximately 33 km south-east of Drumheller.

The name for this post office, when it was established 1 February 1908, was taken after the first and only baby born in the district at that time, Dorothy Wilson, daughter of Jack Wilson, an early rancher.

Douglas Creek (creek)

72 L/13 - Wardlow
18-23-14-W4
50°57′N 111°57′W
Flows south-east into Red Deer River, approximately. 133 km north-west of Medicine Hat.

This feature was named for the original owner of the land through which this creek flows. No other information about this individual is available.

Drifting Sand Hills (hills)

82 I/14 - Gleichen
21-22-W4
50°49′N 113°00′W

Approximately 80 km east south-east of Calgary.

The descriptive term for these hills is a direct translation of the Blackfoot name, *ispatsik-way*.

Drowning Ford (river crossing)

72 L/7 - Watching Hill
23-17-5-W4
50°27′N 110°35′W
Approximately 45 km north of Medicine Hat.

The precise origin for the name of this feature is unknown.

Drumheller (city)

82 P/7 - Drumheller
11-29-20-W4
51°28′N 112°42′W
Approximately 100 km north-east of Calgary.

Drumheller, 1918

This city was named after Samuel Drumheller (1864-1925), a pioneer in the Alberta coalfields. He was born in Walla Walla, Washington and came north to Canada with a herd of cattle. Drumheller bought the land in 1910 on which the townsite is now located from Thomas B.

Greentree, the original homesteader. Drumheller's name was applied to the post office which opened 1 April 1911 although rail service was not available until 1912. Drumheller was incorporated as a village in 1913, as a town in 1916, and as a city in 1930. Samuel Drumheller was the promoter of the location with the Northern Townsite Company (a subsidiary of the Canadian Northern Railway Company). A Committee, naming the town, recommended that it be named after Samuel, the founder of the Drumheller Land Company.

Dry Coulee (coulee)

82 J/1 - Langford Creek
13-12-1-W5
50°00′N 114°00′W
Flows north-east into Trout Creek, approximately 30 km west of Claresholm.

Officially approved 3 December 1941, the name for this coulee is likely descriptive.

* Drywood (former railway point)

82 H/5 - Pincher Creek
24-4-29-W4
49°18′N 113°47′W
Approximately 81 km south-west of Lethbridge.

(see Drywood Creek)

Drywood Creek (creek)

82 H/5 - Pincher Creek
15-4-28-W4
49°18′N 113°41′W
Flows east into Waterton Reservoir, approximately 78 km south-west of Lethbridge.

This creek also has a local Indian name in Blackfoot, *ohsakisitoti*, or "backfat," from the fat on the back of a buffalo. The well-established name, Drywood Creek, was made official 8 July 1954.

Dubois Hill (hill)

72 L/7 - Watching Hill
32-16-7-W4
50°23′N 110°56′W
Approximately 40 km north of Medicine Hat.

The precise origin for the name of this feature is unknown.

Duchess (village)

72 L/12 - Brooks
32-20-14-W4
50°43′N 111°55′W
Approximately 117 km north-west of Medicine Hat.

Named for the Duchess of Connaught, wife of the Duke of Connaught and Strathearn. The Duke owned a large amount of land in the Brooks area and was appointed Governor-General of Canada in succession to Earl Grey in 1911. Many of the communities in this area are named after members of the royal family.

Dunbar Coulee (coulee)

72 L/14 - Halsbury
16-21-11-W4
50°18′N 110°29′W
Runs south into Red Deer River Valley, approximately 97 km north-west of Medicine Hat.

Named for J.M. Dunbar and family, early homesteaders who operated a ranch in the immediate area. Mr. Dunbar referred to the coulee as the Big Coulee, and named his ranch "Big Coulee Ranch."

Dunmore (hamlet)

72 E/15 - Seven Persons
3-12-5-W4
49°58′N 110°36′W
Approximately 5 km south-east of Medicine Hat.

Named for the 7th Earl of Dunmore, Charles A. Murray, who visited the west in

1883. The Earl was a major stockholder in the Canadian Agricultural Coal and Colonization Company. The post office here was known as "Coleridge" between 1905 and 1957.

Dunphy (locality)

82 P/7 - Drumheller
14-29-21-W4
51°28′N 112°52′W
Approximately 10 km north-west of Drumheller.

The precise origin for the name of this feature is unknown.

Dunshalt (locality)

82 P/3 - Strathmore
20-25-24-W4
51°09′N 113°18′W
Approximately 50 km east of Calgary.

Archibald McLean and his family were the first settlers here arriving in 1901. They came from the Falkland Islands and homesteaded approximately 2 km south of where Nightingale is now. The railway lines went through this area circa 1910-11, and it is at this point where the two railways intersect. Archibald named the station after his former home town in Scotland, Dunshelt, Fife. The post office operated from 15 August 1914 through 20 May 1926.

Durward (railway point)

82 I/5 - Nanton
30-15-27-W4
50°18′N 113°43′W
Approximately 75 km south of Calgary.

This former Canadian Pacific Railway station (1913-16) was named for *Quentin Durward*, a novel by Sir Walter Scott.

■ Eagle Butte (locality)

72 E/9 - Elkwater Lake
36-7-4-W4
49°36′N 110°26′W

Approximately 50 km south south-east of Medicine Hat.

The post office here opened 1 May 1900 and was closed 15 July 1963. It is named for its proximity to a long-abandoned nesting ground for eagles located on top of a prominent butte. Local residents have suggested that because of this feature's elevation, it provides an "eagle's view" of the surrounding area.

Eagle Hill (hill)

82 I/14 - Gleichen
21-23-24-W4
50°58′N 113°17′W
Approximately 45 km east of Calgary.

In the past, eagles used the summit of this hill for nesting. The Blackfoot call the hill *petoomoxecing*, translating to "many eagles have been killed," the Cree word is *ki-hi-a-watis* and the Stoney name is *mha-moos-ni-bin*. Apparently, many eagles disappeared from the area in 1898 after a great forest fire. During World War I, a beacon was affixed to the top of the hill, and in 1975, there was still a cairn of rock and cement at its peak.

Eagle Lake (lake)

82 P/3 - Strathmore
32-23-24-W4
51°00′N 113°19′W
Approximately 50 km east of Calgary.

(see Eagle Hill)

Eagle Springs (springs)

72 L/6 - Alderson
36-16-9-W4
50°22′N 111°06′W
Within the Suffield Military Reserve, approximately 50 km north north-west of Medicine Hat.

The precise origin for the name of this feature is unknown.

East Arrowwood Creek (creek)

82 I/14 - Gleichen
9-21-23-W4
50°46′N 113°07′W

Flows north into Bow River, approximately 66 km south-east of Calgary. This creek is named for its proximity to Arrowwood

(see Arrowwood)

East Berry Creek (creek)

72 L/13 - Wardlow
26-22-12-W4
50°55′N 111°36′W
Flows south into Berry Creek, approximately 113 km north-west of Medicine Hat.

This creek is named for its position as a tributary to Berry Creek.

(see Berry Creek)

East Berry Reservoir (reservoir)

72 M/6 - Plover Lake
26,27-11-W4
51°16′N 111°24′W
Approximately 91 km east south-east of Drumheller.

The reservoir is likely named for its proximity to East Berry Creek.

East Coulee (hamlet)

82 P/8 - Dorothy
28,29-27-18-W4
51°20′N 112°29′W
Approximately 18 km south-east of Drumheller.

The descriptive name for this hamlet refers to the combination of its position in the Red Deer River Valley, east of Drumheller, and that it is near a coulee, a steep-sided valley or ravine, usually dry, that has been worn away by heavy rains or melting snow. The post office opened 1 June 1929.

East Fork McAlpine Creek (creek)

72 E/16 - Irvine
NE1/4-3-10-2-W4
49°47′40″N 110°11′03″W
Flows north-west into McAlpine Creek, approximately 47 km south-east of Medicine Hat.

The creek is named for its position as a tributary to McAlpine Creek. The Water Survey of Canada placed a number of gauging stations around the province, and requested that the creeks on which they are situated, some dry for most of the year, be named.

(see McAlpine Creek)

Easy Coulee (coulee)

72 L/10 - Easy Coulee
19-6,7-W4
50°39′N 110°52′W
Approximately 50 km north of Medicine Hat.

The precise origin for the name of this feature is unknown.

Easy Lake (lake)

72 L/10 - Easy Coulee
17-18-6-W4
50°31′N 110°48′W
Approximately 50 km north of Medicine Hat.

The precise origin for the name of this feature is unknown.

Eight Mile Lake (lake)

82 H/15 - Picture Butte
NE-31-9-20-W4
49°47′N 112°41′W
Approximately 13 km north-east of Lethbridge.

The lake is about 12.8 km (the equivalent of eight miles) north-east of Lethbridge "as the crow flies." The area is a natural depression and was a prominent lake at one time. The area was to be completely drained and the land reclaimed but local ecologists objected because the area is used by many species of birds and ducks. The lake is now partially drained and the rest is a small slough.

Eladesor (locality)
82 P/7 - Drumheller
12-28-19-W4
51°24′N 112°35′W
Approximately 12 km south-east of Drumheller.

The precise origin for the name of this former Canadian Pacific Railway siding is unknown. Art O'Dwyer had a small mine here and the siding was likely established to handle the coal. The trains stopped here only once a day to collect the coal.

Elbow River (river)
82 O/1 - Calgary
14-24-1-W5
51°03′N 114°02′W
Flows north-east into Bow River, in the middle of the city of Calgary.

The name for this river is descriptive and refers to the point at which it abruptly turns northward and enters the Bow River. David Thompson refers to it as "Hokaikshi" in 1814, and Arrowsmith's map of 1859 labels it "Hokaikshi" or "Moose River." The Cree call it *o-too-kwa-na*, and according to Tyrrell, the Stoney refer to it as *mn-no-tho-ap-ta*. Until 1880, it was often called "Swift Creek," after the speed of its watercourse.

* Elcan (former locality)
82 H/16 - Taber
4-10-17-W4
49°48′N 112°14′W
Approximately 40 km east of Lethbridge.

---
*denotes rescinded name or former locality.

The name reflects the influence that Mormon settlers had on this area, and southwestern Alberta generally. The name is derived from the word tabernacle, one of which was built in Cardston. "Elcan" contains the last five letters of the word "tabernacle," spelled backwards. Taber, the first five letters, is the name of the next station down the line. A post office was established at Elcan from 1 April 1910 through 31 October 1924.

Elkwater (hamlet)
72 E/9 - Elkwater Lake
24-8-3-W4
49°40′N 110°17′W
Approximately 45 km south-east of Medicine Hat.

The Blackfoot name for this area is *ponokiokwe*, and refers to the many species of deer that congregated at Elkwater Lake. With the arrival of white settlers, the original elk population was hunted to extinction before the turn of the century. A new herd of elk were re-introduced to the area in 1938, to provide settlers some variety in their diet. With the establishment of the Cypress Hills Provincial Park, the elk have become a nuisance for many ranchers, destroying hay and forage supplies.

Elkwater Lake (lake)
72 E/9 - Elkwater Lake
23,25-8-3-W4
49°39′N 110°18′W
Approximately 43 km south-east of Medicine Hat.

(see Elkwater)

Eltham (locality)
82 I/12 - High River
4-19-26-W4
50°35′N 113°33′W

Approximately 45 km south-east of Calgary.

The precise origin for this name is not known; however, it may be taken from the district of Eltham, in London, England.

Emerson Lake (lake)
82 I/12 - High River
6-5-19-28-W4
50°35′45″N 113°51′00″W
Approximately 46 km south of Calgary.

This is a relatively new feature and was named for George Emerson, one of the early ranchers in the district. George Emerson was a prospector, Indian trader, financier, and Hudson's Bay man and helped lead trail herds into the Canadian West. Emerson contributed extensively to the opening of the west in its most colourful and adventurous days. The dates of his birth and death are unknown.

Empress (village)
72 L/16 - Bindloss
13-23-1-W4
50°57′N 110°00′W
Approximately 108 km north north-west of Medicine Hat.

Named in 1913 for Queen Victoria, Empress of India (1821-1901). This title was given the British Monarch after the crushing of the Indian uprising known as the Indian Mutiny (1856-57). Many communities in this part of Alberta are named after members of royal families.

Empress Creek (creek)
72 L/16 - Bindloss
8-24-23-1-W4
50°58′N 110°00′W
Flows south-east into Red Deer River, approximately 115 km north north-east of Medicine Hat.

(see Empress)

Enchant (hamlet)

82 I/1 - Vauxhall
17-14-18-W4
50°10′N 112°25′W
Approximately 56 km north-east of
Lethbridge.

The name may indicate the feelings of the
area's first settlers: they may have been
impressed or "enchanted" with their new
life. A post office, previously known as
"Lost Lake," opened under the name
"Enchant" 1 February 1915.

* Endon (former post office)

72 E/6 - Foremost
14-6-9-W4
49°29′N 110°06′W
Approximately 65 km south of Medicine
Hat.

(see Etzikom)

Ensign (hamlet)

82 I/6 - Vulcan
31-17-25-W4
50°28′N 113°26′W
Approximately 60 km south-east of
Calgary.

The national flag, the Red Ensign, was the
recognized flag of Canada until 1965. It was
based on the ensign flown by British
merchant ships. The post office here
opened 15 June 1911 and commemorated
the name of the flag. The post office closed
31 January 1986.

Entice (locality)

82 P/6 - Carbon
14-29-24-W4
51°29′N 113°17′W
Approximately 40 km west of Drumheller.

The Canadian Pacific Railway line came
through this area in 1921, on its route from

Acme to Drumheller. The name Entice was
chosen for this station by railroad officials,
in hopes of encouraging settlement in the
district. Kneehill Creek, which flows
through Entice, was dammed in the early
1920s to provide water to refill steam
engines.

Erickson Coulee (coulee)

72 E/7 - Manyberries
9-5-7-W4
49°22′N 110°53′W
Runs north-west into Irrigation Creek,
approximately 78 km south of Medicine
Hat.

Named for John Erickson, an early settler
in the region, who applied for the water
rights for this coulee because it ran through
his property.

Etzikom (hamlet)

72 E/6 - Foremost
14-6-9-W4
49°29′N 111°06′W
Approximately 67 km south-west of
Medicine Hat.

Homesteaders arrived to this area as early
as 1909, five years before the Canadian
Pacific Railway staked its Foremost-
Weyburn line. In order to facilitate farming,
the railway placed stops approximately 16
km away from each other, easing the
travelling burden, particularly for outlying
farmers, and simultaneously giving each
community a chance to grow. Etzikom was
one of the stops established by the railway.
It is a Blackfoot term meaning "valley."
This place was also known by the Blackfoot
as *misloonsisco*, translating "crows springs,"
because Crow Indian parties used to water
their horses at the creek which flows
through Etzikom Coulee. Just as the town
began growing in 1915, a controversy over
its name developed. Someone in the post
office department decided that Etzikom
was not a suitable name, and arbitrarily

changed it to "Endon." The officials with
the railway had it changed back within the
year.

■ **Etzikom Coulee** (coulee)

82 H/8 - Warner
19-6-16-W4
49°28′N 112°08′W
An east-west trending coulee, approximately 51 km south-east of Lethbridge.

(see Etzikom)

* Ewelme (former post office)

82 H/6 - Raley
6,7-6-26-W4
49°27′N 113°29′W
Approximately 55 km south-west of
Lethbridge.

The post office here operated from 1 May
1905 through 29 February 1928 and was
named after a village in Oxfordshire,
England.

Excel (hamlet)

72 M/7 - Cereal
13-28-5-W4
51°23′N 110°35′W
Approximately 154 km east of Drumheller.

The name was suggested by Mr. A.E.
Wetheral at what was probably the community's first Board of Trade meeting that
took place at the home of Arthur
Gulleckson. The name was suggested on
the basis of the community's excellent
geographical location and for the ambitious
plans that had been suggested for the
townsite. Apparently, Mr. A.E. Wetheral,
who would be the first postmaster, made
the comment, "let us excel." A post office
was established in June 1911.

Excoffin Bottom (bottom)

82 H/10 - Lethbridge
W-16-8-22-W4
49°38′50″N 112°55′50″W

---

*denotes rescinded name or former locality.

Approximately 9 km south-west of
Lethbridge.

Named for John Excoffin, a bachelor who
came to the Lethbridge area from France,
prior to the 1902 flood, and settled along
the river with several other bachelor
squatters. In 1903, he filed on a homestead
and obtained possession in 1907. Excoffin
raised grain and cattle on his homestead
until the late 1940s. Throughout the years,
he gained a reputation for being somewhat
eccentric. One of his peculiarities included
playing the French horn to call his cattle in
at the end of the day—apparently, they
came running when they heard the music.
On days when certain atmospheric conditions existed, Excoffin's horn playing could
be heard for several miles.

Expanse Coulee (coulee)

82 H/16 - Taber
12-16-W4
49°58′N 112°05′W
Runs south into Oldman River, approximately 57 km north-east of Lethbridge.

This coulee is known locally as both
"Rocky Coulee," a descriptive name
common to many of these types of features,
and "Perry Coulee," after Eber Perry. Mr.
Perry was a rancher who settled in the area
in 1904, and when he became too old to be
useful as a rancher, it is said that he killed
himself. Since 1924, however, this feature
has been known descriptively as Expanse
Coulee, and it is this name that has survived
over the years.

* Eyremore (former post office)

82 I/8 - Scandia
9-17-17-W4
50°26′N 112°14′W
Approximately 90 km north north-east of
Lethbridge.

(see Bow City)

---

*denotes rescinded name or former locality.

Faith (post office)

72 E/6 - Foremost
6-4-9-W4
49°17′N 111°13′W
Approximately 90 km south-west of
Medicine Hat.

James Sergeant operated this post office
which was opened in 1911. Sergeant named
the post office after his daughter.

Fareham (post office)

82 H/3 - Cardston
16-1-23-W4
49°02′N 113°02′W
Approximately 73 km south-west of
Lethbridge.

(see Whiskey Gap)

Farrow (locality)

82 I/11 - Arrowwood
9-20-25-W4
50°41′N 113°24′W
Approximately 53 km south-east of
Calgary.

The name is taken from the family name of
the wife of A. Halkett, a former General
Superintendent of the Canadian Pacific
Railway. A post office opened 15 January
1931 and closed 15 November 1959.
Originally known as "Glenview," it was
also called "Randle" for a short time.

* **Fieldholme** (former locality)

72 M/4 - Pollockville
6-24-14-W4
51°02′N 111°56′W
Approximately 72 km south-east of
Drumheller.

Named after the first postmaster, G.S.
Field. The name was changed in 1911. (see
Hutton)

_____
*denotes rescinded name or former locality.

Fifteen Mile Butte (butte)

82 H/7 - Raymond
20-6-20-W4
49°30′N 112°38′W
Approximately 24 km south of Lethbridge.

The name describes this feature's distance
south from Lethbridge.

Fincastle (locality)

82 H/16 - Taber
7-10-15-W4
49°48′N 112°00′W
Approximately 60 km east of Lethbridge.

Viscount Fincastle is a title of the Earl of
Dunmore. (see Dunmore)

Fincastle Lake (lake)

72 E/13 - Grassy Lake
16-10-15-W4
49°50′N 111°59′W
Approximately 62 km east of Lethbridge.

(see Fincastle)

Finn Coulee (coulee)

72 E/7 - Manyberries
9-6-5-W4
49°27′N 110°37′W
Runs south-west into Manyberries Creek,
approximately 64 km south of Medicine
Hat.

Officially approved 12 January 1968, this
coulee was named for the large number of
Finnish settlers in the area.

Finnegan (locality)

82 P/1 - Finnegan
18-25-15-W4
51°07′N 112°04′W
Approximately 55 km south-east of
Drumheller.

John Finnegan (1842-1924), after whom
this locality is named, was Gleichen's first
carpenter who built some of the first

buildings in Gleichen. Finnegan came from
Selkirk, Scotland and worked with the
Canadian Pacific Railway carpenters until
business slowed down. At this point, John
began homesteading on the Red Deer River
where he operated a ferry which was also
named for him. The post office here opened
under the name Finnegan 1 August 1930.

Fish Creek (creek)

82 P/8 - Drumheller
8-28-16-W4
51°23′N 112°12′W
Flows south into Little Fish Lake, approximately 35 km east south-east of
Drumheller.

The precise origin for the name of this
feature is unknown.

Fish Creek Provincial Park

(provincial park)
82 J/16 - Priddis
3-23-1-W5
50°55′30″N 114°04′00″W
Within the city limits of Calgary.

The name was officially approved in 1975
and was revised in 1978. This park is named
for the creek which runs through it. Fish
Creek is Calgary's 18 km long "backyard"
where one may see beaver dams, coyote
dens and a heron colony, where deer roam
the park and hawks soar overhead. The
park offers facilities for swimming, cycling,
jogging, horseback riding, and picnicking.
In winter, one could choose to go tobog-
ganing or cross-country skiing.

Fish Lake (lake)
82 G/8 - Beaver Mines
36-4-1-W5
49°20′N 114°00′W
Approximately 17 km south-west of
Pincher Creek.

This lake has been known by this name
since 29 August 1884, when it abounded in
trout weighing from three to five kilo-
grams.

* Fishburn (former locality)
82 H/5 - Pincher Creek
29-5-28-W4
49°25′N 113°44′W
Approximately 71 km west south-west of
Lethbridge.

Named for Mr. A.M. Fish, one of the
community's earliest settlers. A post office
operated here from 1 November 1894
through 31 August 1942.

Fitzgerald (locality)
72 E/15 - Seven Persons
7-11-6-W4
49°53′N 110°50′W
Approximately 10 km south-west of
Medicine Hat.

Named for Edward Fitzgerald, a part-time
Purchasing Agent for the Canadian Pacific
Railway.

Five Mile Creek (creek)
82 H/12 - Brocket
10-9-29-W4
49°43′N 113°51′W
Flows south into Beaver Creek, approximately 73 km west of Lethbridge.

The descriptive name for this creek refers to
its length. The name was officially approved 8 July 1954.

Flagpole Hill (hill)
82 P/7 - Drumheller
5-20-29-20-W4
51°21′45″N 112°47′25″W
Approximately 6 km north-west of
Drumheller.

The hill was named when James Russell, a
local rancher, erected a flagpole on top of
the hill to commemorate the coronation of
King George V in 1910. A steel flagpole has
been put in the place of the original
wooden one. The property still belongs to
the Russell family.

* Florann (former locality)
72 E/6 - Foremost
2-4-11-W4
49°16′N 111°24′W
Approximately 97 km south-west of
Medicine Hat.

The name was suggested to federal surveyors by an early settler, Leo J. Grady. His
wife, Ann, and her sister, Florence
Whitney, operated a small store in the area
and referred to it as Florann, a combination
of their first names.

* Flowerdale (former locality)
72 M/5 - Sunnynook
1-28-12-W4
51°22′N 111°34′W
Approximately 79 km east of Drumheller.

Named by Annie Twelvetree for the
abundance of wild flowers growing along
the banks of Berry Creek and the adjacent
fields. A post office was opened 15 May
1911 and operated until 31 March 1917.

Fly Lake (lake)
72 E/9 - Elkwater Lake
17-8-3-W4
49°39′N 110°23′W
Approximately 45 km south-east of
Medicine Hat.

The name is likely descriptive of the vast
number of very large horse flies around the
lake in the summer months.

Foothill Creek (creek)
82 H/5 - Pincher Creek
29-5-27-W4
49°25′N 113°35′W
Flows north-east into Waterton River,
approximately 64 km south-west of
Lethbridge.

The name for this creek may refer to its
location in the foothills, but its precise
origin is unconfirmed. There is some local
use for the name "Dryfork Creek;"
however, its origin is unknown as well.

* Forcin (former post office)
72 M/5 - Sunnynook
23,24-28-14-W4
51°24′N 111°52′W
Approximately 60 km east of Drumheller.

The precise origin for the name of this
feature is unknown. The name was changed
from "Rose Lynn #1."

■ **Foremost** (village)
72 E/6 - Foremost
17-6-11-W4
49°29′N 111°25′W
Approximately 80 km south-west of
Medicine Hat.

In January of 1910, the area around what is
now Foremost was opened for the filing of
homesteads and soon attracted the attention
of settlers. A post office was opened at
"Webber," two miles south of the present
village, to serve the incoming settlers. In
1913 the Canadian Pacific Railway an-
nounced that a railway would be built from
Lethbridge to Weyburn, Saskatchewan. The
steel reached Foremost in October of that
year. With its arrival a new townsite was
laid out and grew rapidly. The station was
named Foremost and this was as far as the

_____
*denotes rescinded name or former locality.

railway went for two years. When Fore-most post office was opened 15 January 1914, the one at Webber closed. The people of Foremost claim that their community is the friendliest to be found, and this, with their will to succeed, has given the village its optimistic name.

Forest Lawn (locality)
82 P/4 - Dalroy
24-29-W4
51°02'N 113°58'W
Within the city limits of Calgary.

This locality is now a subdivision of Calgary, and has been since 31 December 1961. The name is taken after the famous Hollywood Cemetery, an exclusive spot in Los Angeles, California which boasts beautiful trees and gardens. The name Forest Lawn was chosen by two American real estate promoters, Mr. McCullough and Mr. Smythe, who used the reputation of the name to promote the area as prime residen-tial land. To further encourage sales and development, the two men laid down railway ties in order to convince investors that a rail line would pass through here, even though there were no official plans to do so. A post office operated here from 1 December 1913 through 1 October 1959, during which time the provincial govern-ment combined the three districts of Hubalta, Albert Park and Forest Lawn into the village of Forest Lawn, which eventu-ally developed into the town.

Forster Reservoir (reservoir)
72 L/13 - Wardlow
28-23-13-W4
50°59'N 111°47'W
Approximately 124 km north-west of Medicine Hat.

This reservoir was constructed by the Prairie Farm Rehabilitation Administration on deeded land held by J.W. Forster and family since the early 1900s. These early homesteaders owned several quarter sections of land in 23-13-W4. The name for this reservoir was officially approved 6 December 1968.

Fort Macleod (town)
82 H/11 - Fort Macleod
12-9-26-W4
49°43'N 113°25'W
Approximately 40 km west of Lethbridge.

Named for Lieutenant-Colonel James Farquharson Macleod (1836-1894) who established a North West Mounted Police fort here in 1874. The original fort was built on an island in the Oldman River, but was later moved to the present site of the town of Fort Macleod following several floods. Macleod was admitted to the bar of Upper Canada in 1860. Receiving promotion and credit during the suppression of the 1869-70 North West Rebellion, he was selected to be second in command of the "Great March of 1874" carried out by the first contingent of the NWMP. Besides working his way up to the position of Commis-sioner in 1877, Macleod also attained the level of a puisne judge of the Supreme Court of the Northwest Territories in 1887. The Blackfoot word for Fort Macleod is *stamix otokan-okowy*, which translates to "home of a head of a bull." Colonel Macleod was known to the Indians as "Bull's head" because he had a buffalo head over the entrance to his residence. The crest of the Macleod clan in Scotland is also a bull's head, which may further explain the existence of this feature over the door of his home.

Forty Mile Coulee (coulee)
72 E/11 - Maleb
7-10-W4
49°33'N 111°12'W
Runs south-west into Seven Persons Coulee, approximately 65 km south-west of Medicine Hat.

The name for this coulee describes its length.

Foster Creek (creek)
82 O/7 - Wildcat Hills
19-29-5-W5
51°29'N 114°42'W
Flows north into Little Red Deer River, approximately 67 km north-west of Calgary.

Charles Foster, after whom this creek and nearby hill were officially named 11 June 1930, was born in 1865 in Escanda, Michi-gan. He came to the area in 1919.

Foster Hills (hill)
82 O/7 - Wildcat Hills
7-29-5-W5
51°28'N 114°42'W
Approximately 66 km north-west of Calgary.

(see Foster Creek)

Four Mile Creek (creek)
72 L/16 - Bindloss
8-24-23-1-W4
50°58'N 110°01'W
Flows south-east into Red Deer River, approximately 115 km north north-east of Medicine Hat.

The name "Empress Creek" was submitted in 1920 by the Department of the Interior Reclamation Services. Four Mile Creek was the local name for this creek because it is that distance from the fork of the Red Deer and the Saskatchewan rivers. Since this type of name was being discouraged in 1921 the name "Empress" was approved, but it has since been changed.

Fourways Creek (creek)
72 E/7 - Manyberries
35-6-7-W4
49°25'N 110°50'W

Flows south into Irrigation Creek, approximately 65 km south-west of Medicine Hat.

The precise origin for the name of this feature is unknown.

* Fox (former locality)

72 E/9 - Elkwater Lake
20-7-1-W4
49°34'N 110°06'W
Approximately 65 km south south-east of Medicine Hat.

The post office operated here from 1 July 1912 through 7 March 1964 and was named after its first postmaster, James H. Fox.

Fox Creek (creek)

82 P/7 - Drumheller
9-29-20-W4
51°28'N 112°46'W
Flows south into Red Deer River, immediately west of Drumheller.

The name for this creek which begins out of a large slough at Munson refers to the fact that the coulee is a gathering place for the many foxes in the area. The name has been in use since the early part of the century.

Frank Lake (lake)

82 I/12 - High River
25-18,19-27,28-W4
50°34'N 113°43'W
Approximately 49 km south of Calgary.

Previously known as "Begg Lake," "Green Lake," "Windsor Lake" and "Big Lake," this lake was given its current name in 1926. Christopher E. Frank took up residence in the locality which was eventually named Frankburg (after him) in 1902. He served as postmaster in 1905. In 1910, he was made Bishop of the Mormon Church for the area. He originally came to the area for the

purpose of locating land for the Church of Jesus Christ of Latter -day Saints' settlement. He served as Bishop from 1910 to 1923 and from 1926 to 1930. Frank died in Calgary in 1962.

* Frankburg (former locality)

82 I/12 - High River
21-18-27-W4
50°32'N 113°38'W
Approximately 55 km south south-east of Calgary.

Named for Christopher E. Frank, who came to the area from Utah with his brother John, in 1902. Christopher served as the first postmaster, and he and his brother were the first members of the Mormon church to settle near High River. In 1911, Bishop Frank opened Frankburg Hall which served the community as both a meeting place and a church. By the mid-1930s, many townspeople had dispersed to other areas.

* Fraserton (former locality)

72 M/5 - Sunnynook
27-27-14-W4
51°20'N 111°54'W
Approximately 58 km east of Drumheller

Named for Robert Ross Fraser (1882-1963), the area's first storekeeper and postmaster. Fraser was well-known in the area for his unique round barn.

Fricke Creek (creek)

82 O/7 - Wildcat Hills
21-28-5-W5
51°25'N 114°39'W
Flows south-east into Dogpound Creek, approximately 60 km north-west of Calgary.

Henry Fricke arrived in the area in 1910 from Rochester, New York. The creek was officially named after him on 11 June 1930.

Frog Ponds (pond)

72 L/7 - Watching Hill
15-6-W4
50°17'N 110°46'W
Approximately 25 km north of Medicine Hat.

The precise origin for the name of this feature is unknown.

Frozenman Coulee (coulee)

82 O/7 - Wildcat Hills
19-29-6-W5
51°30'N 114°43'W
Approximately 70 km north-west of Calgary.

The name was officially approved 23 April 1940. The precise origin for the name of this feature is unknown.

* Furman (former locality)

82 H/13 - Granum
2-12-30-W4
49°58'N 113°59'W
Approximately 89 km north-west of Lethbridge.

A post office was established here 1 June 1911 and was named after John Furman, an early settler to this locale. The post office closed 31 March 1944.

Furman Lake (lake)

82 H/3 - Cardston
34-1-26-W4
49°04'N 113°24'W
Approximately 80 km south-west of Lethbridge.

The name for this lake was suggested by a Mr. Lowrie, in a submission by the Department of the Interior's Reclamation Service in the 1920s. (see Furman)

Gahern (locality)

72 E/6 - Foremost
30-4-8-W4
49°19'N 111°05'W

Approximately 80 km south-west of Medicine Hat.

The name Gahern was derived by combining H.G. Ahern's middle initial "G" and his last name. Mr. Ahern was the first postmaster.

Galarneau Creek (creek)

82 P/1 - Finnegan
3-25-15-W4
51°07′N 112°01′W
Flows west into Red Deer River, approximately 65 km south-east of Drumheller.

(see Galarneauville)

Galarneauville (locality)

82 P/1 - Finnegan
23-25-15-W4
51°09′N 112°00′W
Approximately 60 km south-east of Drumheller.

This locality was named after Gaspard P. Galarneau, an early rancher and homesteader who was the first postmaster. He came to the area from Lewiston, Idaho in 1911. The post office operated from 1 November 1914 through 31 January 1932.

Galt Island (island)

72 L/2 - Medicine Hat
7-13-6-W4
50°04′N 110°49′W
Immediately west of Medicine Hat.

This island, located in the South Saskatchewan River, is named after the Galt family, originally of Ontario, later of Lethbridge, who provided the capital to develop the valuable coal resources of southern Alberta and branched out to river shipping and railroad building. Sir Alexander Tilloch Galt (1817-1893), and Elliott Torrance Galt built 571 km of irrigation canals throughout southern Alberta, and developed coal mines with a daily capacity of over 2,000 tons. Sir

Alexander Galt was a father of Canadian Confederation, and was the moving spirit behind the organization of finances for the family's ventures. Galt was Finance Minister in the Canadian government for several years following Confederation, and served as Canada's first high commissioner to Great Britain from 1880 to 1883. It was during Sir Alexander's residence in London that he organized the North Western Coal and Navigation Company, Limited, formed in 1882 with British capital, to develop and market the coal of this area. The company began its operations in 1883 in the area around Lethbridge, then known as "The Coal Banks." Galt's son, Elliott Torrance, and son-in-law, Charles Alexander Magrath, also helped lay the foundations for the family's Lethbridge operations. The Galt interests, numbering eight companies altogether, helped develop southern Alberta. The North Western Coal and Navigation Company, Limited, later became the Alberta Railway and Coal Company in 1884. It was absorbed by the Alberta Railway and Irrigation Company in 1904, the Lethbridge Land Company, Limited which was formed in 1888 was also incorporated into the AR&ICo. in 1904. Great Falls and Canada Railway Company, formed in 1889 to build the Sweetgrass–Great Falls portion of a narrow gauge railway, was sold to J.J. Hill of the Great Northern Railway in 1901. St. Mary's River Railway Company, formed in 1898 was absorbed into the AR&ICo. in 1904. All other Galt companies were amalgamated into the AR&ICo., which was eventually purchased outright by the Canadian Pacific Railway on 1 January 1912. The CPR maintained the corporate name, Alberta Railway & Irrigation Company.

Gardner Springs (spring)

72 E/12 - Skiff
NW-5-8-14-W4
49°37′20″N 111°52′35″W
Approximately 68 km east of Lethbridge.

This spring was named for Samuel Gardner who settled near the feature in 1895. This feature was an important navigational landmark used by ranchers. Its water was also vital for the survival of their farming and ranching operations.

Gatine (locality)

82 P/7 - Drumheller
7-29-21-W4
51°28′N 112°55′W
Approximately 20 km west of Drumheller.

The Canadian Pacific Railway station was named after the Gatine family, originally from France. They arrived in Manitoba in the 1890s, and eventually moved into the Rosebud area in 1898 to homestead. Mrs. Gatine was a housekeeper for railway construction crews. Rene Gatine (1861-1930) was the area's first and only postmaster, who operated the post office from 14 February 1910 through 1 January 1913.

Gayford (locality)

82 P/3 - Strathmore
28-26-25-W4
51°11′N 113°26′W
Approximately 45 km north-east of Calgary.

A Canadian Pacific Railway station was established here in 1911 and was named "Swastika," a Sanskrit word, signifying a form of primitive cross. The name was changed during World War II, to Gayford, possibly after James Gay (1810-1891), a Canadian poet.

Gem (hamlet)

82 I/16 - Bassano
8-23-16-W4
50°57′N 112°11′W
Approximately 134 km east of Calgary.

Early settlers believed that the name was appropriately descriptive of the general area. The post office opened under the name 1 August 1914.

* Ghent (former locality)

82 H/10 - Lethbridge
5-9-21-W4
49°42′N 112°48′W
Within the city limits of Lethbridge.

A Canadian Pacific Railway station here was named for the city of Ghent in Belgium.

Ghost Lake (reservoir)

82 O/2 - Jumpingpound Creek
26-6-W5
51°12′N 114°45′W
Approximately 15 km west of Cochrane.

This feature is named after the Ghost River which flows south into it.

Ghost Lake (summer village)

82 O/2 - Jumpingpound Creek
10-26-6-W5
51°12′N 114°46′W
Approximately 40 km north-west of Calgary.

Incorporated 31 December 1968, the name for this community was made official 3 November 1965, and is taken from the nearby Ghost River and Lake.

Ghost River (river)

82 O/2 - Jumpingpound Creek
13-26-6-W5
51°13′N 114°43′W
Flows south-east into the Bow River, approximately 40 km north-west of Calgary.

Palliser's map of 1860 shows this feature as "Dead Man River." Several explanations have been given for the name. One legend says that a ghost was seen going up and down the river, picking up the skulls of the dead who had been killed by the Cree. Another states there are many Indian graves on the river. The third, and the one the

---

Indians say is the true explanation, is due to the fact that many years ago there used to be a wild white horse running through the hills and they could never catch it, finally deciding it must only be a ghost.

Gladys (locality)

82 I/12 - High River
29-20-27-W4
50°43′N 113°42′W
Approximately 25 km south-east of Calgary.

Named for Gladys Harkness, who with her husband, W.S. Harkness, homesteaded in this area in 1884 and operated the community's first post office from 1890 to 1894 although there is some contention as to the exact location of the post office. The location for the post office that closed on 15 June 1938 is 18-21-27-W4.

Gleddie Marsh (marsh)

72 L/5 - Tilley
36-17-13-W4
50°28′N 111°40′W
Approximately 85 km north-west of Medicine Hat.

The precise origin for the name of this feature is unknown.

Gleichen (town)

82 I/14 - Gleichen
13-22-23-W4
50°52′N 113°03′W
Approximately 65 km east south-east of Calgary.

On 15 June 1939, Baron von Stuterheim, a German newspaper correspondent, injected a bit of romance into this frequently mispronounced place name. On that fine morning the Baron got off the train at Gleichen, not to view the town but to see some Indians. The name of Gleichen made him curious and his first remark on meeting Indian Agent Gooderham was, "Ah, Mr. Gutterheim (giving the German pronuncia-

tion), do you know how it got that name?" When told, Stuterheim interjected, "No, no, not good enough. I'll tell you the rest of the story. In the eleventh century the first Count Gleichen, a crusader whose castle was in my native province of Schleswig-Holstein, near a place called Gottingham got into the Turkish Court at Constantinople. He was there for some time and his family did not accompany him; the favourite daughter of the Sultan became his constant companion. The Sultan was pleased and everyone was happy till the day the Count was ordered to return to his homeland. The Sultan voiced his regrets, but stated there was now a strong bond between the two countries since his daughter would be Gleichen's wife. The Count was in a dilemma; a wife and family awaited his return to Germany! He pondered the situation and finally wrote to his wife and told her everything and added that if she wanted to see him again it must be with another woman, the Sultan's daughter. She understood and accepted his condition. On returning he built a second castle and the two castles are still to be seen."

Glenbow (locality)

82 O/1 - Calgary
29-25-3-W5
51°10′N 114°23′W
Approximately 28 km west north-west of Calgary.

The name for this Canadian Pacific Railway station that was established here in 1907 is descriptive and refers to its location: it lies in a glen on the Bow River. The name is a combination of the two words. The post office operated from 1 September 1908 through 15 October 1920.

Glenbow Lake (lake)

82 O/1 - Calgary
7-25-3-W5
51°07′N 114°24′W

Approximately 26 km west north-west of Calgary.

(see Glenbow)

Glenmore Reservoir (reservoir)

82 J/16 - Priddis
23-1-W5
50°59′N 114°08′W
Located within the city limits of Calgary.

The name was officially approved 3 March 1960. The reservoir was created when the Glenmore Dam was built (1930-31) to regulate the flow of the Elbow River, and to provide a water supply to the city of Calgary. Prior to this construction, floods were quite prevalent.

Glenwood (village)

82 H/5 - Pincher Creek
1-5-27 W4
49°22′N 113°31′W
Approximately 61 km south-west of Lethbridge.

Named in 1908 for Glen, son of Edward J. Wood, who served as President of the Alberta Stake (the Cochrane Ranche after its purchase by the Latter Day Saints in 1906 for six million dollars). George M. Cannon, a church authority from Salt Lake City, suggested that the village located near the old Cochrane Ranche headquarters should be named Edwood after Edward Wood. Mr. Wood declined the honour, and instead, suggested the place be named after his first born son, Glen. The name was changed from Glenwoodville by request from the post office in 1979. The name Glenwood was made official 27 July 1979.

* Glenwoodville (former hamlet)

82 H/5 - Pincher Creek
1-5-27-W4
49°22′N 113°31′W

---

*denotes rescinded name or former locality.

Approximately 61 km south-west of Lethbridge.

(see Glenwood)

Glover's Lake (lake)

72 M/8 - Sibbald
19-29-1-W4
51°29′30″N 110°08′10″W
Approximately 181 km east of Drumheller.

This lake is named for Edwin Glover on whose land it is situated. It was a popular recreation spot for local people during the 1920s. The lake dried up almost completely during the 1930s, and has been filling and draining intermittently ever since.

* Goddard (former locality)

72 E/5 - Legend
27-4-12-W4
49°24′N 111°32′W
Approximately 102 km south-east of Lethbridge.

This locality was named for Ernest Goddard who emigrated to Canada from England. As early settlers to the community, Goddard and his family homesteaded and operated a general store and the post office. Ill health and an extended economic recession prompted Goddard to move to British Columbia, and eventually back to England.

* Gold Spur (former locality)

72 L/15 - Buffalo
1-23-6-W4
50°54′N 111°43′W
Approximately 97 km north of Medicine Hat.

The precise origin for the name of this former locality is unknown.

Goose Lake (lake)

82 H/5 - Pincher Creek
32-5-29-W4
49°26′N 113°52′W

Approximately 80 km west south-west of Lethbridge.

Possibly named after an unusual goose, or the presence of geese found in the area. The name was made official 3 October 1942.

Graburn Creek (creek)

72 E/9 - Elkwater Lake
13-8-1-W4
49°38′N 110°01′W
Flows north-east into Battle Creek, approximately 60 km south-east of Medicine Hat.

This creek was named for North West Mounted Police Constable Marmaduke Graburn who was shot to death by an unknown assailant near a horse camp located north-west of Fort Walsh 17 November 1879. Some have suggested that the murderer was a Blood Indian who vowed revenge for the death of his daughter, who had died while in the care of a white man. If she was not to survive, he swore he would send a white man "to the beyond" in her company. Graburn was the first of a significantly few members of the force who died violently while bringing law and order to the West.

Grainger (locality)

82 P/6 - Carbon
20-29-24-W4
51°30′N 113°20′W
Approximately 45 km west of Drumheller.

Frank William Grainger (1848-?) came to Canada in 1904 to homestead. When the Grand Trunk Pacific Railroad crossed his land in 1913, Grainger was asked to choose a name for the new station. He chose the name of his birthplace in England a place called Badminton; however, when the station was erected, the name Grainger was painted on it. The Canadian National Railway later took over the Grand Trunk, but this made little difference to the growth of the small hamlet of Grainger. The post office operated from 1 December 1912 through 5 January 1966.

Grand Forks, The (river junction)
72 E/13 - Grassy Lake
27-11-13-W4
49°56′N 111°42′W
Approximately 86 km east of Lethbridge.

The descriptive name for this feature refers to the junction of the Oldman and Bow rivers. The two rivers approach one another from opposite directions until just before the confluence where they both turn south and join, making the "stem of the fork." Local residents usually shorten the name to "The Forks" or "The Bow."

Grand Valley Creek (creek)
82 O/2 - Jumpingpound Creek
13-26-5-W5
51°13′N 114°34′W
Flows south into Bow River, approximately 30 km north-west of Calgary.

The name for this creek is taken from the unofficial name of the valley, which was given by Donald McEachen who exclaimed "Aye! It's a grand valley." The creek was officially named 12 December 1939.

* Granlea (former locality)
72 E/11 - Maleb
2-8-9-W4
49°37′N 111°08′W
Approximately 55 km south-west of Medicine Hat.

The name Granlea is a combination of the words "grain" and "lea," suggesting the rich agricultural value of the region. "Grain" refers to the wheat grown in the area, and "lea" refers to the large tracts of

pastureland used by cattle ranchers. The post office in Granlea opened 1 August 1928 and was closed in April 1962.

Grant Creek (creek)
72 E/8 - Thelma Creek
29-5-1-W4
49°25′N 110°06′W
Flows south-west into Middle Creek, approximately 75 km south-east of Medicine Hat.

Named after the Grant family, who owned a ranch in the vicinity before they moved to Battle Creek.

* Granta (former station)
82 I/15 - Cluny
13-22-19-W4
50°52′N 112°31′W
Approximately 95 km south-east of Calgary.

The name for this Canadian Pacific Railway station, established in 1913, was suggested by two Cambridge graduates who lived in the area, Van Shaik and Fairburn. They chose the name of a stream which flowed through Cambridge known by the old Saxon name, Granta. The watercourse is now called Cam.

Grantham (locality)
82 I/1 - Vauxhall
8-13-15-W4
50°04′N 112°00′W
Approximately 68 km north-east of Lethbridge.

A Canadian Pacific Railway station was established here in 1913. A combination of drought and its proximity to Vauxhall contributed to the community's demise. It boasted no more than about 24 people at its peak. Grantham was named for a town and borough in Lincolnshire, England. The post office operated from 1 January 1928 through 18 November 1961.

Granum (town)
82 H/13 - Granum
31-10-26-W4
49°52′N 113°30′W
Approximately 50 km north-west of Lethbridge.

The land in this area was first surveyed in 1883. The process was slow until the construction of a branch of the Canadian Pacific Railway. This site on Willow Creek became a stopping point between Calgary and points south, and was known as "Leavings" or the "Leavings Switch." The name "Leavings" is descriptive of the place's location: it is at the point on the Fort Benton, Montana–Calgary Trail which left the banks of Willow Creek. In 1886, a chain of detachments from Calgary south to Fort Macleod was erected, and three constables of the North West Mounted Police were stationed at the "leavings" of the Willow Creek Detachment. As the settlement in the area grew, it became necessary to start a community newspaper, and in 1905, the *Leavings Star* was born. The settlement is surrounded by some of the best wheat growing land in Alberta. This fact prompted the late Malcolm McKenzie, Memeber of Parliament to suggest another name for the town. The Latin word for grain, *granum*, was chosen, and was used to refer to the place beginning in 1906, and was made official 1 October 1907. The community won the World's Wheat Crown prior to its name change, and several winners of other awards for wheat have emerged from the town which was incorporated 7 November 1910.

Grassy Island (island)
82 I/8 - Scandia
15-17-17-W4
50°26′N 112°16′W
Approximately 91 km north-east of Lethbridge.

---

*denotes rescinded name or former locality.

The name for this island located in the Bow River is likely descriptive.

Grassy Lake (lake)

72 E/1 - Cripple Creek
3-1-2-W4
49°00'N 110°12'W
Approximately 115 km south-east of Medicine Hat.

This body of water straddles the Alberta-Montana border. The name that was well-known locally in the early years was "Wild Horse Lake." It was, at one time, a much larger lake which subsequently partially dried up, forming two distinct bodies of water. The name Milk River Lake was applied to the larger more westerly lake and the name "Wild Horse Lake" was applied solely to the smaller feature straddling the international boundary. Some confusion occurred and in 1974, the name Grassy Lake was officially applied to this feature, to comply with local usage in Montana.

Grassy Lake (village)

72 E/13 - Grassy Lake
16-10-13-W4
49°49'N 111°43'W
Approximately 80 km east of Lethbridge.

The name is derived from the Blackfoot word *moyi-kimi*, translating to "grassy waters." In the translation to English, the name became known as Grassy Lakes. The natives originally applied the name "Grassy Waters" to the area because in the 1800s they referred to the south central area of Alberta as "much grass." This name was derived from the existence of all the long prairie grass common to this region at that time.

Grease Creek (creek)

82 O/7 - Wildcat Hills
35-28-6-W5
51°27'N 114°44'W
Flows south-east into Little Red Deer River, approximately 65 km north-west of Calgary.

This creek is abundantly framed by notched-leaved, or black birch brush, familiarly known as "greasewood." The Stoney Indian name for the stream is *to-muna*. The name Grease Creek was officially approved for this feature 23 April 1940.

Green Lake (lake)

72 E/8 - Thelma Creek
13-6-1-W4
49°28'N 110°01'W
Approximately 79 km south-east of Medicine Hat.

The well-established name for this lake may be descriptive of the long green grass which grows in abundance around it. Another local name by which this lake is known is "Egg Lake," but its precise origin is unknown. The official name has been in use since at least 1958.

Green's Lake (lake)

72 M/8 - Sibbald
33-27-2-W4
51°21'20"N 110°13'20"W
Approximately 174 km east of Drumheller.

Named for Errol C. Green who arrived in the Sibbald area to homestead in 1910. The lake is located on the land upon which Mr. Green originally settled. The lake was a popular spot during the summer for local residents and continues to be a good spot for game bird hunting.

Greenan Lake (lake)

72 L/8 - Hilda
23-17-1-W4
50°27'N 110°02'W
Approximately 70 km north-east of Medicine Hat.

The name was originally proposed by the Department of the Interior's Reclamation Service in 1920. Its precise origin is not known, but the name was officially approved 5 January 1967. Since its naming, local field research has discovered that this lake is also known as "Montgomerie Lake," after Tom S. Montgomerie (1887-1961) a Scottish immigrant who arrived in Canada in 1908. Montgomerie settled in Medicine Hat in 1913, and joined the 175th Battalion of the Canadian Army, serving through World War I. Mr. Montgomerie married Grace MacDougall, a nursing sister in the war, in 1920 and moved to the Hilda district shortly after that. They plowed up the quarter section upon which this lake is located, after acquiring the homestead in 1923. "T.J." was postmaster of Hilda from 1924 until 1946, and also served as police magistrate. The Montgomeries' daughter, Shirley, was drowned in this lake.

* Grierson (former post office)

82 P/7 - Drumheller
18-27-21-W4
51°18'N 112°57'W
Approximately 25 km south-west of Drumheller.

The post office which operated from 1 July 1890 through 30 April 1909, was named after the first postmaster, James Grierson. (see Rosebud)

* Griesbach (former post office)

82 I/14 - Gleichen
12-22-25-W4
50°51'N 113°28'W
Approximately 40 km east south-east of Calgary.

The original post office was opened 15 May
1913 and operated until 1 December 1914.
It was named after its first and only
postmaster, Emil Griesbach. The name was
later changed. (see Carseland)

Gros Ventre Creek (creek)
72 E/16 - Irvine
14-11-3-W4
49°54′N 110°19′W
Flows north-east into Ross Creek, approximately 25 km south-east of Medicine Hat.

Named to commemorate an attempted
Atsina raid in 1868 on a band of Blackfoot
Indians encamped along this creek. The
Atsina thought they were attacking a small
band but the Blackfoot encampment was
much larger than they had anticipated. As a
result, the Atsina were chased into the
Cypress Hills. The Atsina were Arapaho
Indians, part of the Algonkian-speaking
nation of the western plains. Residents of
the southern prairies during the 18th
century, the Atsina moved south into
Montana as a result of pressure from the
Assiniboine and Plains Cree. The Atsina
were known by whites as the *Gros Ventres*,
the French for "big bellies," which is an
approximate translation of the symbol by
which they were designated in the inter-
tribal sign language used on the Plains.

* Groton (former locality)
72 E/3 - Aden
5-3-10-W4
49°11′N 111°18′W
Approximately 103 km south-west of
Medicine Hat.

Albert J. Peterson, a homesteader and the
first postmaster, applied for permission to
name this post office and chose Groton,
after his home town in North Dakota. The
post office opened in February 1913 and
closed in February 1961.

---

*denotes rescinded name or former locality.

H~I

* Hacke (former post office)

82 H/2 - Shanks Lake
10-1-20-W4
49°02'N 112°36'W
Approximately 70 km south south-east of
Lethbridge.

The post office here was named after the
first postmaster, William Hacke and
operated from 1914 to 1922 when the name
was changed. (see Twin River)

Halifax Coulee (coulee)

82 H/5 - Pincher Creek
35-5-29-W4
49°25'N 113°47'W
A north-west/south-east trending coulee,
approximately 76 km south-west of
Lethbridge.

This coulee contains a creek which flows
into Halifax Lake (see Halifax Lake). The
submission to have this feature officially
named was made in 1920 by the Department of the Interior's Reclamation Service.

Halifax Lake (lake)

82 H/5 - Pincher Creek
7-6-28-W4
49°27'N 113°46'W
Approximately 71 km west south-west of
Lethbridge.

This lake and the surrounding area in
general, was named for the Halifax Ranch
Company. The company was named
because its owners, including J.E. Chipman
were from Halifax, Nova Scotia. The
company was granted a lease of 40,470
hectares (100,000 acres) near the lake in
May 1882.

Halliday (station)

72 M/5 - Sunnynook
7-28-12-W4
51°22'N 111°40'W

Approximately 71 km east of Drumheller.

Named for Howard Hadden Halladay
(1878-?) who was the Member of Parliament for the riding of Bow River from 1917
until 1921. Halladay had a varied background which included jobs in insurance,
local politics, and farming. The Canadian
National Railway station was established
here in 1920.

* Halsbury (former railway point)

72 L/14 - Halsbury
18-21-8-W4
50°47'N 111°07'W
Approximately 85 km north north-west of
Medicine Hat.

Named in 1914 after Giffard Hardinge
Stanley (1823-1921), who served as
Lord Chancellor of Britain from 1885 to
January 1886, July 1886-?, and from 1895 to
1905. He was a prominent Conservative
and a respected member of the bar. When
he was appointed Lord Chancellor in 1885,
he took the title of Baron Halsbury of
Halsbury, in the parish of Parkham, Devon,
one of the former seats of the Giffard
family. Shortly before the railway point
was named for him, Halsbury lead a group
of Lords (in the House of Lords) in
opposing reductions to the powers of that
House. His "die hards," as they were called,
lost after an exciting political battle.

Hamilton Hill (hill)

72 L/16 - Bindloss
35,36-23-1-W4
50°59'40"N 110°01'50"W
Approximately 114 km north north-west of
Medicine Hat.

The hill is locally known under this name
due to its location on land once owned by
E. Hamilton. The Hamiltons moved to the
area in the spring of 1913.

Hamlet (locality)

82 P/3 - Strathmore
26-25-24-W4
51°10'N 113°14'W
Approximately 55 km east of Calgary.

Hamlet was built in the early 1920s as a
result of competition among grain companies. Swen Swenson owned approximately
2 or 3 sections of land and was considered
an important farmer in the area. Swenson
wanted to haul his grain and Atlantic &
Pacific Grain Co., always in competition
with the Parrish & Heimbecker Grain Co.,
built an elevator to handle, among others,
Swenson's grain. The closest elevator was
about 2 km away, but it belonged to P & H,
and it was along the Canadian National
Railway line. So, the Canadian Pacific
Railway built a siding to accommodate the
new A & P elevator. Hamlet, which was
about 14 km from Rockyford, was named
after William Hamlet, a railway employee
from Fort William. He won the Croix de
Guerre in World War I.

Hammer Hill (hill)

82 I/14 - Gleichen
15-23-23-W4
50°57'N 113°08'W
Approximately 50 km east of Calgary.

The Blackfoot call this hill *poxatsis*,
translating "stone hammer," after an
incident in which a sleeping Cree Indian
was killed by an Indian woman with a
hammer. Another legend states that a Cree
group, intruding into Blackfoot territory
and camped here, was discovered and killed
at this spot by a Blackfoot force wielding
war hammers. It is also noted that a stone

shaped like a hammer lay on top of the hill, which was used as a buffalo jump by the Blackfoot. Until it was moved to Ottawa via Gleichen in 1912, the Blackfoot worshipped at this rock.

Hand Hills (hills)

82 P/8 - Dorothy
28,29-18-W4
51°30′N 112°17′W
Approximately 33 km east of Drumheller.

The name for these hills, one of the more prominent features of southeastern Alberta, is a translation of a native name; however, the origin attached to the name has more than one focus. Tyrrell noted: "They are called by the Crees *michichi ispatinan* or 'hand hills' on account of their resemblance to the outstretched fingers of the hand, the top of the table land not being flat but composed of five ridges which radiate from a center lying to the south-east." Tyrrell mentions them as being called *o-chun-um-bin* in Stoney. Another version is that the name means "little hand." A Blackfoot chief who was killed on one of these hills had one small hand, according to Peter Erasmus and John Leech. This chief was born crippled, his hand resembled the claw of an animal, and the other children in his band, while he was growing up, threw stones at him, and called him "Little Hand." He grew up compensating for his disability and became a great warrior.

Handhills Lake (lake)

82 P/8 - Dorothy
13-29-15,16-W4
51°30′N 112°07′W
Approximately 40 km east of Drumheller.

(see Hand Hills)

Hanson Creek (creek)

72 E/7 - Manyberries
20-4-6-W4
49°18′N 110°46′W
Flows north-west into Ketchum Creek, approximately 83 km south of Medicine Hat.

The precise origin for the name of this feature is unknown.

* Hants (former station)

82 I/15 - Cluny
22-21-19-W4
50°48′N 112°33′W
Approximately 120 km south-east of Calgary.

A Canadian Pacific Railway station was in operation here from 1909 to 1912 and was named for the county of Hampshire, also known as Hants, located in south-central England, on the English Channel.

Hardieville (locality)

82 H/10 - Lethbridge
18-9-21-W4
49°45′N 112°51′W
Approximately 1 km north of Lethbridge.

A post office was established nearby in 1910 and was named for W.D.L. Hardie (1863-1942), who served as the Superintendent of the Galt Coal Mine when it opened at this location in 1909. In 1912, he served as the Mayor of Lethbridge.

Harland Lakes (lake)

82 H/5 - Pincher Creek
22-4-29-W4
49°19′N 113°50′W
Approximately 82 km south-west of Lethbridge.

This feature was probably named for Edwin Harland (1845-1923) who moved to the Twin Butte area with his family in 1899. Harland was originally from Ontario and operated a mill there prior to heading west.

He established the Ranch X in 1899 and operated it until 1919 when he moved to the west coast.

Hartleyville (locality)

82 H/5 - Pincher Creek
5-5-27-W4
49°22′N 113°37′W
Approximately 67 km south-west of Lethbridge.

Named for James Hartley, Social Credit Member of the Legislative Assembly for Macleod from 1935 to 1967. Hartley served as Deputy Speaker of the Legislature and in 1955 he was appointed to Premier Ernest Manning's cabinet as Minister of Public Works. The name was officially approved 12 December 1939. The post office closed 29 April 1968.

Hatfield Hill (hill)

82 H/5 - Pincher Creek
3,4-28-W4
49°16′N 113°45′W
Approximately 82 km south-west of Lethbridge.

Named for Herbert M. Hatfield (1855-1946) who, with Lionel Brooke, owned the Chinook Ranch near Pincher Creek. In 1899, he sold his interest in the operation, and bought a ranch near the Waterton River, where he developed an extensive operation. The name for this hill was made official 31 October 1942.

* Haven (former locality)

72 M/1 - Acadia Valley
9-26-3-W4
51°13′N 110°22′W
Approximately 132 km north of Medicine Hat.

A post office of the same name, taken from a rancher who had grazing leases in the valley, was established on this site 1 November 1922, and operated until 31 July 1953.

* **Hawick** (former locality)

82 P/3 - Strathmore
21-25-25-W4
51°08′N 113°26′W
Approximately 35 km east of Calgary.

(see Ardenode)

Hays (hamlet)

72 L/4 - Hays
24-13-14-W4
50°06′N 111°48′W
Approximately 80 km west of Medicine Hat.

One source suggests that this hamlet was named in 1912 after the late Charles Melville Hays, President of the Grand Trunk and Grand Trunk Pacific Railway. Another suggests that the name was selected by Prairie Farm Rehabilitation Administration officials to honour David Hays, manager of the former Canada Land and Irrigation Company, long active in the promotion of irrigation.

■ **Head-Smashed-In Buffalo Jump**

(buffalo jump)
82 H/12 - Brocket
8-9-28-W4
49°42′14″N 113°39′17″W
Approximately 67 km west of Lethbridge.

The descriptive name is a direct translation of *itsipa-sikkih kinih-kootsiya-opi*. The aboriginal peoples of this continent used this spot, and several areas like it for thousands of years, as a means to capture and kill large numbers of buffalo, the mainstay of their survival. The animals were driven over steep cliffs such as this, and a majority of them were killed on impact, their top-heavy shapes plunging them head-first to their death. A provincial historic site and interpretive centre is located at this buffalo jump.

According to Peigan Blackfoot legend, a young man wanted to witness the plunge to death of countless buffalo driven over the sandstone cliffs. The "jump" was the culmination of intense planning and the rounding up of the shaggy beasts toward the precipice where the herd was frightened into a headlong stampede resulting in a final plunge over the cliff edge. The young warrior, standing under the shelter of a ledge, watched the great beasts cascade past him with the dead and wounded piling up in a large mass. But, as the bodies mounted, he became trapped between the animals and the cliff. He was later found by his people with his skull crushed by the weight of the buffalo. Thus they named the place in the Blackfoot language: *itsipa-sikkih kinih-kootsiya-opi* or "where-he-got-his-head-smashed-in."

Heathdale (post office)

72 M/3 - Big Stone
27-26-8-W4
51°15′N 111°03′W
Approximately 120 km east of Drumheller.

The precise origin for the name of this feature is unknown. The post office operated from 15 November 1914 through 15 November 1947.

Helm (station)

72 M/5 - Sunnynook
SW-7-29-12-W4
51°26′50″N 111°48′30″W
Approximately 70 km east of Drumheller.

This station was named in memory of a former Superintendent of Transportation in Calgary. Mr. John K. Helm joined the Canadian National Railway at Edmonton in 1936 as a Callboy, saw active service in the Royal Canadian Navy from 1941 to 1945, and rejoined CN after the war. He filled various positions in the Transportation Department in Edmonton, Edson, Hanna, and Jasper. He was appointed Superintendent in Calgary in 1963 and died

in 1966. The station is at Mileage 15.5 on the Sheerness Subdivision serving an Alberta power plant.

* **Helmer** (former locality)

82 P/7 - Drumheller
33-27-20-W4
51°21′N 112°46′W
Approximately 12 km south of Drumheller.

This post office which operated from 16 June 1927 to 4 May 1932 was named after Ivan Helmer, the first postmaster. The name was later changed. (see Taylor)

Helmsdale (locality)

72 M/2 - Cappon
36-25-6-W4
51°11′N 110°42′W
Approximately 130 km north of Medicine Hat.

This locality was named by Murdock Mackay, the first postmaster on the site 15 April 1927. He chose the name of his birthplace in Scotland for the first post office, and handed the title of postmaster down through his family until the office's closure 1 May 1962. Helmsdale is a word that originated with the Norse *Hjalmundda*, later changed to Holmsdale in the 1200s and further mutated to Helmsdaill in 1513. Its literal meaning is "valley of the helmet."

Helmsdale (locality)

82 O/8 - Crossfield
2-28-1-W5
51°22′N 114°02′W
Approximately 38 km north of Calgary.

Both localities are named after Helmsdale, Highland, Scotland. The one north of Calgary was originally the name of the Canadian Pacific Railway station while the one south-west of Oyen was named by Murdock MacKay after his birthplace in Scotland and was the name of the post office which he opened in April, 1913. (see Helmsdale)

Henderson Lake (lake)

82 H/10 - Lethbridge
32,33-8-21-W4
49°41′N 112°48′W
Within the city limits of Lethbridge.

Named for William Henderson (1857-1909) who came to the Lethbridge area in 1882 from Edinburgh, Scotland, where he was born, and had apprenticed and contracted as a carpenter. Henderson built a number of hotels, the North West Mounted Police barracks in Fort Macleod, and invested almost all his money (reported to be a quarter of a million dollars) in various ventures in the Lethbridge area. A well-known and highly esteemed man, Henderson also served as mayor of the city for two years, retiring just prior to his death.

Heningers Reservoir (reservoir)

72 E/4 - Coutts
16-3-12-W4
49°12′N 111°34′W
Approximately 100 km south south-west of Medicine Hat.

Named after John Taylor Heninger who arrived in Alberta from the U.S.A. in 1900, and built a home in the Magrath area to start his sheep-ranching operation. Due to lack of water in the southern regions during the 1920s, Heninger applied for and received permission from the government to build a dam diverting water from Etzikom Coulee for irrigation purposes. Heninger became a strong advocate of water conservation and supported construction of an irrigation system for southern Alberta. He built a number of small dams over the next two decades and tackled his largest project, creating Heningers Reservoir in 1945-46. He died in

1949. The name was made official 14 June 1968.

Herronton (hamlet)

82 I/11 - Arrowwood
20-19-25-W4
50°38′N 113°25′W
Approximately 56 km south-east of Calgary.

Named for John (Honest John) Herron (1853-1936), an original member of the North West Mounted Police that came west in 1874. Herron joined the force as a blacksmith, and helped with the building of Fort Macleod. He served a total of four years before he left the NWMP to return to Ottawa. In 1881, he returned to the Pincher Creek area, leased a large amount of land, and founded the Stewart Ranch Cattle Company. Herron was elected as Conservative Member of Parliament of the Macleod constituency in both 1904 and 1908, retiring from the cattle business in 1908 and from politics in 1911. In 1912, he was responsible for the establishment of the community's first post office. It was named in his honour. Herron lived his remaining years in the Pincher Creek area, and his grave is located there.

Hesketh (hamlet)

82 P/7 - Drumheller
12-29-22-W4
51°28′N 112°58′W
Approximately 20 km west of Drumheller.

A Canadian Pacific Railway station was established here in 1921 and was named after Colonel J.A. Hesketh, Assistant Division Engineer of the C.P.R. in Winnipeg. He was a graduate of the Royal Military College in Kingston in 1883. The post office operated from 1 December 1921 through 14 May 1969.

High River (town)

82 I/12 - High River
6-19-28-W4
50°35′N 113°52′W
Approximately 40 km south of Calgary.

Named for its proximity to the Highwood River (see Highwood River). The site of the present town of High River was known to the white settlers of the 1880s as "The Crossing," since it was used as a crossing point on the Highwood River.

Highwood River (river)

82 I/13 - Dalemead
26-21-28-W4
50°49′N 113°47′W
Flows north into Bow River, approximately 12 km south-west of Calgary.

The descriptive name for this river, spitzee, in Blackfoot, or "tall timber," refers to the level of the river. It appears to be on the same level as the prairie, without a "bottom." This caused the trees which grow along its banks to appear as though they are higher than usual. The Blackfoot name for the upper portion of the river is sapow or "wind" river. This river appears on the 1865 Palliser map as "High-wood River" (Ispasquehow), an English translation of the Stoney name. It appears as "Spitchee" on the David Thompson map of 1814. It is known on the Arrowsmith map of 1859 as "Spitchi" or "Ispasquehow." Blakiston called it the "High Woods River."

Hilda (hamlet)

72 L/8 - Hilda
35-17-1-W4
50°28′N 110°03′W
Approximately 63 km north-east of Medicine Hat.

The original post office was named for Hilda Dorothy Koch-Murray, by her father, S. Koch. He was appointed postmaster in 1910, and named this station after his one-year-old daughter. Originally from Oklahoma, Hilda's family came to this region in 1910 and remained until 1917 when they moved to Medicine Hat. In 1923, the family moved to Fresno, California.

Hill Spring (village)
82 H/5 - Pincher Creek
18-4-27-W4
49°17'N 113°38'W
Approximately 70 km south-west of Lethbridge.

Named by residents of the community for the number of water springs that flowed from the nearby hill, especially a large one on the north end of the hill that supplied the village with water for many years. The hill was traditionally known by cowboys and settlers as "Spring Hill," but because this name had already been used for a town in the province, it was decided to name the hill and village Hill Spring.

Hillside Coulee (coulee)
82 I/4 - Claresholm
34-12-29-W4
50°03'N 111°52'W
Runs into Lyndon Creek, approximately 85 km north-west of Lethbridge.

An intermittent creek flows through this coulee which likely has a descriptive name.

Hoenig's Hill (hill)
72 M/8 - Sibbald
SW-19-28-1-W4
51°24'15"N 110°08'40"W
Approximately 178 km east of Drumheller.

Named after Andrew Hoenig (?-1977) who owned and operated a lumberyard in nearby Sibbald. He attempted ranching in Iowa in 1910, but gave it up that year and

went to Haywarden, Saskatchewan, where he worked for Rogers Lumberyard. He came to the Sibbald area in 1915 and in the next decade bought Ed Callin's land where he remained.

Hogsback, The (ridge)
72 L/7 - Watching Hill
16-6-W4
50°21'N 110°44'W
Approximately 35 km north of Medicine Hat.

The name for this feature is likely a descriptive one.

Hollis Coulee (creek)
82 H/12 - Brocket
20-9-29-W4
49°45'N 113°54'W
Flows south into Beaver Creek, approximately 75 km west of Lethbridge.

Possibly named for an original squatter who settled on the land through which this coulee runs.

Home Coulee (coulee)
82 P/7 - Drumheller
0,9-7-20-19-W4
51°21'00"N 112°38'20"W
Runs north-east into Rosebud River, approximately 5 km south of Drumheller.

A number of Indian families lived near the mouth of the coulee south of Wayne during the 1890s. They called the coulee home—hence the name. The name has been in use since the turn of the century and was officially approved 6 March 1986.

Homestead Creek (creek)
82 P/1 - Finnegan
33-25-16-W4
51°11'N 112°10'W
Flows south-west into Red Deer River, approximately 48 km south-east of Drumheller.

The precise origin for the name of this stream is unknown; however, this part of the province was a popular settling place for homesteaders and its name may reflect this fact.

Hooper Creek (creek)
72 E/7 - Manyberries
20-4-6-W4
49°19'N 110°47'W
Flows north-west into Ketchum Creek, approximately 80 km south of Medicine Hat.

Named for Sydney Hooper who came to the Manyberries area in the late 1880s to ranch. His ranch was later known as the Fiddleback Ranch. The creek flows through an area once known as the Hooper School District, established in 1918. Hooper originally came from England and lived at one time in the Fort Kipp area. (see Cronkhite Coulee)

Horsefly Lake Reservoir (reservoir)
82 H/9 Chin Coulee
11,12-9-16-W4
49°43'N 112°04'W
Approximately 54 km east of Lethbridge.

This watering hole is named for the large number of flies that followed livestock to it. Prior to the building of the reservoir, this natural depression was known as "Rocky Lake" for the large number of glacial rocks and boulders found within the vicinity. The name was changed to this other descriptive one when the reservoir was built to ensure a supply of water for ranchers as they increasingly populated the prairies in the late 19th and early 20th centuries.

Horseshoe Canyon (canyon)
82 P/7 - Drumheller
28,29-21-W4
51°27'N 112°53'W
A north-south trending coulee, perpendicular to Kneehills Creek, approximately 6 km east of Drumheller.

The descriptive name for this feature was officially approved 20 January 1955. The name has been in use since the late 1800s.

* Howie (former locality)

72 L/14 - Halsbury
25-22-10-W4
50°54′N 111°16′W
Approximately 100 km north north-west of Medicine Hat.

Named in 1913, after James Howie, the first postmaster. The post office closed 31 March 1946.

Hubalta (railway point)

82 P/4 - Dalroy
24-29-W4
51°02′N 113°57′W
Within the city limits of Calgary.

This railway point is now a subdivision of Calgary (#69), but was once a unique settlement, established in 1912. The name was suggested by a Mr. William Lowry, owner of the land, who advertised it as the "centre of progress" or "hub" of Alberta (often abbreviated as "Alta"). This area, along with Albert Park, joined Forest Lawn to form a single village in the 1930s. The post office operated from 1 April 1912 through 21 December 1915, and from 1 April 1924 through 20 February 1961.

Humphrey's Coulee (coulee)

72 E/4 - Coutts
W1/2-25-1-13-W4
49°04′N 110°34′W
Approximately 115 km south-east of Lethbridge.

Ted Humphrey was a homesteader on section 36-1-13-W4 circa 1912. This bachelor collected many artifacts of the Police and local natives which were found in the Writing-on-Stone area. Most of these have disappeared since his death.

Hunting Hill (hill)

72 L/13 - Wardlow
22-13-W4
50°51′N 111°49′W
Approximately 121 km north-west of Medicine Hat.

The Blackfoot word for this feature is *sahamisapikawaghway* and the Cree word is *onachewassawapewin*. Indian hunters watched for buffalo from the summit of this hill. Both words translate to an equivalent of Hunting Hill.

Hussar (village)

82 P/2 - Hussar
14-24-20-W4
51°03′N 112°41′W
Approximately 47 km south of Drumheller.

Hussar was settled by a group of German settlers known as the German-Canadian Farming Company. They bought a sixteen-section block of land from the Canadian Pacific Railway in 1910-11 to establish colonization farms in the area. This group of settlers were once officers in the German Hussars, and they brought their uniforms, spiked helmets and guns with them to Canada, and displayed them in their homes. By 1914, 4,000 acres of land had been broken and ready to seed, and four sets of buildings had been erected. By the outbreak of World War I, most of the settlers, including the manager, Captain Schultz, attempted a return to Germany, but few were successful in their efforts.

Hutton (locality)

72 M/4 - Pollockville
6-24-14-W4
51°02′N 111°56′W
Approximately 72 km south-east of Drumheller.

Named in 1911 for the manager of the Northern Crown Bank of Calgary, Mr. Hutton, who lent Oregon land promoter, A.H. Willet the money to purchase a townsite near the Fieldholme post office (see Fieldholme). Willet and Hutton's goal was to make Hutton the "Gold Grain Town of Sunny Alberta," as well as serving as the northern terminus for an American railway belonging to James J. Hill, an American railway magnate.

Iddesleigh (hamlet)

72 L/11 - Jenner
34-20-10-W4
50°44′N 111°18′W
Approximately 89 km north-west of Medicine Hat.

This settlement was named in 1914 after Sir Walter Stafford Northcote, Earl of Iddesleigh (1818-1887) who served as Governor of the Hudson's Bay Company from 1869 to 1874. He was the son of the 7th Baronet of Pynes, in the county of Devon, and on graduating from Oxford, he became the private secretary of William Gladstone, the great Liberal statesman. He was in charge of the detailed arrangements for the Great Exhibition of 1851. He was returned to the House of Commons at Westminster in 1855, and became a Cabinet Minister in Lord Derby's third government eleven years later as the president of the Board of Trade. He was elected Chairman of the Hudson's Bay Company in 1869, a position he held for the next five years. He persuaded the company to accept £300,000 in return for the transfer of the vast Prince Rupert's Land to the Canadian Government. Alberta was created from part of this territory in 1905. Northcote was appointed Chancellor of the Exchequer in Disraeli's cabinet in 1874. He became leader of the Conservative Party in the House of Commons when Disraeli became a lord. Many of the communities in this area are named after members of the royal family.

---

*denotes rescinded name or former locality.

* Illingworth (former locality)

72 L/3 - Suffield
21-13-11-W4
50°07′N 111°27′W
Approximately 50 km west of Medicine Hat.

This former Canadian Pacific Railway station was established in 1914 and was named after W.J. Illingworth, sometime Director of the railway.

Immigration Gap (gap)

82 H/3 - Cardston
SW1/4-1-1-24-W4
49°00′00″N 113°05′45″W
Approximately 78 km south-west of Lethbridge.

In 1884 Charles Ora Card (see Cardston) led homesteaders to Canada on a trail through this gap which also was very near the border. It then became well-known as Immigration Gap. The route was used by many who settled in Canada. It was an old Indian trail and was also used by ranchers to drive cattle to the big ranches in Canada. A road was built to the border here on the Canadian side but it was not continued by the American government.

Improvement District of Badlands #7

(improvement district)
82 P/7 - Drumheller
27-29-18-20-W4

This naming request, submitted by the Improvement District Manager, C.R. Dompnier, was the unanimous choice of the Advisory Council and was the most popular choice among local residents. The Advisory Council held a *Name the I.D.* contest, and Badlands was chosen because it denotes the ruggedness of the area; ever since the time of the occupation of the First

Nations peoples, the area has been commonly known as the Badlands. The name is not duplicated in Alberta. The name was officially approved 5 May 1987.

Indian Lake (lake)

82 I/10 - Queenstown
22-21-20-W4
50°42′N 112°49′W
Approximately 87 km south-east of Calgary.

The precise origin for the name of this feature is unknown.

Indianfarm Creek (creek)

82 H/5 - Pincher Creek
6-29,30-W4
49°30′N 113°54′W
Flows north into Pincher Creek, approximately 85 km west south-west of Lethbridge.

The name for this stream is derived from its proximity to the Dominion Government's project aimed at demonstrating agricultural techniques to the native Indians of the area. The Indian farm was established in 1879 and is mentioned in the Mounted Police histories; however, it was not very successful and closed down after a few years. Local people began calling the creek "Chipman Creek," after a Mr. Chipman, partner with a Mr. Harris, who established the Halifax Ranching Company. In 1942, the name Indianfarm Creek was officially adopted, in order to avoid duplication.

Indus (hamlet)

82 I/13 - Dalemead
35-22-28-W4
50°55′N 113°47′W
Approximately 17 km south-east of Calgary.

The name was suggested in 1914 to the Canadian Pacific Railway by Dr. J.M.

Fulton, as the shortened form of "industry." When the rail line reached this area, Dr. Fulton envisioned industrial growth for the region. Indus is also a Sanskrit word, meaning "constellation of the stars." There appears to be no direct connection of this name to the Sanskrit word. It is the name of an Aryan group that came to what is now northern India and pushed out the original inhabitants. The word is the root of Hindus and thus Hindustan, an early name for India. There is also the River Indus in India. The Indus Valley in north India was named thus because the Indus people settled there.

Inner Rainy Hill (hill)

72 L/11 - Jenner
20-10-W4
50°41′N 111°17′W
Approximately 80 km north-west of Medicine Hat.

The name is a translation of the Blackfoot word, "pistssotahyghkimikway." (see Rainy Hills)

Inverlake (locality)

82 P/4 - Dalroy
13-24-27-W4
51°03′N 113°38′W
Approximately 27 km east of Calgary.

The precise origin for the name of this Canadian Pacific Railway station which was established in 1910, is unknown.

Inversnay (station)

72 E/14 - Bow Island
9-11-10-W4
49°53′N 111°18′W
Approximately 46 km west of Medicine Hat.

A Canadian Pacific Railway station operated here from 1912 to 1914 and was named after Inversnaid, Scotland.

---

*denotes rescinded name or former locality.

Ireland Hill (hill)

82 O/7 - Wildcat Hills
36-27-6-W5
51°21′N 114°43′W
Approximately 57 km north-west of
Calgary.

This hill was named after an early home-steader of the area, Mr. John Ireland.

Iron Springs (hamlet)

82 H/15 - Picture Butte
21-11-20-W4
49°56′N 112°41′W
Approximately 25 km north north-east of
Lethbridge.

Named after the mineral deposits found in
the Blackspring Ridge. The post office
opened at this site 1 February 1908.

Irricana (village)

82 P/5 - Irricana
21-27-26-W4
51°19′N 113°37′W
Approximately 42 km north-east of
Calgary.

Present day Irricana lies in what was the
western section of the Bow Valley Irrigation Block. This was land transferred from
the Dominion Government to the Canadian Pacific Railway in 1894, on the
condition that an irrigation system using
the water from the Bow River be developed. This water was diverted to a
man-made reservoir now known as
Cherstermere Lake. The C.P.R. developed
a massive advertising campaign geared
toward the United States, inviting pioneers
to homestead "the most desirable land in
America." The name Irricana, whose post
office opened 1 January 1909, is a combination of the words "irrigation" and "canal."
It is on or near the site of the 1859 Buffalo
Slaughter Camp where members of the
Palliser Expedition killed seventeen buffalo.
It is not known who the first family in

Irricana was, but in 1900, William Dennis
had a roadhouse on the old Carbon Trail,
immediately east of Irricana. Hughy Miller
had the first store, in a tent, circa 1908.
Despite the fact that the original irrigation
plan was not successful for a number of
reasons, the settlement here continued to
grow into a village. The irony of the place is
that no irrigation canal ever came through
to within 8 km of a town that was named
after one.

Irrigation Creek (creek)

72 E/7 - Manyberries
9-5-7-W4
49°22′N 110°54′W
Flows south-west into Pakowki Lake,
approximately 75 km south of Medicine
Hat.

The precise origin for the name of this
feature is unknown. (see Cronkhite Coulee)

Irvine (town)

72 E/16 - Irvine
31-11-2-W4
49°57′N 110°16′W
Approximately 30 km east south-east of
Medicine Hat.

Named for Colonel A. Irvine (1837-1916),
Commissioner of the North West Mounted
Police from 1880 to 1886, member of the
Northwest Council of the Northwest
Territories and appointed Warden of the
Stoney Mountain Penitentiary, Manitoba,
in 1892.

Irwin Hill (hill)

82 O/7 - Wildcat Hills
33-26-5-W5
51°15′N 114°40′W
Approximately 47 km west north-west of
Calgary.

James Lamon Irwin was originally from
Nova Scotia. He worked as a lumberjack in
British Columbia before settling in the

Cochrane area in 1914. In 1919, he
homesteaded on SW 1/4 32-26-5-W5,
raising a few cows. Just before Christmas of
1929, he was burnt to death in his log cabin.
The big hill to the south-east on part of his
property was officially named Irwin Hill in
June, 1930. Some local residents refer to
this as "Beaupre Hill" because it is located
directly north-west of the old Beaupre
cabin site.

J~K

Jackass Canyon (canyon)

82 O/7 - Wildcat Hills
31-26-5-W5
51°16'N 114°40'W
Approximately 48 km west north-west of
Calgary.

The precise origin for the name of this
feature is unknown; however, when the
Canadian Pacific Railway came through in
the 1880s, mules were used for building the
roadbed and many mules were wintered in
this canyon.

Jackfish Bay (bay)

72 L/5 - Tilley
8-17-14-W4
50°25'N 111°54'W
Approximately 96 km north west of
Medicine Hat.

This bay was named in 1959 for the
Northern Pike, commonly known as
Jackfish, found in Newell Lake, and many
other Alberta lakes.

Jackson Hill (hill)

72 L/16 - Bindloss
29,30-23-1-W4
50°59'00"N 110°07'10"W
Approximately 107 km north north-west of
Medicine Hat.

Mr. George Jackson (1883-1973)
homesteaded the land on which the hill is
located. Originally from England, Jackson
came to Canada in 1907, settling in the
Olds-Didsbury area, and moving to this
region in 1912.

Jamieson Creek (creek)

82 O/7 - Wildcat Hills
27-26-6-W5
51°15'N 114°46'W

Flows north-east into Ghost River,
approximately 55 km west north-west of
Calgary.

This tributary of the Ghost River was
named after Alexander Jamieson and his
family, early homesteaders to the area.
Jamieson came to the Calgary district in
1890 from Ontario. In 1891, he took up a
homestead in the area south of Shepard. He
passed away in 1936 and his wife died in
1949.

Jamieson Lake (lake)

72 L/12 - Brooks
16-19-14-W4
50°37'N 111°53'W
Approximately 107 km north-west of
Medicine Hat.

The precise origin for the name of this
feature is unknown.

Janet (hamlet)

82 P/4 - Dalroy
5-24-28-W4
51°01'N 113°52'W
Approximately 10 km east of Calgary.

Janet was a siding and flag station built by
the Canadian National Railway when the
railroad went through. A station was
erected in 1912, and it is believed that the
Harry Whittaker family was one of the first
settlers here. Whittaker built a house about
0.2 km from the crossing. The Columbia
Grain Co. built an elevator here in 1928 and
rented it to Parrish and Heimbecker. It
carried the Columbia name for many years
thereafter. The precise origin for the name
is unknown.

* Jaydot (former station)

72 E/1 - Cripple Creek
33-3-1-W4
49°15'N 110°05'W
Approximately 92 km south-east of
Medicine Hat.

The station received its name from the
adjacent Jaydot Ranch. The ranch was
owned by J.L. Peacock, who was a livestock dealer, and Bill Babb, a horse rancher.
They trailed in hundreds of horses from
Babb's Cold Spring Ranch near Cypress
Hills, to be broken for the purpose of trade
and the brand they used on the trail was a
"j." The ranch still carries this brand.

* Jefferson (former locality)

82 H/3 - Cardston
36-1-24-W4
49°05'N 113°05'W
Approximately 69 km south-west of
Lethbridge.

(see Owendale)

Jenner (hamlet)

72 I/11 - Jenner
33-20-9-W4
50°45'N 111°11'W
Approximately 85 km north-west of
Medicine Hat.

This one-time village, previously known as
"Websdale" after the first postmaster, was
renamed in 1913 after the famous English
physician, Dr. Edward Jenner (1749-1823),
who discovered the vaccine for the prevention of smallpox in 1796 using matter
drawn from the lesions of cowpox, a mild
disease, that prevented a person from
contracting smallpox. The practice of
vaccination for the prevention of smallpox
soon became widespread and Jenner won
world-wide recognition, including cash
awards from the British Parliament in 1802
and 1806.

Jensen (locality)
72 E/14 - Bow Island
6-11-10-W4
49°52′N 111°21′W
Approximately 52 km west of Medicine Hat.

This feature is named for Mr. Christian Jensen, Chairman of the Board of Trustees of the Magrath Irrigation District for more than twenty years.

Jensen Dam (dam)
82 H/7 - Raymond
4-22-W4
49°20′N 112°54′W
Approximately 37 km south of Lethbridge.

(see Jensen Reservoir)

Jensen Reservoir (reservoir)
82 H/7 - Raymond
21-4-22-W4
49°18′N 112°54′W
Approximately 40 km south of Lethbridge.

The name was proposed in 1948 by Ben Russel, Director of Water Resources, after Christian Jensen (1868-1958) who moved to the Magrath area from the United States in 1903. With his brothers, Jensen acquired large tracts of land for the purpose of grain farming and sheep ranching. His name was chosen because of his commitment to water management, serving as Chairman of the Board of Trustees of the Magrath Irrigation District for more than twenty years. He was also involved in City Council and the School Board, the Alberta Wheat Pool and other agricultural associations. The dam and reservoir were given individual names, but both commemorate Christian Jensen.

Jerry the Bird's Bottom (bottom)
82 H/10 - Lethbridge
9-9-22-W4
49°38′20″N 112°55′50″W

Approximately 8 km south-west of Lethbridge.

This riverbottom on the Blood Indian Reserve was officially named 5 May 1987 after a man whose name was Jerry the Bird who ranched there. It is not known if he filed a claim or merely squatted. It is believed, however, that he was one of the Métis who interpreted for the treaty of 1883 and that he fled from Batoche, Saskatchewan to the Lethbridge area. He is said to have spoken Cree, Blackfoot and English fluently. It is further believed that he died in Montana.

Jethson (locality)
72 M/4 - Pollockville
16-26-12-W4
51°13′N 111°38′W
Approximately 78 km south-east of Drumheller.

The precise origin for the name of this feature is unknown. (see Carolside)

Johnson Creek (creek)
82 I/4 - Claresholm
13,14-30-W4
50°09′N 114°00′W
Flows north-east into Willow Creek, approximately 95 km west north-west of Lethbridge.

This creek was presumably named after Link Johnson who arrived from Montana about 1903. He was a steam engineer and owned a portable steam engine. He went to work on the north fork of Willow Creek and worked for several years at the mill. He returned to Montana circa 1915.

Johnson Island (island)
82 I/14 - Gleichen
31-21-25-W4
50°50′N 113°27′W
Approximately 35 km south-east of Calgary, in the Bow River.

The precise origin for the name of this feature is unknown.

Johnson Lake (lake)
72 L/12 - Brooks
9-19-14-W4
50°36′N 111°53′W
Approximately 106 km north-west of Medicine Hat.

The precise origin for the name of this feature is unknown.

Johnson Reservoir (reservoir)
72 L/5 - Tilley
13-16-14-W4
50°20′N 111°48′W
Approximately 85 km west north-west of Medicine Hat.

The precise origin for the name of this feature is unknown.

Judson (locality)
82 H/9 - Chin Coulee
34-6-18-W4
49°32′N 112°21′W
Approximately 38 km south-east of Lethbridge.

This Canadian Pacific Railway station was named for Judson Bemis, owner of the Bemis Bag Company.

Jumping Buffalo Hill (hill)
82 I/10 - Queenstown
20-19-W4
50°43′N 112°35′W
Approximately 100 km south-east of Calgary.

The name for this hill is a direct translation of the Blackfoot word, *oteschiksisapaghkio-teseh.*

* **Jumping Pound** (former locality)
82 O/2 - Jumpingpound Creek
30-24-4-W5
51°04′N 114°33′W
Approximately 45 km west of Calgary.

(see Jumpingpound Creek)

Jumpingpound Creek (creek)
82 O/2 - Jumpingpound Creek
4-26-4-W5
51°11′N 114°30′W
Flows north-east into Bow River, approximately 38 km west north-west of Calgary.

The Blackfoot name for this creek is *ninapiskan*, translating "men's pound." In Stoney, the name is *to-ko-jap-tab-wap-ta*. Both names are descriptive and refer to the high steep bank near the mouth where buffalo were driven over and killed. This was known as a "buffalo pound," in contrast to a "buffalo jump." (see Head-Smashed-In Buffalo Jump or Old Women's Buffalo Jump)

Juniper Flats (flat)
72 L/7 - Watching Hill
17-5,6-W4
50°27′N 110°42′W
Approximately 40 km north of Medicine Hat.

The name for these flats is likely descriptive.

Juno (locality)
72 E/13 - Grassy Lake
18-10-12-W4
49°49′N 111°36′W
Approximately 87 km east of Lethbridge.

Established by the Canadian Pacific Railway in 1894, this station was named for the mythical character Juno, both the sister and wife of Jupiter and the goddess of marriage and childbirth. This ancient Roman queen of heaven (the highest deity in the Roman pantheon next to Jupiter) was identified with the Greek goddess, Hera.

Kathyrn (hamlet)
82 P/4 - Dalroy
16-26-27-W4
51°13′N 113°42′W
Approximately 25 km north-east of Calgary.

Neil McKay, a large local landowner of the area, named this hamlet after Kathryn, his daughter. He had offered some of his land to the Grand Trunk Pacific Railway Company in 1911 for a townsite, on the provision that he be permitted to give it a name. When the station was finally built in 1913, apparently the painter who was in charge of the sign misspelled the name Kathryn and the settlement became known as Kathyrn. The post office opened 1 January 1919.

Keho Lake (lake)
82 H/15 - Picture Butte
11-22,23-W4
49°57′N 112°59′W
Approximately 25 km north-west of Lethbridge.

Keho Lake was derived from the name Dan Keough who was a wolfer and whisky trader and came to the area in the early 1870s. He also mined coal near the lake and sold it to the North West Mounted Police forts Macleod and Kipp. Keough came to Canada in search of hides and in order to catch his prey, Keough would kill a buffalo, poison the meat with strychnine and leave it for the wolves. As would be expected, a number of other animals died from eating the poisoned meat, including many dogs owned by Indians. This resulted in poor relations between wolfers and the natives. In order to endear himself to the police, Keough mined coal at Scabby Butte and hauled it to Fort Macleod. Despite these efforts to remain on good terms with the Mounties, who arrived in Western Canada in 1874, Keough and other wolfers and whisky traders soon found that their welcome had run out. Despite his less-than-pure reputation, the nearby School District and this lake were named after him, although the name was spelled incorrectly.

Keith (locality)
82 O/1 - Calgary
5-25-2-W5
51°06′N 114°15′W
Within the city limits of Calgary.

A Canadian Pacific Railway station was established here in 1884 and was named by Donald Smith, Lord Strathcona, after Keith, a town in Banffshire (now Grampian), Scotland.

Kennedy Coulee (coulee)
72 E/2 - Comrey
2,3-1-6-W4
49°00′N 110°43′W
Runs south-east into the U.S., approximately 110 km south of Medicine Hat.

The name Kennedy Coulee was adopted by the Canadian Permanent Committee on Geographical Names in July 1974, to standardize the name with that section of this feature located in Montana. This procedure has since been discontinued in Canada. Alternate names are "Canada Coulee" or "Canadian Coulee." The origin of the name Kennedy is unknown. The coulee contains Kennedy Creek.

Kennedy Creek (creek)
72 E/2 - Comrey
2-1-6-W4
49°00′N 110°43′W
Flows south-east into the U.S., approximately 110 km south of Medicine Hat.

(see Kennedy Coulee)

Kennedy's Coulee (coulee)

72 L/16 - Bindloss
16-23-2-W4
50°59'20"N 110°15'00"W
Approximately 104 km north north-west of Medicine Hat.

This feature's name is derived from a local ranching family, the Kennedys, who held the water rights on the coulee. Fergus Kennedy and his family operated a Hereford ranch located at the mouth of the coulee.

Keoma (hamlet)

82 P/4 - Dalroy
13-26-27-W4
51°13'N 113°39'W
Approximately 37 km north-east of Calgary.

Keoma is a native word which translates to "far away." The hamlet was settled in 1910 when the Canadian Pacific Railway opened up land for irrigation. It is assumed that the C.P.R. named the site, but this is not definitive. The post office was in operation from 15 January 1910 through 27 June 1986.

Kerfoot Creek (creek)

82 O/7 - Wildcat Hills
10-27-5-W5
51°18'N 114°36'W
Flows east into Grand Valley Creek, approximately 49 km west north-west of Calgary.

William Duncan Kerfoot, (ca. 1852-1908) was born in Virginia and came to the Calgary district in 1880 as the Manager for the British American Ranche Co. He settled here in 1884, and resided here until his death. Three of his sons apparently still live in the district.

Kersey (locality)

82 P/5 - Irricana
9-28-27-W4
51°24'N 113°49'W
Approximately 38 km north north-east of Calgary.

This site was the result of a Canadian Pacific Railway colonization scheme. In 1911, the C.P.R. recruited settlers from England and Scotland, offering 80-acre farms as incentive. However, there was a bad hailstorm the following year, and most of the homesteaders packed up and returned to their homeland. The individuals who stayed behind were able to absorb the land the others had abandoned. Between 12 and 15 families remained, and the surrounding area became known locally as "the English Colony." The name Kersey was taken after a village in Suffolk, England. The post office opened 1 October 1912 and was run out of the Howden home. It operated until 31 December 1937.

Ketchum Creek (creek)

72 E/7 - Manyberries
21-4-7-W4
49°20'N 110°52'W
Flows west into Pakowki Lake, approximately 80 km south-west of Medicine Hat.

Likely native in origin, the name Ketchum Creek was changed by whites to Catchem when the area's first school district was established in the early 1900s. The original spelling was adopted in 1939 when the name was made official. The precise origin of the name is unknown.

Kettles Creek (creek)

82 H/5 - Pincher Creek
4-25-6-30-W5
From 49°24'10"N 113°57'00"W
to 49°29'50"N 113°55'28"W
Flows north into Pincher Creek, approximately 80 km west south-west of Lethbridge.

This creek was officially named 6 March 1986 after Charles Kettles of the North West Mounted Police. He was born near Ottawa in 1851 and at the age of 19, joined the militia and received a service medal. By 1878, Charles Kettles had worked his way to Pincher Creek, where he and his family established themselves as respected members of the community. The butcher shop which opened in 1883 became a healthy success for Charles Kettles and his family. Many descendants of the original Kettles clan still reside in the area and the name is well established locally.

Keystone Hills (hill)

82 O/7 - Wildcat Hills
29-27-6-W5
51°22'N 114°48'W
Approximately 64 km west north-west of Calgary.

Keystone was the name of an American oil company that drilled in this area circa 1930. These hills may take their name from it.

Kimball (hamlet)

82 H/3 - Cardston
31-1-24-W4
49°05'N 113°12'W
Approximately 71 km south-west of Lethbridge.

Named for Herber C. Kimball whose grandsons were early settlers of the Cardston area. This locality was known as "Colles" prior to 1903, after Henry Cope Colles and his wife, who homesteaded and operated the post office and a small trading post. Other sources suggest that the area was organized in 1900 by the Latter Day Saints Church in Salt Lake City, Utah into an L.D.S. ward and named after the many descendants of Herber C. Kimball, who resided within the locale. The Kimball Ward was closed down in 1948 with its responsibility taken over by the Aetna Ward.

Kinbrook Island (island)

72 L/5 - Tilley
19-17-14-W4
50°27′N 111°55′W
Approximately 98 km north-west of
Medicine Hat, in Lake Newell.

The name, approved in 1959, is a combination of the first three letters of the word Kinsmen, and the name of the nearby town of Brooks. This name was chosen because the Kinsmen Club of Brooks was instrumental in originally developing this island as a picnic and recreation centre. The 95 acre island has since been developed by the provincial government into a well-known, widely used provincial park. This required the building of a causeway, levelling, ditching, planting trees, the creation of a beach, a campsite and many other projects.

Kinbrook Island Provincial Park

(provincial park)
72 L/5 - Tilley
19-17-14-W4
50°27′N 110°54′W
Approximately 98 km north-west of
Medicine Hat.

The Kinsmen had a major role in inspiring the formation of the 38.44 hectare park, created by Order-in-council 147/71. It is suggested that the root of this name acknowledges their involvement. All other islands in Lake Newell are also part of this provincial park. (see Kinbrook Island)

Kininvie (railway point)

72 L/6 - Alderson
29-16-11-W4
50°22′N 111°28′W
Approximately 65 km north-west of
Medicine Hat.

This railway point was named in 1884 after Kininvie House, Banffshire (now Grampian), Scotland.

Kinmundy (post office)

72 M/3 - Big Stone
7-25-8-W4
51°06′N 111°06′W
Approximately 120 km east south-east of
Drumheller.

This post office, opened 1 May 1913 was named after the hometown of its first postmaster, Walter Flagg who hailed from Kinmundy, Illinois.

Kipp (locality)

82 H/15 - Picture Butte
30-9-22-W4
49°45′N 112°57′W
Approximately 7 km north-west of
Lethbridge.

Named for Fort Kipp, which in turn, was established by Joseph Kipp (1847-1913), son of James Kipp. Joseph Kipp was born at Fort Union, an American Fur Company post, and was a resident of Montreal. His partner, Charlie Thomas, came to Canada to avoid American authorities for trading whisky at Fort Benton. They built Fort Kipp in 1870 at the confluence of the Oldman and Belly rivers, so that they could continue with their whisky trading. Built with its back to the river, the North West Mounted Police found little more than a few roofless buildings when they arrived in the West. The present village of Kipp is actually several kilometres east of the original fort.

Kipp Coulee (coulee)

82 H/7 - Raymond
5-19-W4
49°25′N 112°30′W
A south-west/north-east trending coulee, approximately 35 km south-east of Lethbridge.

(see Kipp)

Kippenville (post office)

72 E/4 - Foremost
34-2-12-W4
49°03′N 111°32′W
Approximately 110 km south-east of
Lethbridge.

A post office was established here 1 October 1913, and was named after the first postmaster, D. Kippen.

Kirkcaldy (hamlet)

82 I/6 - Vulcan
9-16-24-W4
50°20′N 113°14′W
Approximately 87 km south-east of
Calgary.

Named by an unknown Scotsman in 1911 after Kirkcaldy, Fife, Scotland, this post office was opened 15 January 1915 and closed 9 February 1970. Kirkcaldy may have been this person's hometown.

Kirkpatrick (locality)

82 P/7 - Drumheller
24-29-21-W4
51°30′N 112°50′W
Approximately 9 km west north-west of
Drumheller.

The Canadian Pacific Railway established a station here in 1921 and named it after Major W.M. Kirkpatrick, Foreign Traffic Manager for the C.P.R. The name means "church of St. Patrick."

* Kitsim (former locality)

82 I/8 - Scandia
27-17-16-W4
50°27′N 112°07′W
Approximately 98 km north-east of
Lethbridge.

The precise origin for the name of this feature is unknown.

---

*denotes rescinded name or former locality.

* Knappen (former locality)

72 E/3 - Aden
15-1-11-W4
49°02′N 111°24′W
Approximately 122 km south south-west of
Medicine Hat.

Named in honour of Mr. A.J. Knappen, the
first postmaster who served from 1913 to
1917. The post office remained open from
March 1913 through July 1968.

Kneehill (locality)

82 P/7 - Drumheller
SE-9-29-20-W4
51°28′N 112°44′W
Approximately 3 km west of Drumheller.

This locality is named for its proximity to
Kneehills Creek, which in turn was named
after the Knee Hills. The creek begins in the
Knee Hill Valley, approximately 85 km to
the north-west. The Knee Hills were
descriptively named, as they resemble the
shape of a knee. In Cree, the name is
rendered *mi-chig-wun*; and in Stoney, *che-
swun-de-ba-ha* (Tyrrell).

Kneehills Creek (creek)

82 P/7 - Drumheller
24-29-21-W4
51°30′N 112°50′W
Flows south-east into Red Deer River,
approximately 2 km west of Drumheller.

(see Kneehill)

Knight Creek (creek)

82 H/2 - Shanks Lake
20-2-20-W4
49°09′N 112°39′W
Flows south-east into North Milk River,
approximately 61 km south of Lethbridge.

This creek was named after the Knight
Ranch, owned by Raymond Knight who
came to southern Alberta in 1901 when his
father purchased several large parcels of
land. The town of Raymond was also
named after Mr. Knight.

Kohler Coulee (coulee)

82 I/4 - Claresholm
29-13-29-W4
50°07′45″N 113°53′50″W
A north-south trending coulee, approximately 93 km north-west of Lethbridge.

This feature was named for Hans Kohler
who came to the area in 1903 where he
ranched until 1912, when he returned to his
native Switzerland to marry. The Kohler
family lived in various places in the United
States for some years but eventually
returned to the Stavely area where Mr.
Kohler died in 1977. Kohler Coulee School
District #1198 was established in 1909, and
was also named after Hans Kohler.

Kuntz Creek (creek)

82 I/4 - Claresholm
11-14-30-W4
50°09′N 113°58′W
Flows south into Willow Creek, approximately 98 km north-west of Lethbridge.

This creek was named for Henry Kountz
(or Kounts), a pioneer settler who was
described as a real frontiersman. He arrived
in Alberta in 1871, but before that he had
been a buffalo hunter in the United States.
On his arrival in Alberta he freighted
between Fort Benton and the Blackfoot
Reserve but lost his outfit in a poker game.
He then commenced ranching at the
"Leavings" where the trail north left
Willow Creek (see Granum). His ranch
became a famous stopping place. In 1882 he
sold out to the Oxley Ranching Co. and
later located further west; he later staked a
claim on a coal seam but this failed to be
productive.

Kyiskap Creek (creek)

82 H/13 - Granum
11-10-27-W4
49°48′N 113°33′W
Flows east into Willow Creek, approximately 53 km west of Lethbridge.

The origin for the name of this feature is
unknown.

---

*denotes rescinded name or former locality.

* **Lake McGregor** (former locality)

82 I/7 - McGregor Lake
18-22-W4
50°30'N 112°58'W
Approximately 80 km south-east of
Calgary.

This former locality was named for His
Honour James Duncan McGregor (1860-
1935), who with his family, travelled west
from Brandon, Manitoba in 1877. For three
decades, he farmed, ranched and served as a
mining license inspector in Dawson, Yukon
territory. McGregor was a shareholder in
the Grand Forks Cattle Company and
when it was taken over by the Southern
Alberta Land Company, an English firm,
he was appointed the firm's Canadian
manager. Shortly after the turn of the
century, McGregor envisioned the need for
irrigation and in 1909, the S.A.L. Co. began
construction on a dam across what was
then known as Snake Valley and is now
filled with water forming the reservoir. The
original Snake Lake, in Snake Valley, was
enlarged, and the dam was completed in
1918. McGregor left the company in 1912
and went on to become a very successful
cattle breeder and was eventually appointed
Lieutenant-Governor of Manitoba in 1929.
McGregor founded this community in
1909. (see McGregor Lake)

Lane Creek (creek)

82 I/4 - Claresholm
6-14-29-W4
50°08'N 113°57'W
Flows south into Willow Creek, approximately 99 km north-west of Lethbridge.

This creek was named after George Lane
(1856-1925), who became internationally
known as a result of his ranching and
breeding operations. Lane worked as a
ranch hand and manager in the United

States until 1884, when he came to Alberta.
Here, he worked as foreman and manager
of the Bar U Ranch for the North West
Cattle Company near High River, and later
worked for the Pat Burns Company. In
1902, Lane and some partners, purchased
the Bar U, and by 1920 was its sole owner.
He became famous for breeding world class
Percheron stallions, and with Guy Weadick
and others, for founding the Calgary
Stampede. Lane also invested in several
large grain farms. In 1913, George Lane was
elected to the Alberta Legislature for the
riding of Bow Valley. This feature is also
known to some local residents as "Coon
Creek," after the abundance of raccoons
located in the vicinity of the creek.

Lanfine (hamlet)

72 M/7 - Cereal
7-28-5-W4
51°23'N 110°42'W
Approximately 146 km east of Drumheller.

The post office here, established 15 May
1912, was named by the first postmaster,
William Davidson, for a county seat near
his home town called Lanfine House in
Ayrshire (now Strathclyde), Scotland. The
post office closed 31 October 1968.

Langdon (hamlet)

82 I/13 - Dalemead
23-23-27-W4
50°58'N 113°40'W
Approximately 18 km east of Calgary.

This hamlet was named for R.B. Langdon
of Langdon and Shepard, Canadian Pacific
Railway sub-contracting firm who built a
section of the line just east of Calgary. Both
the Langdon and Shepard stations took
their names from these men. Langdon was
one of two people to turn the first sod in
the settlement in 1882. A year later, a
railway station was set up in a boxcar and
named after him. A post office was established 1 January 1890. The community of

Langdon became known as the "good luck
town," because in the twenty-five years
between 1883 and 1908 there was not one
death. It was also considered lucky because
it was situated on the railroad's horseshoe-
shaped turnaround.

* **Langevin** (former railway point)

72 L/6 - Alderson
20-15-10-W4
50°17'N 111°20'W
Approximately 53 km north-west of
Medicine Hat.

(see Alderson)

Larmour (station)

72 E/16 - Irvine
30-11-1-W4
49°56'N 110°08'W
Approximately 35 km east of Medicine
Hat.

This station was named for R.E. Larmour,
general freight agent for the Canadian
Pacific Railway during the early years of
this century.

Lathom (locality)

82 I/9 - Cassils
29-20-17-W4
50°43'N 112°20'W
Approximately 117 km north-east of
Lethbridge.

A Canadian Pacific Railway station opened
at this site in 1884 and was named after
Edward George Bootle Wibraham, 2nd
Earl of Lathom (1864-1910). He was the
director of the Oxley Ranch Company, and
travelled over the Canadian Pacific with

---

*denotes rescinded name or former locality.

other directors in 1883. A post office operated from 15 June 1912 through 30 June 1946.

Lathom Lake (lake)
82 I/9 - Cassils
21,28-20-17-W4
50°43′N 112°18′W
Approximately 116 km north-east of Lethbridge.

(see Lathom)

* **Lawsonburg** (former locality)
82 P/8 - Dorothy
22-29-16-W4
51°29′N 112°10′W
Approximately 37 km east of Drumheller.

The post office which was established 1 June 1909, was named after Dr. L.L. Lawson, the first doctor in the area. Mail service was conducted out of Dr. & Mrs. Lawson's home and it remained in operation until 31 May 1929.

Layton Creek (creek)
82 H/6 - Raley
25-5-26-W4
49°24′N 113°23′W
Flows north into Bullhorn Coulee, approximately 60 km south-west of Lethbridge.

This stream was officially named in July 1942; however, its precise origin is not known.

* **Leavings** (former locality)
82 H/13 - Granum
31-10-26-W4
49°52′N 113°30′W
Approximately 50 km north-west of Lethbridge.

(see Granum)

Leavitt (hamlet)
82 H/3 - Cardston
31-2-26-W4
49°10′N 113°27′W
Approximately 80 km south-west of Lethbridge.

Named after T.R. Leavitt, an original pioneer in the area. The post office opened here 1 January 1900 and closed 30 April 1968.

Lee Creek (creek)
82 H/3 - Cardston
23-3-25-W4
49°13′N 113°16′W
Flows north-east into St. Mary River, approximately 61 km south-west of Lethbridge.

Named for William Samuel Lee who came to this area in 1867 from Fort Benton, Montana, and established a fur-trading post on an Indian trail near a ford of the creek, west of the present-day townsite of Beazer. This ford was known as "Lariat Cross," and was shown as well on the 1883 Department of the Interior Map. In Blackfoot, it was known as *sakemahpenei*, translating as "rope across," because the Indians used to stretch a rope across the creek at this point, when the water level was high.

Legend (locality)
72 E/5 - Legend
19-6-12-W4
49°25′N 111°36′W
Approximately 90 km south-east of Lethbridge.

The origin of the name Legend may be found in the two words, "leg" and "end," which at one time described this locality's place at the end of a leg of the railroad. The name Legend is pronounced "Lee-gend," after the practice of early Canadian Pacific Railway conductors during the late 1800s and early 1900s.

Legend Coulee (creek)
72 E/6 - Foremost
24-5-12-W4
49°24′N 111°30′W
Runs south into Etzikom Coulee, approximately 85 km south-west of Medicine Hat.

(see Legend)

Lehigh (hamlet)
82 P/7 - Drumheller
31-27-18-W4
51°21′N 112°32′W
Approximately 19 km south-east of Drumheller.

The railway went through Lehigh circa 1928, though it is believed there never was a station here. Jessie Gouge opened the first mine around 1929 which was called the Maple Leaf Mine. At its peak, Lehigh boasted a population of approximately 50 individuals. The precise origin for the name is unknown. There is a river in East Pennsylvania by the same name which flows south into Delaware River and it has been suggested that some settlers were from this state.

* **Lenzie** (former locality)
82 H/10 - Lethbridge
10-9-22-W4
49°43′N 112°55′W
Approximately 4 km west of Lethbridge.

A Canadian Pacific Railway station was established here circa 1914 and was named for Lenzie, a suburb of Kirkintilloch, near Glasgow, Scotland.

Lethbridge (city)
82 H/10 - Lethbridge
9-21-W4
49°42′N 112°49′W
Approximately 180 km south-east of Calgary.

This city was named for William Lethbridge (1824-1901), first President of the North Western Coal and Navigation Company, Limited, which was formed in 1882 to mine coal from the banks of the Oldman River to sell to the Canadian Pacific Railway (see Galt Island). After the opening of the Sheran mine in 1872, the area and settlement growing there was called "The Coal Banks" but the name was changed to Lethbridge ca. 1882. There was, however, already a Lethbridge in Ontario and the postal authorities therefore changed the name to "Coalhurst." In 1885, the Postmaster General restored the name Lethbridge. Many native descriptive names have also been associated with the region. The area was first known as *siko-ko-to-ki*, a Blackfoot word translating to "black rocks," after the coal outcroppings in the area. The Bloods called it *mek-kio-towaghs*, or "medicine stone," after a large granite boulder on the city's site upon which they placed offerings of beads and various trinkets. It was also known as *ashsoysem*, or "steep banks." Another native name for this area was *assini-etmotchi*, translating, "where they slaughtered the Crees," commemorating the Indian Battle of October 1870 when the Blackfoot killed 300 Crees. This incident is commemorated in Indian Battle Park.

* **Lexion** (former railway point)
82 H/10 - Lethbridge
23-8-21-W4
49°39'30"N 112°44'15"W
Approximately 4 km south-east of Lethbridge.

The precise origin for the name of this feature is unknown.

Lime Kiln Lake (lake)
82 H/5 - Pincher Creek
28-5-30-W4
49°25'10"N 113°59'30"W
Approximately 89 km west south-west of Lethbridge.

Named because Alphie Primeau's father, one-time owner of the land upon which the lake is situated, made lime at a kiln in the early 1890s. The site of the original kiln can still be recognized on the shore of the lake. This name has been used locally since the time that the kiln was built. The name was officially approved 15 February 1978.

Linquist Coulee (creek)
72 E/14 - Bow Island
7-12-10-W4
49°58'N 111°22'W
Flows west into South Saskatchewan River, approximately 50 km west of Medicine Hat.

Likely named for Mr. Albert Alfred Linquist and family. Albert and his wife, Anne, were born in Sweden, married in Fargo, North Dakota in 1879 and came to Canada in 1886. They chose the Boundary Creek area in which to settle. Three years later they established the A.P. Ranch on the south shore of the South Saskatchewan River, in the vicinity of Cherry Coulee just west of the town of Bow Island. By 1900 they were running 400 head of cattle and 700 horses. Several of their sons homesteaded and, in 1911, Albert sold the A.P. Ranch and laid claim to a homestead near those of his sons.

Little Bow Lake (reservoir)
82 I/2 - Travers
28-14-20-W4
50°12'N 112°40'W
Approximately 57 km north north-east of Lethbridge.

(see Bow River)

Little Bow Provincial Park
(provincial park)
82 I/2 - Travers
2-15-22-W4
50°13'N 112°56'W
Approximately 53 km north of Lethbridge.

This 109.9 hectare (271.57 acres) park was established by Order-in-council 1392/72. It was named for its location on the Little Bow River drainage. (see Bow River)

Little Bow River (river)
82 H/16 - Taber
12-11-19-W4
49°53'N 112°29'W
Flows south-east into Oldman River, approximately 30 km north-east of Lethbridge.

Named as a tributary to Bow River. (see Bow River)

Little Dogpound Creek (creek)
82 O/7 - Wildcat Hills
33-28-4-W5
51°26'N 114°30'W
Flows east into Dogpound Creek, approximately 53 km north-west of Calgary.

(see Dogpound)

Little Fish Lake (lake)
82 P/8 - Dorothy
8-28-16-W4
51°22'N 112°14'W
Approximately 34 km east south-east of Drumheller.

The descriptive name for this lake refers to its size and its apparent abundance of fish. It was originally known as "Lake of the Little Fishes" and appears to have been a plentiful source of fish for the Indians, as extensive remains of their encampments have been found here.

Little Fish Lake Provincial Park
(provincial park)
82 P/8 - Dorothy
9-28-16-W4
51°22′N 112°12′W
Approximately 38 km east south-east of
Drumheller.

This provincial park was established by
Order-in-council 570/79, is 61.19 hectares
(151.21 acres) in area, and is located on the
east shore of Little Fish Lake. It takes its
name from the lake.

Little Fox Hill (hill)

82 I/10 - Queenstown
20-19-W4
50°43′N 112°37′W
Approximately 102 km south-east of
Calgary.

The name for this hill first appeared on the
map of the Blackfoot Reserve, published in
1909. The likely descriptive name was
submitted for approval by the Geographic
Board of Canada in 1911.

* Little Plume (former locality)

72 E/10 - Bulls Head
14-9-5-W4
49°44′N 110°34′W
Approximately 30 km south of Medicine
Hat.

This former locality was named for the
South Peigan Indian Chief (Tom) Little
Plume. Born in Brocket in 1889, Tom
served overseas in World War I with the
192nd Battalion, Canadian Expeditionary
Force, and was always considered a close
friend of the white settlers. Chief Little
Plume spent most of his life in Brocket and
died in 1971.

Little Rolling Hills (hill)
72 L/5 - Tilley
15-14-W4
50°17′N 111°53′W
Approximately 72 km east north-east of
Medicine Hat.

The descriptive name for these hills is a
translation of a Blackfoot Indian term,
pekisko, or "hilly country."

Little Sandhill Creek (creek)

72 L/13 - Wardlow
7-21-11-W4
50°46′N 111°31′W
Flows north into Red Deer River, approximately 98 km north-west of Medicine Hat.

The name is descriptive as the creek flows
from a small sandy hill.

Loblaw Creek (creek)

82 O/7 - Wildcat Hills
24-28-7-W5
51°25′N 114°51′W
Flows north into Atkinson Creek, approximately 75 km north-west of Calgary.

The precise origin for the name of this
feature is unknown.

* Lochend (former locality)

82 O/8 - Crossfield
26-27-3-W5
51°21′N 114°19′W
Approximately 38 km north north-west of
Calgary.

The descriptive name for this former
locality refers to its position: it is located at
the end of the lake (loch). There are six
Lochends in Scotland and the first postmaster, J.K. Laidlaw, suggested the name. The
post office operated here from 1 June 1905
through 31 December 1929.

Lochend Lake (lake)

82 O/8 - Crossfield
26-27-3-W5
51°20′N 114°19′W
Approximately 40 km north north-west of
Calgary.

(see Lochend)

Lodge Creek (creek)

72 E/1 - Cripple Creek
24-3-1-W4
49°13′N 110°00′W
Flows south-east into the province of
Saskatchewan, approximately 100 km
south-east of Medicine Hat.

The precise origin for the name of this
feature is unknown.

Lomond (village)

82 I/7 - McGregor Lake
14-16-20-W4
50°21′N 112°39′W
Approximately 72 km north north-east of
Lethbridge.

The name for this village, incorporated 16
February 1916, was named after Loch
Lomond in Dunbartonshire (now in both
Central and Strathclyde) Scotland. It was
previously known as "Brunette." One local
resident posits that Lomond was named
after Lomond Dugal McCarthy, who
homesteaded on the townsite.

Lone Eagle Butte (butte)

72 L/7 - Watching Hill
17-6-W4
50°28′N 110°44′W
Approximately 45 km north of Medicine
Hat.

The precise origin for the name of this
feature is unknown.

Lonebutte (locality)
82 P/8 - Dorothy
32-27-15-W4
51°21'N 112°09'W
Approximately 45 km south-east of
Drumheller.

The post office opened here 1 November
1910 as this descriptive name which was
derived from the only noticeable hill
located for miles around. It is located in a
fairly level strip of country between the
Hand Hills and the Red Deer River. The
early ranchers and cowboys who arrived
before this part of the country was surveyed likely used this conspicuous butte as
a landmark. The post office closed 9
September 1943.

Lonely Valley Creek (creek)
82 H/2 - Shanks Lake
28-2-20 W4
49°09'N 112°37'W
Flows south-east into Milk River, approximately 60 km south of Lethbridge.

This creek was named because nobody but
ranchers and cowboys used the valley for
cattle drives. No one lives in the area and
the valley is long and barren except for this
creek.

Lonesome Coulee (coulee)
72 L/15 - Buffalo
7-20-22-4-W4
50°53'00"N 110°31'00"W
Runs south into Red Deer River, approximately 92 km north of Medicine Hat.

The name may be descriptive of the fact
that it is the only coulee north of the Red
Deer River that is noticeable. Alkali Creek
flows through the coulee into the Red Deer
River.

Lonesome Lake (lake)
82 I/8 - Scandia
21,28-16-17-W4
50°22'N 112°17'W
Approximately 83 km north-east of
Lethbridge.

The precise origin for the name of this
feature is unknown.

Long Coulee (creek)
82 I/2 - Travers
32-14-22-W4
50°13'N 112°58'W
Flows south-east into Little Bow River,
approximately 55 km north of Lethbridge.

This creek is named for either Robert Long
and his family who became large landown-
ers within close proximity of the feature, or
the name is descriptive of the creek's 30 km
length.

Long's Lake (lake)
82 H/1 - Milk River
12-1-17-W4
49°01'30"N 112°09'55"W
Approximately 85 km south south-east of
Lethbridge.

This lake is likely named for an early
homesteader, Mr. John Long, who owned
land along its east shore.

Lookout Butte (butte)
82 H/12 - Brocket
11-9-27-W4
49°43'N 113°33'W
Approximately 53 km west of Lethbridge.

The name for this feature is likely descriptive. In Blackfoot, the butte was known as
ickemochsoking, which translates to "Salt
Butte."

Lost Creek (creek)
72 E/2 - Comrey
4-1-7-W4
49°00'N 110°52'W

Flows south into the U.S.A., approximately
113 km south of Medicine Hat.

The precise origin for the name of this
feature is unknown.

* **Lost Lake** (former post office)
82 I/1 - Vauxhall
10-14-18-W4
50°10'N 112°18'W
Approximately 62 km north-east of
Lethbridge.

A post office operated here from 1 August
1909 through 1 February 1915, and was
named after the nearby lake. The name was
later changed. (see Enchant)

Lost Lake (lake)
82 I/1 - Vauxhall
6-14-17-W4
50°09'N 112°18'W
Approximately 54 km north-east of
Lethbridge.

The precise origin for the name of this
feature is unknown.

Lost Lake (lake)
82 O/7 - Wildcat Hills
31-28-5-W5
51°27'N 114°42'W
Approximately 60 km north-west of
Calgary.

The precise origin for the name of this
feature is unknown.

■ **Lost River** (river)
72 E/1 - Cripple Creek
2-1-4-W4
49°00'N 110°17'W
Flows south-east into the U.S.A., approximately 112 km south south-east of Medicine Hat.

According to William Heydlauft, a local
resident of 68 years, Indian legend had it

that the Cree Indians attempted to find the source of this river, but it changed direction when they started to follow it. This incident led them to call it the equivalent of "river that got lost."

Lott Creek (creek)

82 O/1 - Calgary
16-33-23-2-W5
51°00′N 114°13′W
Flows east into Elbow River, within the city limits of Calgary.

This creek was likely named after Herbert S. Lott and family, who were early homesteaders in the area. Lott was born in England in 1864, and by 1888, owned land close to the creek. By 1907, the whole family had moved to Victoria and they remained in British Columbia.

Louisiana Lakes (lake)

72 L/12 - Brooks
18-12-W4
50°32′N 111°35′W
Approximately 85 km north-west of Medicine Hat.

Named for the Louisiana Gun Club, who, in association with Ducks Unlimited and the Alberta Government built these lakes and marshland areas as part of their waterfowl land reclamation project. The state of Louisiana was named in 1682 when La Salle, an early explorer, claimed the land for Louis XIV of France.

* Lucky Strike (former locality)

72 E/3 - Aden
30-3-11-W4
49°14′N 111°29′W
Approximately 115 km south-west of Medicine Hat.

Although the origin for this name is difficult to corroborate, two theories exist. While surveying the area for homesteads on a very wet blustery day, one man decided to light his pipe. Despite the rain and gusting winds, he was able to light his pipe with the only match the group had. They all decided that it had been a very "lucky strike." Another account suggests that the post office was named by a Mr. Jochem. Apparently, it was his belief that anyone fortunate enough to own land in the general vicinity had made a "lucky strike."

Lumpy Butte (butte)

82 H/3 - Cardston
24-3-24-W4
49°14′N 113°07′W
Approximately 54 km south-west of Lethbridge.

The name for this butte is descriptive and refers to the varying levels of elevation of the hills north-east of Woolford. The most prominent of these hills is locally named "Bald Hill."

* Lyall (former locality)

82 P/4 - Dalroy
SW-8-25-26-W4
51°07′N 113°36′W
Approximately 28 km east of Calgary.

(see Lyalta)

Lyalta (hamlet)

82 P/4 - Dalroy
SW-8-25-26-W4
51°07′N 113°36′W
Approximately 28 km east of Calgary.

The name for this locality, formerly known simply as "Lyall," is a contraction of the name Lyall and Alberta. Mr. Harry A. Parsons, of the Lyall Trading Company, suggested this alternative, to avoid duplication with another Lyall also located in Alberta. The original charter for construc-

tion of the line was awarded to Alberta Midland Railway, but the line became incorporated into the Canadian National Railway before its completion. The post office here opened 2 July 1923.

Lynch Lakes (lake)

82 H/5 - Pincher Creek
22-5-30-W4
49°24′N 113°57′W
Approximately 87 km south south-west of Lethbridge.

Named for Mr. James Stephen Lynch (1884-1962) who farmed and owned the land upon which this lake is located from 1909 to at least 1919. He came from his home in St. Jacques, New Brunswick in 1908. He went on to become a prominent individual in the community.

Lyndon (locality)

82 I/4 - Claresholm
34-12-29-W4
50°02′N 113°53′W
Approximately 83 km north-west of Lethbridge.

A post office was opened here in 1893 and was named after its first postmaster, Charles A. Lyndon, an early settler to the community. He arrived in the area in 1881.

Lyndon Creek (creek)

82 H/13 - Granum
11-12-29-W4
49°59′N 113°51′W
Flows south into Trout Creek, approximately 79 km north-west of Lethbridge.

(see Lyndon)

* Macbeth (former locality)

72 L/12 - Brooks
14-18-14-W4
50°32'N 111°50'W
Approximately 98 km north-west of
Medicine Hat.

This former locality was named for Hugh
Macbeth of the North Western Coal and
Navigation Company. Macbeth was a
Canadian Pacific Railway station from 1912
to 1914.

MacDonald Creek (creek)

72 E/3 - Aden
14-2-11-W4
49°07'N 111°25'W
Flows north-east into Milk River, approximately 120 km south south-west of
Medicine Hat.

Donald, Archie, and Sam, the three
McDonald brothers, took up homesteads in
the area of the headwaters of this creek. The
creek was later named for them, although it
was misspelled when the name was made
official. The McDonalds stayed for a short
time and then left for the U.S.A.

MacKay Creek (creek)

72 E/16 - Irvine
12-12-1-W4
49°59'N 110°00'W
Flows north into Boxelder Creek, approximately 45 km east of Medicine Hat.

Originating in the Cypress Hills, this creek
was named for Edward MacKay, a mixed
blood trader who settled on the creek in
1895.

MacMillan Creek (creek)

82 I/5 - Nanton
8-17-29-W4
50°25'N 113°57'W

Flows south-east into Mosquito Creek,
approximately 58 km south of Calgary.

This creek was named for Robert
Langworth MacMillan of Prince Edward
Island who came west in 1902 and took up
work on the Heartz and Henderson ranch
to learn the business. In 1910 he bought
them out and immediately sold a large
amount of the land, maintaining the land
within township seventeen. MacMillan
farmed, ranched and raised feed on this land
until 1937 when he sold his land and moved
to Calgary where he died in 1954.

Mackie Creek (creek)

82 H/1 - Milk River
19-2-18,19-W4
49°08'N 112°25'W
Flows south-east into North Milk River,
approximately 67 km south-east of
Lethbridge.

This creek was named for Colonel A.T.
Mackie, who, until selling out to the Pat
Burns Company in 1910, leased more than
60,705 hectares (150,000 acres) of short
grass country in this area.

Macklin Lake (lake)

82 H/1 - Milk River
24-1-16-W4
49°03'N 112°02'W
Approximately 92 km south-east of
Lethbridge.

The precise origin for the name of this
feature is unknown.

Macleod Island (island)

82 H/11 - Fort Macleod
19-9-25-W4
49°44'N 113°22'W
Approximately 40 km west of Lethbridge,
in the Oldman River.

Probably named because this island was the
original site of the North West Mounted

M~N~O

Police post built by Lieutenant-Colonel
Macleod in 1874 (see Fort Macleod)

* Macson (former locality)

72 E/15 - Seven Persons
10-12-5-W4
49°58'N 110°36'W
Approximately 3 km south-east of Medicine Hat.

The name for this locality is derived from
the combination of the names McArthur
and Jamieson, who were Superintendents
for the Canadian Pacific Railway.

Madden (hamlet)

82 O/8 - Crossfield
31-28-2-W5
51°26'N 114°17'W
Approximately 46 km north north-west of
Calgary.

This hamlet was named after Bernard
Madden, an early and prominent rancher
who arrived in the area in 1876. The post
office was opened 1 May 1931.

Magrath (town)

82 H/7 - Raymond
26-5-22-W4
49°25'N 112°52'W
Approximately 30 km south of Lethbridge.

This town was named in 1899 for Charles
A. Magrath (1860-1949) who was the Land
Commissioner of the locally-prominent
North Western Coal and Navigation
Company, Limited from 1885 to 1906 (see
Galt Island). When the various activities of
the company such as mining coal, operating
riverboats and stagecoaches, and lumbering,
did not make acceptable levels of profits for

---

*denotes rescinded name or former locality.

the company, he decided to sell some of the company's large land holdings to the Mormon community. In 1899, he, a former Dominion Topographical Surveyor, surveyed the townsite of Magrath and of Stirling, as these two towns were to be service centres at each end of the settlement project. At that time, C.A. Magrath also served as Member of the Northwest Legislature for the Lethbridge District. He later served as Member of Parliament for Medicine Hat (1908-11) and Mayor of Lethbridge (1891). When he retired to Ontario, early in the twentieth century, he was appointed member of the Canadian section of the International Joint Commission (1911-36), Canadian Fuel Controller (1917-20), Chairman of the Ontario Hydro Electric Commission (1925-31) and Member of the Newfoundland Royal Commission (1933).

■ **Maher Coulee** (coulee)
72 E/7 - Manyberries
1-6-6-W4
49°26'N 110°41'W
Runs south-west into Irrigation Creek, approximately 66 km south of Medicine Hat.

This coulee was named after an early irrigator, a Mr. J.O. Maher. (see Cronkhite Coulee)

Majestic (locality)
72 L/15 - Buffalo
31-21-6-W4
50°51'N 110°50'W
Approximately 90 km north north-west of Medicine Hat.

This locality takes its name from that of an office building in Detroit which was chosen by Mrs. W.C. Hand as the name of the school district. The school district was

established 25 September 1911, and the Canadian Pacific Railway station was established at this location in 1914. The name is also descriptive of the surrounding land. The Hands came from Ontario and homesteaded in 1910 in the area and helped to organize the school district two years later.

* **Major** (former post office)
82 I/10 - Queenstown
20-19-20-W4
50°38'N 112°42'W
Approximately 100 km south-east of Calgary.

Previously known as "Liberty," the post office operated under the name Major from 1 August 1911 through 1 May 1915. One of the postmasters, D.H. Shaw, was an army major. The name was changed in 1915. (see Majorville)

Majors Lake (lake)
72 M/3 - Big Stone
25-9-W4
51°08'N 111°10'W
Approximately 113 km east south-east of Drumheller.

The precise origin for the name of this feature is unknown.

Majorville (locality)
82 I/10 - Queenstown
27-19-20-W4
50°38'N 112°42'W
Approximately 100 km south-east of Calgary.

Originally, this community was given the name "Liberty," when a post office opened on a trial basis. Once permanent status was achieved, a problem arose with mail delivery between Liberty, Saskatchewan and this station. Oddly, at the same time the post office here changed its name to "Major," so too did the post office in

Saskatchewan. The name of this post office, "Major," was changed to Majorville by the Post Office authorities in 1915, to avoid this continuing confusion with mail delivery to Major, Saskatchewan.

Makepeace (locality)
82 I/15 - Cluny
8-23-19-W4
50°56'N 112°37'W
Approximately 95 km east of Calgary.

This Canadian Pacific Railway station was established in 1913 and was named after William Makepeace Thackery, an English novelist. The post office was in operation from 1 July 1917 through 26 October 1951.

Maleb (locality)
72 E/11 - Maleb
24-8-10-W4
49°40'N 111°15'W
Approximately 55 km south-west of Medicine Hat.

This locality is named after a post office which was renamed to a re-arranged combination of the initials of Postmistress Amy Elizabeth Bowen and her husband, Morley Lorne. This post office was first located at 16-8-10-W4 and later moved to its present location. The couple settled in the area in 1910 and the post office opened under the name of Maleb in June 1911. It should be noted that Conquerville is the name of the school and community hall for this same area. The centralization of schools in 1945 amalgamated a number of school districts. At the time, Conquerville, being centrally located, was chosen the site for the large consolidated school over Maleb. The new school was built on 24-8-10-W4, the original Robert Conquergood homestead from whom the name Conquerville received its origin in 1913.

Mallow (locality)
82 I/16 - Bassano
16-22-16-W4
50°52'N 112°10'W
Approximately 136 km east of Calgary.

The precise origin for the name of this feature is unknown.

Mami Creek (creek)
82 H/4 - Waterton Lakes
19-3-27-W4
49°13'N 113°38'W
Flows north into Belly River, approximately 63 km south-west of Lethbridge.

The name for this creek comes from the nearby lake from which it flows. The name Mami Lake was changed to the more commonly known Paine Lake; however, the name for the creek remained. Its precise origin is unknown. (see Paine Lake)

Many Island Lake (lake)
72 L/1 Many Island Lake
13-1-1-W4
50°08'N 110°03'W
Approximately 50 km east of Medicine Hat.

The name for this lake is a descriptive one, and is a translation of the Cree Indian name *aka-amuskie-skway*, or *aka-naywass*, translating to "many islands."

Manyberries (hamlet)
72 E/7 - Manyberries
24-5-6-W4
49°24'N 110°42'W
Approximately 72 km south of Medicine Hat.

This name is derived from the Blackfoot word *akoniskway*, and is descriptive, meaning "many berries." Generations of First Nations peoples came to the area every autumn to pick an assortment of berries, including saskatoons and chokecherries. They used them to make pemmican and to supplement a diet heavily dependent upon meat. This name was chosen for the post office in 1911 and was officially adopted for the hamlet in 1939.

■ **Manyberries Creek** (creek)
72 E/7 Manyberries
8-5-7-W4
49°20'N 110°53'W
Flows south-west into Pakowki Lake, approximately 75 km south of Medicine Hat.

(see Manyberries)

Maple Leaf (Sitook-Spagkway) (hill)
82 I/12 - High River
32-19-29-W4
50°40'N 113°58'W
Approximately 25 km south of Calgary.

The name *sitook-spagkway* is an Indian term translating to "middle heights," and dates back to G.M. Dawson's map of 1884. The name is used on topographical maps and by some geologists. It refers to the high points of land between Mosquito Creek and the Highwood River. The district became known as Maple Leaf when the school was built. The school was shared by Methodists and Mennonites as a place of worship until 1902 when a Methodist church building was constructed. The church became a farm residence in 1911. The school continued in use until 1953 and was dismantled in 1956.

Margaret Lake (lake)
82 H/5 - Pincher Creek
1-4-30-W4
49°16'N 113°55'W
Approximately 94 km south-west of Lethbridge.

This lake may have been named after the wife of J.R. Akins, a Dominion Land Surveyor.

Marr Lake (lake)
82 H/5 - Pincher Creek
28-4-29-W4
49°19'N 113°51'W
Approximately 85 km south-west of Lethbridge.

This lake was named for the Marr family. Walter (1867-1960) and John (1879-1947) took up a homestead on the land near this lake in 1901. They were both born in Kincardine, Ontario, and, when they first came west in 1900, they worked at McClaren's Lumber Camp and Dobbies Livery Barn, and also delivered water. The two brothers raised Shire horses and Shorthorn cattle on the homestead. Their parents, Edwy Ryerson and Sarah Clark Marr came to the area in 1910 and located nearby.

Mary Lake (lake)
82 H/3 - Cardston
12-1-25-W4
49°01'N 113°13'W
Approximately 75 km south south-west of Lethbridge.

The precise origin for the name of this lake, officially approved 8 July 1954, is unknown. Miss Mary Robertson once owned land approximately 6 km north-west of this lake and it may be for her that this lake was named.

Masinasin (post office)
72 E/4 - Coutts
28-2-13-W4
49°09'N 111°40'W
Approximately 150 km south south-west of Medicine Hat.

The name for this post office established 1 August 1909 was suggested by a Mounted Policeman posted in the Milk River region. *Masinasin* is the Cree Indian word for "writing on stone," and refers to the carvings along the sandstone banks of the

Milk River valley. (see Writing-on-Stone Provincial Park)

Massacre Butte (butte)

82 G/9 - Blairmore
27-7-1-W5
49°35'20"N 114°03'00"W
Located at the south end of Porcupine Hills, approximately 90 km west of Lethbridge.

Legend has it that in 1867 twelve members of the Fiske Expedition, who had left the main party in Montana, were making their way north in what is now Alberta to look for gold. Apparently, while camped at this site, they were massacred and all twelve members died.

Mattoyekiu Lake (lake)

82 P/1 - Finnegan
SE-16-25-18-W4
51°08'N 112°28'W
Approximately 35 km south-east of Drumheller.

The descriptive name for this feature is a native term which translates to "grassy lake."

Matzhiwin (locality)

82 I/16 - Bassano
32-21-15-W4
50°50'N 112°03'W
Approximately 140 km east of Calgary.

The precise origin for the name of this feature is unknown.

Matzhiwin Creek (creek)

72 L/13 - Wardlow
1-22-14-W4
50°50'N 111°49'W

Flows south-east into Red Deer River, approximately 119 km north-west of Medicine Hat.

The precise origin for the name of this feature is unknown.

* Maunsell (former locality)

82 H/12 - Brocket
4-7-29-W4
49°32'N 113°52'W
Approximately 79 km west of Lethbridge.

A former Canadian Pacific Railway station, this locality was named for Edward Maunsell (1854-1923) who was a member of the first contingent of North West Mounted Police that marched west from Fort Garry to Fort Macleod in 1874. Maunsell left the force in 1877 to operate the Ivy Ranch with his brothers and was also made an honorary Peigan Chief, and given the name Sa-Sas-ke.

May Creek (creek)

82 O/1 - Calgary
4-24-2-W5
51°01'N 114°14'W
Flows south into Elbow River, within the city limits of Calgary.

This creek was likely named after an early homesteader and rancher, Ernest G. May and his family who came to the Calgary area from England in 1886. Ernest and his cousin W.H. Boorne established the first photography business in Calgary. He then took up ranching and named his land the "Stanford Ranch" after his birthplace in England.

* Maybutt (former locality)

82 H/10 - Lethbridge
32-6-19-W4
49°32'N 112°31'W
Approximately 24 km south-east of Lethbridge.

Maybutt was established in 1893 when the Canadian Pacific Railway bought the Alberta Railway & Irrigation Company (see Galt Island), converted it to standard gauge and built a junction point for lines to Raymond and Foremost. At this point, one mile north of Stirling, New Stirling, also known as "New Town" in contrast to the "Old Town" of Stirling, grew. In 1912, the settlement was named after May Butt, Mr. W. Fisher's wife. Mr. Fisher was the original owner of the land on which the townsite was built, and was the first owner of the local hotel.

Mayme Coulee (coulee)

82 O/7 - Wildcat Hills
13-29-6-W5
51°29'N 114°43'W
Runs east into Little Red Deer River, approximately 68 km north-west of Calgary.

The precise origin for the name of this feature is unknown.

Mazeppa (locality)

82 I/12 - High River
30-19-27-W4
50°38'N 113°44'W
Approximately 35 km south-east of Calgary.

A Canadian Pacific Railway station was established here in 1912 and was named after the hero of Lord Byron's poem of the same name. Mazeppa was a Cossack hetman (a Polish or Cossack military commander). The post office was in operation from 1 November 1913 through 30 November 1955.

McAlpine Creek (creek)

72 E/16 - Irvine
2-11-1-W4
49°53'N 110°03'W

---

*denotes rescinded name or former locality.

Flows north-east into MacKay Creek, approximately 45 km south-east of Medicine Hat.

Named for Duncan McAlpine and his family who emigrated from Scotland and settled west of the Walsh area in the early 1900s. Working as a sheep foreman for J.A. Grant, a local rancher, McAlpine was killed in a wagon accident. Duncan and his wife had five sons and two daughters, and his son Duncan Jr., took over the family sheep-ranching operation. Duncan Jr. was known for his apparent ability to shear a hundred or more sheep in half a day.

McBride Lake (lake)
82 H/11 - Fort Macleod
21-7-26-W4
49°34′N 113°28′W
Approximately 49 km west of Lethbridge.

The name for this lake was made official 8 July 1954. Its precise origin is unknown.

McBride Reservoir (reservoir)
72 M/6 - Plover Lake
28-27-10-W4
51°21′N 111°22′W
Approximately 93 km east of Drumheller.

The precise origin for the name of this feature is unknown.

McConnell Coulee (coulee)
82 P/8 - Dorothy
23-28-18-W4
51°24′N 112°26′W
Runs south into Willow Creek, approximately 18 km east of Drumheller.

The precise origin for the name of this feature is unknown.

McDonald Hills (hill)
82 O/7 - Wildcat Hills
11-27-6-W5
51°19′N 114°45′W

Approximately 55 km west north-west of Calgary.

At the time of naming these hills, ca. 1930, McDonald was the name of the local rancher. These hills may be named for him.

McDonald Lake (lake)
82 P/4 - Dalroy
2-26-29-W4
51°12′N 113°55′W
Approximately 20 km north of Calgary.

The precise origin for the name of this feature is not known; however, there was a W.A. McDonald that once owned property in the area close to this lake and it may be for him that the lake is named.

McGregor Lake (reservoir)
82 I/10 - Queenstown
19-15,16-21,22-W4
50°25′N 112°52′W
Approximately 96 km south-east of Calgary.

This artificial lake near Milo takes its name from James Duncan McGregor (1860-1935). Born in Ontario, he came west with his family in 1877 and for the next three decades he farmed, served as a mining license inspector in the Yukon, and was a horse rancher. He was a shareholder in the Grand Forks Cattle Co. and when that was taken over by the Southern Alberta Land Co. (an English Company), he became its Canadian Manager. The company planned to build a dam across Snake Valley, for irrigation purposes. Work commenced in 1909 and, in spite of financial difficulty and World War I, the dam was completed in 1918. J.D. McGregor was associated with the dam until 1912 when differences between the management and himself led to his dismissal although he continued cattle ranching and showing his prize cattle. In 1929 he became Lieutenant-Governor of Manitoba. In 1961 his portrait was hung in

the Canadian Agricultural Hall of Fame at the Royal Winter Fair at Toronto. (from *Snake Valley*, 1973)

McLennan Creek (creek)
82 O/2 - Jumpingpound Creek
5-26-4-W5
51°12′N 114°32′W
Flows east into Bow River, approximately 38 km west north-west of Calgary.

The name for this creek was suggested by D.A. Nichols and allegedly commemorates an early rancher.

McNab (locality)
82 H/8 - Warner
1-5-18-W4
49°21′N 112°17′W
Approximately 50 km south-east of Lethbridge.

Named for a Mr. McNabb, Master Mechanic of the old narrow-gauge Alberta Railway & Irrigation Company of Lethbridge (see Galt Island), which ran from Lethbridge to Great Falls, Montana and operated from 1890 until it was sold to the Canadian Pacific Railway Company in 1906. The name was corrupted in its original spelling and the new spelling has garnered local usage over the years.

McNab Coulee (coulee)
82 H/11 - Fort Macleod
29-8-25-W4
49°40′N 113°19′W
An east-west trending coulee, approximately 38 km west of Lethbridge.

(see McNab)

McNeill (locality)
72 L/9 - Middle Sand Hills
12-20-1-W4
50°41′N 110°02′W
Approximately 80 km north-east of Medicine Hat.

This Canadian Pacific Railway station was named for Dr. A.K. McNeill (1900-1961) an early homesteader who settled in Empress, north of this locality, in 1926.

McPherson Coulee (coulee)

82 O/8 - Crossfield
25-27-1-W5
51°19′N 114°02′W
Approximately 34 km north of Calgary.

This coulee was named after Addison "Ad" McPherson (1846-1929), of Scottish-American descent. He was born in the eastern United States and as a young man came to Edmonton in 1868, while prospecting for gold. McPherson was a colourful figure who travelled throughout what is now Alberta, tracing, freighting and mining for coal and oil. For a while he had a trading post in the Highwood area, also one near the present town of Crossfield. The coulee named for him is believed to be where he often stopped on his freighting journeys. He also raised sheep in the area. In Blackfoot, the name for the coulee is *namahkanes*, translating "rifle bed" (Nelson) although it is not entirely clear where this name came from.

Meadow Creek (creek)

82 H/13 - Granum
32-11-27-W4
49°57′N 113°39′W
Flows north-east into Willow Creek, approximately 65 km north-west of Lethbridge.

The descriptive name for this creek refers to the good hayland around it. The name was officially approved 8 July 1954.

Medicine Hat (city)

72 L/2 - Medicine Hat
12-5-W4
50°03′N 110°40′W

Approximately 150 km east north-east of Lethbridge.

The site of the present city is so called in the report of the North West Mounted Police for 1882 and it was about this year the first house was erected. Medicine Hat is a translation of the Blackfoot Indian name *saamis* meaning "head-dress of a medicine man." One explanation connects the name with a fight between the Cree and Blackfoot tribes, when the Cree medicine man lost his war bonnet in the river. Another associates it with the slaughter of a party of white settlers and the appropriation by the Indian medicine man of a fancy hat worn by one of the victims. Another explanation is that the name was applied originally to a hill east of the town, from its resemblance to the hat of an Indian medicine man. This hill is styled Medicine Hat on a map of the Department of the Interior dated 1883. Another possibility describes the rescue of a female Indian from the South Saskatchewan River by an Indian brave, upon whose head a well-known medicine man placed his own hat as a token of admiration of the act of bravery of the rescuer. Still another story posits that the name was given to the locality because an Indian chief saw in a vision an Indian rising out of the South Saskatchewan River wearing the plumed hat of a medicine man.

Medicine Hat, 1885

Medicine Lodge Coulee (coulee)

72 E/9 - Elkwater Lake
7-3-W4
49°35′N 110°25′W
Runs south-east, approximately 58 km south-east of Medicine Hat.

This coulee was a place of spiritual ceremony for the Indians. It was here where they held the Sun Dance, before the North West Mounted Police put a stop to it. The Sun Dance was a test of bravery and strength in which all young men participated as a rite of passage before they could become tribal warriors. Medicine Lodge Coulee is located at the western edge of the Cypress Hills.

* Mekastoe (former locality)

82 H/11 - Fort Macleod
9-26-W4
49°43′N 113°28′W
Approximately 45 km west of Lethbridge.

Named for Mekasto (Red Crow), Chief of the southern Bloods, next in rank to the famous Chief Crowfoot. Mekasto, Crowfoot and other Blackfoot Confederacy leaders signed Treaty Number 7 in 1877. This was one of a series of territorially huge treaties that gave up the Indian's sovereign powers over land in exchange for resources, education, agricultural assistance, the prohibition of alcohol on reserves and a recognition of their hunting and fishing rights and was offered in peace because the Blackfoot did not join the North West Rebellion in 1885. Mekasto's body is buried near Stand Off along the Fort Macleod–Cardston Road.

* Mesekum (former locality)

72 L/5 - Tilley
2-17-12-W4
50°25′N 111°33′W
Approximately 73 km north-west of Medicine Hat.

This Blackfoot name, translating as "the land is rich," refers to the rich fertility of the soil in this part of the province. It became the official name in 1912 and was rescinded in 1958 when residents were no longer inhabiting the area. The name has remained in the official historical record.

Michael Coulee (coulee)

82 G/16 - Maycroft
3-10-1-W5
49°47'N 114°04'W
Flows south into Heath Creek, approximately 90 km west of Lethbridge.

The precise origin for the name of this feature is unknown.

Michel Reservoir (reservoir)

72 E/9 - Elkwater Lake
5-7-3-W4
49°32'N 110°22'W
Approximately 53 km south-east of Medicine Hat.

This reservoir was built by the Prairie Farm Rehabilitation Administration in the late 1950s to provide water to ranchers on the south side of the feature in the winter months. It was named for Jimmy Michel, who operated a ranch in the area.

Michichi Creek (creek)

82 P/7 - Drumheller
11-29-20-W4
51°28'N 112°43'W
Flows south-west into Red Deer River, immediately north of Drumheller.

This creek has five branches, which may correspond to the five fingers of a hand. The word *michichi* is Cree for "hand" or "little hand."

Middle Coulee (coulee)

82 H/8 - Warner
31-36-4-18-W4
49°21'N 112°22'W
Runs east/west into Verdigris Coulee, approximately 50 km south-east of Lethbridge.

The name may possibly be descriptive of this feature's location: it is halfway between Verdigris and Kipp coulees.

Middle Creek (creek)

72 E/8 - Thelma Creek
25-5-1-W4
49°25'N 110°00'W
Flows into the Middle Creek Reservoir, straddling the Alberta-Saskatchewan boundary, approximately 80 km south-east of Medicine Hat.

Two long-time residents suggest that the local name is "Middle Fork" rather than Middle Creek because of its position between Lodge Creek and Battle Creek.

Middle Creek Reservoir (reservoir)

72 E/8 - Thelma Creek
24-5-30-W4
49°25'N 110°00'W
Approximately 80 km south-east of Medicine Hat, on the Alberta-Saskatchewan boundary.

The dam built to create this reservoir was constructed by the Prairie Farm Rehabilitation Administration. It was one of the first dams established by this agency in southern Alberta for the purpose of water conservation and irrigation. The reservoir is fed by Middle Creek. (see Middle Creek)

Middle Sand Hills, The (hill)

72 L/9 - Middle Sand Hills
18,19-3,4-W4
50°35'N 110°23'W
Approximately 60 km north-east of Medicine Hat.

The descriptive name for these hills is a direct translation of the Blackfoot word, *sitoko spathcikway.*

Midland Provincial Park (provincial park)

82 P/7 - Drumheller
29-20-W4
51°30'N 112°40'W
Immediately north of Drumheller.

This park, created by Order-in-council 520/79, contains 605.27 hectares (1,495.68 acres). It is located on the Dinosaur Trail. The park encloses the site of the Midland Mine Company's coal mining operation in the Drumheller area. (see Midlandvale)

* Midlandvale (former locality)

82 P/7 - Drumheller
9-29-20-W4
51°28'N 112°43'W
Within the city limits of Drumheller.

This community was once a thriving settlement due to the mining operation of the Midland Coal Company, after which the post office took its name. The post office operated from 1 December 1917 through 12 December 1958. It is now incorporated into the city of Drumheller.

Midnapore (locality)

82 J/16 - Priddis
4-23-1-W5
50°55'N 114°05'W
Within the city limits of Calgary.

The name may have been suggested by a Captain Boynton who lived in the district and who had served with the British Army in India. Midnapore is a large town in India, within the Bengal Province. Whether the local terrain reminded him of that Midnapore or whether he intended to commemorate a specific event is not clear. Another possibility suggests that the local posmaster, John Glenn, who could neither read nor write, grew tired of his position. A letter came misdirected to this place, then called Fish Creek. He handed the letter to his assistant, Mr. Shaw, stating, "that's you." As a result, Shaw became postmaster and Fish Creek became Midnapore.

Milk River (river)

72 E/2 - Comrey
1-1-5-W4
49°00′N 110°33′W
Flows south-east into the U.S.A., approximately 110 km south of Medicine Hat.

The earliest record of this river appears in the *Journals of Lewis and Clark* dated 8 May 1905: "... the waters of the river possess a peculiar whiteness being about the color of a cup of tea with the admixture of a tablespoon of milk. From the colour of its waters we call it Milk River." Lewis and Clark were early American adventurers sent by U.S. President Thomas Jefferson to explore the American West. The Milk River is part of the Missouri drainage system, located in the southeastern-most part of the province. The Blood Indians knew this river as *Kenushsisuht*, translating to "little river." Certain of the tribes of Missouri called the feature "the river that scolds all others." Milk River also appears on the Harmon map of 1820. Daniel W. Harmon (1778-1845) was a fur trader and author born in Vermont and was a member of the North West Company from 1800 until he moved east in 1819. He published his journals and maps, and in his later years, settled on the shores of Lake Champlain. The area of Alberta in which the Milk River may be found was at various times claimed by Spain, France, the United States and Britain.

Milk River (town)

82 H/1 - Milk River
28-2-16-W4
49°09′N 112°05′W
Approximately 80 km south-east of Lethbridge.

(see Milk River)

Milk River, 1912

Milk River Lake (lake)

72 E/1 - Cripple Creek
8-1-2-W4
49°01′N 110°14′W
Approximately 112 km south-east of Medicine Hat.

Milk River Lake was once part of the larger "Wild Horse Lake." The water of Wild Horse Lake partially dried up during the drought of the 1920s and 1930s and resulted in the formation of two smaller lakes. The larger of the two lakes was renamed Milk River Lake so it would not be confused with the smaller lake, which retained the name "Wild Horse Lake" until local usage prompted a name change to Grassy Lake. (see Grassy Lake)

Milk River Ridge (ridge)

82 H/1 - Milk River
3,4-19-W4
49°15′N 112°30′W

Approximately 45 km south-east of Lethbridge.

(see Milk River)

Milk River Ridge Reservoir (reservoir)

82 H/8 - Warner
4,5-19-W4
49°22′N 112°35′W
Approximately 32 km south-east of Lethbridge.

Named for its proximity to Milk River Ridge. (see Milk River)

Mill Coulee (coulee)

82 H/13 - Granum
1-12-30-W4
49°57′N 113°58′W
Runs north into Burke Creek, approximately 85 km north-west of Lethbridge.

The precise origin for the name of this feature is unknown.

Millburn Creek (creek)

82 O/1 - Calgary
17-24-3-W5
51°03′N 114°23′W
Flows north into Elbow River, approximately 25 km west of Calgary.

The precise origin for the name of this feature is unknown.

Millerfield (locality)

82 P/8 - Drumheller
36-27-18-W4
51°21′N 112°25′W
Approximately 23 km east south-east of Drumheller.

This locality was named after John Malcolm Miller (1879-1951), the first postmaster who opened the post office in his home in 1913. Miller was born in Dunnville, Ontario and was a veteran of the Boer War.

---

*denotes rescinded name or former locality.

Millicent (hamlet)

72 L/12 - Brooks
20-20-13-W4
50°42′N 111°46′W
Approximately 104 km north-west of
Medicine Hat.

Millicent was the Christian name of both
the 4th Duchess of Sutherland, who was the
wife of the Duke of Sutherland, and of their
daughter, Rosemary Millicent. The Duke of
Sutherland had extensive land holdings in
the Brooks region, and many of the names
in this area are named after other royalty.

Milo (village)

82 I/10 - Queenstown
31-18-21-W4
50°34′N 112°53′W
Approximately 91 km south-east of
Calgary.

This settlement is named for the first
postmaster, Milo Munroe, who operated
the post office from his home between 1908
and 1909. The post office then moved to its
present location.

* Minda (former post office)

72 E/7 - Manyberries
7-6-5-W4
49° 20′N 110° 42′W
Approximately 64 km south of Medicine
Hat.

This post office operated from 1 February
1910 through 1 May 1917. The origin for
the name is not known.

Minda Coulee (coulee)

72 E/7 - Manyberries
27-5-6-W4
49°25′N 110°44′W
Runs south-west into Irrigation Creek,
approximately 65 km south of Medicine
Hat.

Named for its proximity to the Minda post
office. The precise origin for the name of
this feature is unknown.

Miner's Coulee (coulee)

72 E/3 - Aden
2-11-W4
49°06′N 111°24′W
Runs north from Montana and joins
Macdonald Creek, approximately 120 km
south south-west of Medicine Hat.

This feature originates between Gold and
West buttes, where gold and coal were
respectively once mined. The name was
adopted by the Canadian Permanent
Committee on Geographical Names so that
the Canadian portion of this feature would
coincide with that segment located in
Montana. This practice has since been
discontinued and features that straddle the
border no longer are required to have only
one single name.

Minor Lakes (lake)

72 L/5 Tilley
12-16,17-11,12-W4
50°23′N 111°33′W
Approximately 75 km north-west of
Medicine Hat.

The name for this group of very small lakes,
surrounded by marshland, may be descriptive.

Mitchell Creek (creek)

72 L/2 - Medicine Hat
3-14-5-W4
50°08′N 110°36′W
Flows north into South Saskatchewan
River, approximately 8 km north of
Medicine Hat.

Named for James Mitchell who owned the
land through which this creek flows.

Mitford (locality)

82 O/2 - Jumpingpound Creek
13-26-5-W5
51°13′N 114°34′W
Approximately 40 km west north-west of
Calgary.

This settlement located between Cochrane
and Morley on the banks of the Bow River
was named by Lady Adela Cochrane after
her friend Mrs. Percy Mitford. The town
was abandoned when the Canadian Pacific
Railway established their station at
Cochrane, and later a fire burned the
buildings that remained although some,
such as All Saints Anglican Church, were
moved to Cochrane. The post office
originally opened 1 May 1889, closed 1
April 1899 and was then reopened 15 June
1913 to close again 15 November 1915.

* Mizpah (former locality)

72 M/4 - Pollockville
25-25-14-W4
51°09′N 111°50′W
Approximately 67 km south-east of
Drumheller.

This name, which appears in the Bible, and
means watchtower, is possibly descriptive.
The local post office opened 1 April 1913
and closed 21 August 1931.

Mokowan Butte (hill)

82 H/4 - Waterton Lakes
1-28-W4
49°03′N 113°39′W
Approximately 93 km south-west of
Lethbridge.

(see Mokowan Ridge)

Mokowan Ridge (ridge)

82 H/11 - Fort Macleod
29-6-24-W4
49°30′N 113°13′W
Approximately 36 km south-west of
Lethbridge.

---

*denotes rescinded name or former locality.

This feature is named after the Mokowan River, which is in close proximity. The river is denoted on Arrowsmith's 1810 map. *Mokowanis* is a Blackfoot term and translates to "belly." The Blackfoot named this river for the Atsina Indians, commonly known as the Gros Ventres (in French) or Big Belly (in English) Indians, who frequented this area.

Monarch (hamlet)
82 H/14 - Monarch
7-10-23-W4
49°48′N 113°07′W
Approximately 20 km north-west of Lethbridge.

This hamlet owes its existence to the re-routing of the southern line of the Canadian Pacific Railway. Prior to 1908 the line had meandered down through the coulees, using many bridges and difficult grades after it left Lethbridge. All this was eliminated by the erection of two long steel bridges at Lethbridge and Monarch. When news of the route change became known a townsite was planned. It seems that a meeting was called to select a name and Monarch was chosen, possibly to indicate the hopes of the settlers. As if to emphasize the glowing aspirations for its future, regal names were given to streets: Empress, Victoria, Prince, Alexandra and Princess. Another source suggests that the name Monarch was chosen to fit in well with the other names along the C.P.R.'s "Royal Line" from Bassano to Empress. The names of some of the other towns along the line include Empress, Princess, Patricia, Majestic and Cavendish.

Monarch Hill (hill)
82 P/7 - Drumheller
10,15-19-29-20-W4
51°28′15″N 112°48′20″W
Approximately 6 km west of Drumheller.

_____
*denotes rescinded name or former locality.

The well-established name for this hill was taken from Monarch Coal Company Ltd. which operated its Mine #1473 nearby from 1933 to 1946 and produced a total of 833,520 tonnes of coal.

* Monogram (former locality)
72 L/6 - Alderson
11-16-11-W4
50°18′N 111°21′W
Approximately 60 km north-west of Medicine Hat.

The origin for the name of this former Canadian Pacific Railway station is unknown.

Montana (railway point)
82 H/10 - Lethbridge
4-9-21-W4
49°42′N 112°47′W
Within the city limits of Lethbridge.

The name may be taken from the state of Montana which borders Alberta to the south.

* Montgomery (former locality)
82 O/1 - Calgary
26-24-2-W5
51°04′N 114°10′W
Within the city limits of Calgary.

A post office operated at this site from 1 May 1947 through 3 August 1959 and was named after Hugh J. Montgomery, M.L.A. for the area from 1930 to 1935. It is now a subdivision in the city of Calgary.

Monument Hill (hill)
82 P/3 - Strathmore
7-29-25-23-W4
51°09′30″N 113°10′30″W
Approximately 48 km south-west of Drumheller.

A stone cairn of unknown origin was found atop this small hill by early settlers in the district. Although local residents believe it

to be constructed by natives, both the Glenbow Foundation Archaeological Survey and the Alberta Culture and Multiculturalism Natural and Human History Section (Tudor Site) conclude that it was erected by white men.

Mosquito Creek (creek)
82 I/3 - Carmangay
7-15-25-W4
50°14′N 113°25′W
Flows south-east into Bow River, approximately 73 km north-west of Lethbridge.

According to *Place-Names of Alberta* issued by the Geographic Board of Canada in 1928, the name given this creek by the Blackfoot was *pahmahsois* or "foul water creek." The water was fouled by the buffalo which were very numerous in the early days. The Blackfoot called the lower end of the creek "foul water creek," a good breeding ground for mosquitos. The Stoney called the upper reaches of the creek the equivalent of "white willow place" from the many wolf willows which line its banks. The prevalence of mosquitos likely accounts for the final choice of name. In Blackfoot the translation for Mosquito Creek is *ski-tzee-ta-ta* , and in Stoney it is *sa-po-na-wap-ta*.

Mossleigh (hamlet)
82 I/11 - Arrowwood
30-20-24-W4
50°43′N 113°20′W
Approximately 55 km south-east of Calgary.

One source states that this hamlet was named by Joseph and Elizabeth Moss, after themselves, and for his mother's maiden name, Leigh. Joseph Higginsbothan Saxon Moss came west with a Dominion Government Survey party in 1879. Moss freighted supplies during the North West Rebellion of 1885 and for the I.G. Baker Company of Fort Benton Montana, before settling and farming three quarter sections of land. Another variation of the origin summary posits that the community was named after Leigh Moss, a longtime settler in the region who was married to a Mr. George Moss.

Mountain View (hamlet)
82 H/4 - Waterton Lakes
19-2-27-W4
49°08'N 113°36'W
Approximately 83 km south-west of Lethbridge.

The name is descriptive in that there is a good view of the mountains from this locality.

Mud Lake (lake)
82 H/13 - Granum
24,25-9-27-W4
49°45'N 113°32'W
Approximately 52 km west of Lethbridge.

The name for this lake is likely descriptive of the surrounding terrain, and was officially approved May 1938.

Muddylake Creek (creek)
82 H/13 Granum
27-9-27-W4
49°46'N 113°33'W
Flows south-east into Lethbridge Northern Irrigation Canal, approximately 54 km west of Lethbridge.

The precise origin for the name of this creek is unknown but is very likely descriptive. The name was made official 8 July 1954.

Muddypound Creek (creek)
82 H/13 - Granum
7-11-29-W4
49°53'N 113°53'W
Flows north-east into Meadow Creek, approximately 77 km north-west of Lethbridge.

The precise origin for the name of this creek is unknown. The name was made official 8 July 1954.

Murray Lake (lake)
72 E/15 - Seven Persons
1-10-7-W4
49°48'N 110°56'W
Approximately 27 km south-west of Medicine Hat.

This lake was named for George Murray (1863-1925) who arrived with his family at Cypress Hills in 1897. Three years later, Murray moved to the Seven Persons Creek area, 16 km south of Whitla, and began raising cattle and horses. Originally from Glasgow, Scotland, Murray worked his way west stopping in Winnipeg, Saskatchewan, the Cypress Hills and eventually, Whitla, and began his farming operations with 80 head of cattle. Following Murray's death, the family remained on the original homestead until 1946. By the 1950s, Murray's son operated the largest ranch in Alberta, owning close to 50,000 acres, leasing another 221,000 acres and raising some 6,200 head of cattle and 7,000 sheep.

Myleen (post office)
72 M/8 - Sibbald
10-29-3-W4
51°28'N 110°20'W
Approximately 155 km north north-east of Medicine Hat.

The precise origin for the name of this feature is unknown. The post office operated from 1 September 1914 through 15 July 1927.

Nacmine (hamlet)
82 P/7 - Drumheller
8-29-20-W4
51°28'N 112°47'W
Approximately 5 km west of Drumheller.

The town of Monarch, later renamed Nacmine for its founders, North American Collieries (NAC) and the word mine, established what was thought to be a model town on the site of their mines. The townsite included comfortable accommodation on generous lots, a hotel, running water, a bank, two general stores, a butcher shop, a billiard room, a confectionery and an ice cream parlor. The post office opened 1 April 1919. The Monarch Colliery (hence the original name) was situated on what was then the main highway between Calgary and Saskatoon, since rebuilt further to the south, and was managed by W.J. Dick of Calgary. It was allegedly the deepest mine in the valley.

Namaka (hamlet)
82 I/14 - Gleichen
16-23-24-W4
50°57'N 113°17'W
Approximately 45 km east of Calgary.

A Canadian Pacific Railway station was established in 1884 and was named from the Blackfoot word, *nama*, translating to "bow," and *nietakhtai*, or "river," resulting in the name *namokhtai*, but it was corrupted by those who did not know the language, and later rendered as Namaka. Archdeacon J.W. Tims says: "I think the late General Strange was responsible for the name and probably the spelling of it. I remember his telling me that the C.P.R. had suggested that the station should be called "Strange," but he asked the Company to call it Namaka, as that was the name he had chosen for this ranch on the Bow River and friends would know where to leave the train." The post office operated from 15 June 1908 through 25 August 1969.

Namaka Lake (lake)
82 I/14 - Gleichen
12-23-23,24-W4
50°56'N 113°13'W
Approximately 48 km east of Calgary. (see Namaka)

Nanton (town)

82 I/5 - Nanton
15-16-28-W4
50°21'N 113°46'W
Approximately 65 km south of Calgary.

This hamlet was named in 1893 for Sir Augustus Meredith Nanton (1860-1925) who was involved in a number of land speculation and development projects in western Canada. He was a resident partner in Winnipeg of the financial firm, Osler, Hammond and Nanton, western Canada's largest financial institute. The Canadian Pacific Railway contracted Nanton's firm to plan the townsites on the line running south of Calgary. Nanton was also managing director of Galt's North Western Coal and Navigation Company, Limited (see Galt Island). Nanton directed the Western Patriotic Fund and Victory Loan Campaigns during World War I, and for his efforts, was knighted in 1917. The town of Nanton was originally known as "Mosquito Creek," but changed to Nanton in 1893 with the opening of the post office.

Nanton Creek (creek)

82 I/5 - Nanton
21-16-28-W4
50°22'N 113°47'W
Flows north-east into Mosquito Creek, approximately 60 km south of Calgary.

(see Nanton)

Naphtha (hamlet)

82 J/9 - Turner Valley
28-19-2-W5
50°38'N 114°14'W
Approximately 45 km south south-west of Calgary.

Named for the light gas taken from the gas wells, Naphtha was a boom town which grew as a result of the Turner Valley oil discovery. It came into being in the 1920s and lasted through the early 1940s. In its heyday it had a hotel, dance hall, bowling alley, store, and various other services. It was mainly a residential community for employees of the nearby Home Oil processing plant.

Nateby (locality)

72 L/13 - Wardlow
15-23-13-W4
Approximately 123 km north north-west of Medicine Hat.

A post office was opened here 1 November 1910 and was named after Nateby Triumph, a famous Shire stallion imported from Nateby, England, by J.W. Forster and Sons, residents since 1904 who imported Shire horses to the area. The post office closed 29 February 1932.

Needmore (former post office)

72 E/7 - Manyberries
6-6-6-W4
49°27'N 110°49'W
Approximately 65 km south of Medicine Hat.

The origin is unknown for this locality whose post office opened 15 October 1912. The name was changed to Orion in 1916. (see Orion)

Nemiskam (locality)

72 E/6 - Foremost
22-6-10-W4
49°29'N 111°16'W
Approximately 75 km south-west of Medicine Hat.

The descriptive name is derived from the Blackfoot language and means "between two coulees." The locality of Nemiskam is situated on high ground between Chin

Coulee to the north and Etzikom Coulee to the south. The post office was known as "Bingen" prior to 1916 when the name was changed.

New Dayton (hamlet)

82 H/8 - Warner
33-5-18-W4
49°25'N 112°23'W
Approximately 45 km south-east of Lethbridge.

Named in 1906 by Mr. David Hunter after his hometown of Dayton, Ohio. Hunter and his two brothers purchased a large tract of land and successfully promoted the area for settlement, especially among other Americans from Ohio, the Dakotas and Iowa.

Newcastle Mine (locality)

82 P/7 - Drumheller
10-29-20-W4
51°28'N 112°46'W
Incorporated into the city of Drumheller. The name is derived from the city of the same name in England where coal was also mined. The post office opened under this name on 1 January 1923 and closed 8 October 1976. It was incorporated into the city of Drumheller 1 January 1967.

Newell, Lake (reservoir)

72 L/5 - Tilley
24-17-15-W4
50°26'N 111°55'W
Approximately 90 km north-west of Medicine Hat.

This reservoir was named after a Mr. Newell, who was an early dryland farmer from Boston, Massachusetts. He lived in the area for only a short time, from 1910 to 1914. He appeared to have been wealthy; there was (and still is) a Newell Hotel in the area and he appears to have impressed the Canadian Pacific Railway to have the irrigation reservoir named for him 1914.

---

*denotes rescinded name or former locality.

The county, incorporated in 1952, takes its name from the latter, one of Alberta's largest artificial lakes.

Nicoll Ridge (ridge)

82 O/2 - Jumpingpound Creek
25-45-W5
51°06′N 114°34′W
Approximately 40 km west of Calgary.

An early homesteader and rancher of the area, Louis D. Nicoll, came to Canada from England in 1903, originally to head north for the Klondike. He changed his mind, and in 1905, he and his brother Eugene, came to Calgary and purchased a section of land between them. In later years, they expanded their holdings, formed Nicoll Bros. & Company, and ran a substantial ranching operation. The ranch is still operated by the Nicoll family. This ridge was officially named 12 December 1939.

Nier (locality)

82 O/8 - Crossfield
23-28-2-W5
51°25′N 114°10′W
Approximately 43 km north north-west of Calgary.

Named after "Shorty" Nier, an early rancher who came from Arizona to the Calgary area in the early 1800s. He was a scout in the North West Rebellion, then came south to ride for the Cochrane, Oxley, Flying E, and the Bar U ranches, and was on most of the southern Alberta round-ups. About 1900, Shorty homesteaded seven miles west of Crossfield. The Canadian Pacific Railway spurline to Cremona passed through Shorty's property and the siding at this point eventually was called Nier.

Nier Lakes (2 lakes)

82 O/8 - Crossfield
22,23-28-2-W5
51°24′50″N 114°11′00″W

Approximately 47 km north north-west of Calgary.

(see Nier)

Nightingale (hamlet)

82 P/3 - Strathmore
30-25-24-W4
51°10′N 113°20′W
Approximately 50 km east north-east of Calgary.

This hamlet had its beginnings as a colonization project set up by the Canadian Pacific Railway and the advertisements encouraged many settlers from the British Isles to participate. The area became known as the English Colony in the early 1900s. Early settlers named the community and post office in commemoration of Florence Nightingale (1820-1910), an English nurse and founder of trained nursing as a profession for women. She is celebrated for her participation in the Crimean War in military hospitals and was the first woman ever to receive the Order of Merit (1907). The post office was in operation from 1 January 1911 through 28 February 1957.

Ninastoko (locality)

82 H/3 - Cardston
24-3-26-W4
49°14′N 113°23′W
Approximately 65 km south-west of Lethbridge.

Named for Chief Mountain in Montana, this locality is situated on the Blood Indian Reserve. The word *ninastoko* is from the Blackfoot language, and translates to "Chief Mountain." The centre of the locality was once a Canadian Pacific Railway siding. (see Chief Mountain)

Nine Mile Coulee (creek)

82 H/7 - Raymond
5,6-21-W4
49°26′N 112°47′W

A north-south trending coulee, approximately 26 km south of Lethbridge.

The name is descriptive of this feature's length since it is approximately nine miles long.

Nine Mile Creek (creek)

82 H/12 - Brocket
25-8-29-W4
49°42′N 113°49′W
Flows south into Beaver Creek, approximately 72 km west of Lethbridge.

Officially approved 8 July 1954, the name of this creek may have been taken from the coulee that exists closer to Lethbridge.

Nobleford (village)

82 H/14 - Monarch
3-11-23-W4
49°53′N 113°03′W
Approximately 22 km north-west of Lethbridge.

Named in 1913 after Charles S. Noble (1873-1957), a farmer, organizer and founder of the community known as "Noble" until 1918. Charles Noble originally homesteaded near Claresholm in 1902, but a few years later bought 2,023 hectares (5,000 acres) near Lethbridge and began what was to become a huge farming operation. The Noble Foundation was established and by World War I, 14,164 hectares (35,000 acres) were under cultivation, making his the largest and highest-yielding farmland in the British Empire. The collapse of the post-war wheat market nearly forced Noble out of business, but through the development of revolutionary soil conservation techniques and erosion control, namely the invention of the Noble Blade Cultivator that was capable of cultivating without turning the soil, he was able to save his large-scale operation. Members of the Noble family still reside in the area and have continued to play a prominent role in the community including the operation of the farm business.

* Nolan (former railway point)

82 H/13 - Granum
30-9-26-W4
49°46′N 113°31′W
Approximately 50 km west of Lethbridge.

This former Canadian Pacific Railway station was established and named in 1911 after Patrick James "Paddy"Nolan (1864-1913). He was born in Ireland on 17 March and came to Calgary in 1889 as an advocate lawyer. Nolan was the editor of the *Calgary Herald* from 1900 to 1903 and earned the title "First Associate Editor" in 1904, as dubbed by Colonel G.C. Porter, subsequent editor. P.J. Nolan was well-known for his kindly humour and un-matched wit, and was well respected as a barrister—his specialty was criminal defence law. He was appointed King's Counsel in 1907. In 1908, he was appointed a member of the first Senate of the University of Alberta, and held that position until his death.

Norfolk (locality)

82 P/4 - Dalroy
16-24-27-W4
51°02′N 113°43′W
Approximately 22 km east of Calgary.

The name for this Canadian National Railway station, established in 1914, could have been given by a pioneer from the County of Norfolk, England or from Norfolk in Virginia or in Nebraska. The term Norfolk means "northern people" in contrast to "suffolk," indicating people from the southern part of East Anglia

(Ekwall).

_____
*denotes rescinded name or former locality.

North Easy Coulee (coulee)

72 L/10 - Easy Coulee
19-7-W4
50°37′N 110°52′W
Approximately 60 km north of Medicine Hat.

Named for its proximity to Easy Coulee. (see Easy Coulee)

North Milk River (river)

82 H/1 - Milk River
20-2-18-W4
49°08′N 112°23′W
Flows east into Milk River, approximately 68 km south-east of Lethbridge.

Named as a tributary to Milk River. (see Milk River)

* Northcliff (former railway point)

82 H/3 - Cardston
20-3-26-W4
49°13′N 113°27′W
Approximately 68 km south-west of Lethbridge.

The origin is unknown for the name of this former Canadian Pacific Railway station.

* Norton (former locality)

72 E/16 - Irvine
35-10-4-W4
49°52′N 110°26′W
Approximately 20 km south-east of Medicine Hat.

The post office here was established 1 March 1923, and was named after the first postmaster, Mr. H.A. Norton. Mr. Norton was an early settler who arrived around 1907. It was previously known as "Gros Ventre" after the Indian tribe of the same name.

Nose Creek (creek)

82 O/1 - Calgary
13-24-1-W5
51°03′N 114°01′W

Flows south into Bow River, within the city limits of Calgary.

The name for this creek is taken from the Cree Indian word *os-kewun* which in Stoney is called *tap-o-oi wap-ta* (Tyrrell). Nose Creek is a tributary of the Bow River, and got its name, it is thought, from the Blackfoot tribe of Indians who frequently camped in the area. (see Nose Hill)

Nose Hill (hill)

82 O/1 - Calgary
5,8-25-1-W5
51°07′N 114°08′W
Within the city limits of Calgary.

One theory states that the Indians, looking to the south-east from the buttes, thought of Nose Hill as being a nose on an Indian Chief's face, with the Bow River on one side and Nose Creek on the other. It was common among the early tribes to apply place names according to the topography of the land, and because one word is used by both the Cree and Stoney Indians to describe the place name, this was probably the way in which the name was recorded. A second theory, by a Mrs. E.M. Clayton, which is supported by other pioneers of the district, states: "According to legend, the rather old name is a relic of Indian days. The story is told of a band of Indians camped by the springs who had secured some of the white man's fire-water. The men of the tribe, becoming intoxicated and quarrelsome, began abusing some of the squaws. In the mellee that followed an Indian bit off the end of a squaw's nose." Still another theory, upheld by authorities on Indian life and lore, states that the name comes from the Blackfoot tribes that camped at the Nose Hill and in the Nose Creek vicinity.

Francis Fraser, a student of Indian lore and various tribes, concurs in the Blackfoot source of the name's origin. Two members of the Blackfoot tribe who were reliable sources of information were "Many Owls" (or Mrs. Bad Old-Man) and "the Stump" (or Big Eagle). Listed on the Band Rolls as being 90 and 70 years of age, respectively, in 1942, both agreed that a custom existed in the tribe from which the name could have originated. This custom was that when a society of braves who policed the women found one unfaithful to the tribe, they cut off her nose as an example to the rest. A victim of such torture was the wife of "Skunk" who lived until the 1900s. This practice apparently continued until the 1890s when it was outlawed.

Oakland Lake (lake)

72 M/5 - Sunnynook
13-28-14-W4
51°23'N 111°50'W
Approximately 59 km east of Drumheller.

The precise origin for the name of this feature is unknown.

Ockey Ridge (ridge)

82 H/3 - Cardston
9-2-26-W4
49°06'N 113°25'W
Approximately 77 km south-west of Lethbridge.

Named for John Edward Ockey and his family, who settled in the Beazer area in 1901. John and his wife, Eliza Russel, had a son, Eugene who farmed in the general area from 1925 through 1930.

Ogden (railway point)

82 J/16 - Priddis
23-29-W4
51°00'N 114°00'W
Within the city limits of Calgary.

This Canadian Pacific Railway stop was named after I.G. Ogden, financial Vice-President of the C.P.R.

Okotoks (town)

82 I/12 - High River
28-20-29-W4
50°44'N 113°59'W
Approximately 90 km south of Calgary.

This town began as a Canadian Pacific Railway station in 1894. At that time, it was called "Dewdney," after Edgar Dewdney. This civil engineer and administrator was born in 1835 in Devon, England. The province of British Columbia was his destination in 1859, and he surveyed there for several years. Dewdney was made Indian Commissioner for the Northwest Territories in 1879, and Lieutenant-Governor in 1881. He died in 1916 at Victoria, B.C. The locality of "Dewdney" remained his namesake only until 1897, when it was changed to Okotoks, the Blackfoot name meaning "big rock" or "crossing by that big rock." This name seems more appropriate, because there is a glacial erratic called The Big Rock which lies about eight km west of the town. It has served as a landmark for many years. There is also a game which is played by young Blackfoot boys called "Throwing the Okotoks." Another Indian tribe, the Sarcees, called this place *chachosika*, which translates to "valley of the big rock." Further, the Stoney name is *ipabitungamgay*, which means, "where the big rock is." It is interesting to note that, although each Indian tribe has its own language, the general meaning of their translated forms remains the same. This is quite typical of place names in Alberta whose origins hearken back to old descriptive Indian names.

Old Baldy Hill (hill)

72 E/9 - Elkwater Lake
8-23-8-3-W4
49°39'45"N 110°17'55"W
Approximately 50 km south-east of Medicine Hat.

A descriptive name that is used because the entire south face of this hill is barren, perhaps because the chinook winds remove the snow and moisture that the trees need to grow there.

Old Women's Buffalo Jump

(buffalo jump)
82 I/5 - Nanton
29-17-29-W4
50°28'35"N 113°53'30"W
Approximately 60 km south of Calgary.

The origin of the name concerns the Indian legend of a mythical character named Napi, or Old Man, who was a trickster and the creator of many of nature's wonders. "In the early days of the world," says John Cotton, a Blood Indian Chief, "the men and the women used to travel in separate camps. The men had their chief and the women had theirs. One day Napi called the men together and said: 'Why should we live apart from the women? If we all live together, then we can spend our time hunting and going to war, while the women can do the cooking and tanning of hides.' The men thought it was a good idea, so Napi went in search of the women. He found them near the foothills, where they all lived in a large camp.

Nearby they had a buffalo jump which was their main source of food. This was the Women's Buffalo Jump near Cayley. Napi met the leader of the women and told her the plan. The woman chief agreed, and asked Napi to bring the men to her camp so that each woman could choose a man to be her partner. Napi returned to the men and told them the news. He had noticed many beautiful women in the camp and made plans to get the best one for himself.

When the men moved to the Women's Buffalo Jump, Napi stole from the camp, and dressing himself in women's clothes, went to the women's camp and decided which woman was the most beautiful. Before he had time to return to the men, they arrived, and the women began to choose their partners. The woman of Napi's choice saw a man she liked, but Napi intercepted her and told her to choose him. The woman, however, wanted the other man, and overlooked Napi in favour of him. Napi then went to the next beautiful woman, and the same thing happened. Finally, when all the choosing had been done, Napi was the only one without a woman. In anger, he went to the buffalo jump and changed himself into a pine tree. And there he stood, alone, for many, many years."

The earliest known reference to the Women's Buffalo Jump is in the winter-counts now in possession of Jim White Bull, another Blood Chief. The winter-counts are a calendar system used to keep a record of the years. The winter of 1842-43 was known as the year when the Bloods camped at Women's Buffalo Jump. The name was also recorded by George Dawson, in his list of Blackfoot place names for the Geological Survey of Canada in 1881.

Oldman River (river)

72 E/13 - Grassy Lake
27-11-13-W4
49°57′N 111°42′W
Flows east, joining the Bow River to form the South Saskatchewan River, approximately 86 km east of Lethbridge.

This river was named after the mythical Cree Indian character Wi-suk-i-shak (Old Man) who possessed supernatural attributes. The Old Man's playing ground is marked by several cairns, made from stones and small boulders, and the obscure outlines of rectangles formed from larger stones. These are located near the point at which the Livingstone River (part of the Oldman River system) issues from the

mountains. The rock formations and cairns came into being over an extended period of time by each Indian entering the mountains via this route adding a stone "for luck." The map which accompanied the Palliser report designated this river as the "Old Man" or "Arrow River." This feature was also known to the Blackfoot and Stoney Indians as *apistoki* and *is-sa-goo-win-ih-da-wap-ta* respectively.

Oldman River, 1911

Olsen Creek (creek)

82 H/12 - Brocket
18-8-27-W4
49°39′N 113°40′W
Flows south into Oldman River, approximately 60 km west of Lethbridge.

This creek is possibly named for an original homesteader, although it is now located on the Peigan Indian Reserve.

* Omaktai (former locality)

82 H/5 - Pincher Creek
34-3-27-W4
49°15′N 113°34′W
Approximately 71 km south-west of Lethbridge.

This former railway point is descriptively named for its location next to a large bend on the Belly River. The word comes from

the Blackfoot language and is translated as "big bend."

Onefour (locality)

72 E/1 - Cripple Creek
15-2-4-W4
49°07′N 110°28′W
Approximately 100 km south of Medicine Hat.

Early settlers named the locality for what they believed was the geographical location: township one, range four. The location has since been adjusted to township two, range four but the original name has remained.

Onetree Creek (creek)

72 L/13 - Wardlow
14-21-12-W4
50°46′N 111°35′W
Flows north-east into Red Deer River, approximately 101 km north-west of Medicine Hat.

This creek flows in what is locally called "Onetree Coulee." The name is likely descriptive of the lack of trees in the area; it was officially approved 10 June 1955.

Onetree Reservoir (reservoir)

72 L/12 - Brooks
19-14-W4
50°37′N 111°50′W
Approximately 103 km north-west of Medicine Hat.
The name for this reservoir was taken from the creek.

Orion (locality)

72 E/7 - Manyberries
7-6-6-W4
49°27′N 110°49′W
Approximately 65 km south of Medicine Hat.

This locality was originally called "Needmore," but the name was changed in

1916 to Orion, possibly after the constellation. In Greek mythology, Orion was a giant hunter and the son of Poseidon and Euryale. Orion's hunting partner, Artemis, was tricked by her brother Apollo into sending a giant scorpion to kill Orion. After his tragic death, Artemis placed Orion's image in the sky to be always pursued by the Scorpion.

Orton (hamlet)

82 H/11 - Fort Macleod
13-9-25-W4
49°44′N 113°16′W
Approximately 32 km west of Lethbridge.

The post office was established 1 March 1907 and was named after Josiah Orr, an early settler in the region and the community's first postmaster. It operated until 31 October 1926.

Outer Rainy Hill (hill)

72 L/6 - Alderson
17,18-10-W4
50°27′N 111°17′W
Approximately 63 km north-west of Medicine Hat.

There was a post office which opened 1 December 1912 called Rainy Hills, a translation of the Blackfoot name, *sotaw cheimequan*. A legend involving the "Old Man" caught in a rainstorm near here inspired the name. The post office closed 1 November 1916 and was renamed Denhart. There is another feature called Inner Rainy Hill located 1.6 km north of this feature.

Outpost Lake (lake)

82 H/3 - Cardston
7-1-26-W4
49°01′N 113°28′W
Approximately 88 km south-west of Lethbridge.

Named because the southern shore of this lake was the site of a North West Mounted Police post along the international border, occupied until circa 1905. The southern shore became the northern boundary of Police Outpost Provincial Park in 1971.

Owendale (locality)

82 H/3 - Cardston
1-2-24-W4
49°05′N 113°05′W
Approximately 68 km south-west of Lethbridge.

The locally prominent Owendale Farm was owned by R.H. (Roger) and Owen Owens of Minneapolis. They were shareholders of the O.W. Kerr Co. which had obtained the farm and other parts of the extensive landholdings of the Knight Sugar Co. The local post office was named Owendale when it opened 1 December 1937, a name continuing until its closure 14 January 1972. It was, at one time, known as "Jefferson."

Owl Creek (creek)

82 O/7 - Wildcat Hills
23-28-7-W5
51°24′N 114°53′W
Flows north into Beaver Creek, approximately 73 km north-west of Calgary.

The precise origin for the name of this feature is unknown.

Oxley Creek (creek)

82 I/4 - Claresholm
32-13-28-W4
50°08′N 113°48′W
Flows south-east into Willow Creek, approximately 84 km north-west of Lethbridge.

This watercourse was named after the nearby Oxley Ranch, which was named for Oxley Manor, Wolverhampton, England. Oxley Creek is also known locally as "Beaver Creek," a name associated with the valley through which the creek flows.

Oyen (town)

72 M/8 - Sibbald
34-27-4-W4
51°22′N 110°28′W
Approximately 156 km east of Drumheller.

This town was named for Andrew Oyen (1870-1937), the first of three brothers from Norway who settled in this area in 1909. Andrew originally emigrated to the United States in 1887, at the age of 17. He visited the Oyen area in 1908 and returned for good the following year. Andrew's brother Simon immigrated from Norway in 1911 with his three children and settled on a homestead five km north-east of Oyen. Melkor (Mike) accompanied Andrew to the United States, but later returned to Norway to marry. In 1910 he, his wife and their son emigrated to Saskatchewan and the following year he moved to a homestead 0.4 km north-east of Oyen. The village of Oyen was built on Andrew's land. He was well-known and highly esteemed as one who never turned a wayfarer from his door.

Pageant (locality)

82 I/7 - McGregor Lake
5-18-21-W4
50°29'N 112°51'W
Approximately 87 km north of Lethbridge.

A Canadian Pacific Railway station was established here some time prior to 1928. The precise origin for the name of this feature is unknown.

Paine Lake (lake)

82 H/4 - Waterton Lakes
10-2-28-W4
49°06'N 113°39'W
Approximately 85 km south-west of Lethbridge.

This lake is named after an early homesteader who settled by it, Mr. Frank Payne. A misspelling of his name occurred during the original field work, garnered local usage over the years, and the current spelling was made official 3 November 1942.

Pakowki (locality)

72 E/7 - Manyberries
12-6-8-W4
49°28'N 110°57'W
Approximately 65 km south of Medicine Hat.

When the area was becoming settled and a post office and railway station were established, the name was adopted for the locality from the nearby lake. (see Pakowki Lake)

Pakowki Lake (lake)

72 E/7 - Manyberries
31-4-7-W4
49°20'N 110°55'W
Approximately 70 km south south-west of Medicine Hat.

Pakowki is the Blackfoot word approximately translating as "bad water." The title is still appropriate to this overgrown slough which has no outlet to sweeten the water. In 1855, a traveller by the name of James Doty passed by the lake while looking for the Blackfoot Indians. He noted in his journal that, although the water was clear, it reeked of the offensive odour of "carburetted hydrogen gas." Other Indians have called this *pah-kan-kee* which translates as "unlucky water," from their having lost a number of horses while camped here.

* Pandora (former locality)

72 M/4 - Pollockville
12-24-13-W4
51°02'N 111°42'W
Approximately 85 km south-east of Drumheller.

The name comes from the Greek and means "all giving." This term may reflect the optimism of the early settlers regarding the productivity of the land. The post office opened 1 January 1912 and closed 6 March 1925.

Parflesh Creek (creek)

82 I/15 - Cluny
25-23-21-W4
50°58'N 112°48'W
Flows south-east into Crowfoot Creek, approximately 83 km east of Calgary.

The precise origin for the name of this feature is unknown; however, it may be connected in some way with parboiled meat.

Park Lake (lake)

82 H/15 - Picture Butte
9-10-22-W4
49°48'N 112°55'W
Approximately 12 km north-west of Lethbridge.

P~Q~R

This man-made reservoir was christened by Premier John Edward Brownlee, in office from 1925 to 1934, and the name was made official 16 April 1970. A Provincial Park was established around this lake six years later.

Park Lake Provincial Park

(provincial park)
82 H/15 - Picture Butte
10-22-W4
49°48'N 112°55'W
Approximately 12 km north-west of Lethbridge.

This provincial park was established by Order-in-council 931/76 and measures 223.93 hectares (553 acres). It is named for Park Lake, which it surrounds. (see Park Lake)

* Parkbend (former locality)

82 H/4 - Waterton Lakes
30-3-27-W4
49°15'N 113°37'W
Approximately 93 km west south-west of Lethbridge.

The origin for the name of this former railway station is unknown.

Parkland (hamlet)

82 I/5 - Nanton
16-15-27-W4
50°15'N 113°39'W
Approximately 75 km south of Calgary.

This hamlet was named for W.J. Parkhill of Midland, Ontario, who arrived with his son Herbert Parkhill, later a Calgary Canadian Pacific Railway dispatcher, and his son-in-law, the owner of the Okotoks sawmill.

---

*denotes rescinded name or former locality.

Parkland was originally known as "Parkhill," but when the post office was opened 1 March 1907 in the general store of William D. Sharman, the alternative was chosen to avoid confusion with a post office of the same name located in Ontario.

Parks Creek (creek)
82 O/2 - Jumpingpound Creek
10-25-5-W5
51°07′N 114°37′W
Flows south-east into Pile of Bones Creek, approximately 40 km west of Calgary.

The Park family homesteaded nearby, and this creek and ridge are named after these early settlers.

Parks Ridge (ridge)
82 O/2 - Jumpingpound Creek
25-5-W5
51°09′N 114°39′W
Approximately 43 km west of Calgary.

(see Parks Creek)

Pashley (station)
72 E/16 - Irvine
7-12-3-W4
49°59′N 110°24′W
Approximately 15 km east south-east of Medicine Hat.

Named in 1910, this station bears the maiden name of the wife of David McNicoll (1852-1916). McNicoll was General Manager of the Canadian Pacific Railway in 1900 when the station was built and named and later became first Vice-President of the railway.

Patricia (hamlet)
72 L/12 - Brooks
13-20-13-W4
50°42′N 111°40′W

Approximately 98 km north-west of Medicine Hat.

This hamlet was named in 1914 in honour of Princess Patricia of Connaught (Lady Patricia Ramsey, 1886-1972), daughter of His Royal Highness, the Duke of Connaught (1850-1942), Governor-General of Canada (1911-16), and the grand-daughter of Queen Victoria. Princess Patricia served as honorary Colonel of the Princess Patricia's Canadian Light Infantry from the time that the regiment was formed in 1914 until the time of her death in 1972. The "Pats" were the first Canadian contingent recruited for service in World War I. The Princess presented the corps with its regimental colours, designed and chosen by herself. Many of the communities in this area were named after members of the royal family.

Peace Butte (butte)
72 E/10 - Bulls Head
7-9-6-W4
49°42′N 110°48′W
Approximately 35 km south of Medicine Hat.

The precise origin for the name of this feature is unknown.

Peacock (locality)
82 I/3 - Carmangay
9-13-23-W4
50°05′N 113°05′W
Approximately 45 km north of Lethbridge.

A Canadian Pacific Railway station was located on what was once William Peacock's land. He was the main promoter of the development of the siding built and opened in 1928.

Pearce (locality)
82 H/14 - Monarch
1-10-25-W4
49°48′N 113°16′W

Approximately 32 km west north-west of Lethbridge.

Named in 1910 after William Pearce (1848-1930) who is best known for his participation in the Dominion Lands Survey and for his prominent role in the development of government policy regarding resources in western Canada. A surveyor by trade, Pearce also spent three years apprenticing with an engineering firm in Toronto. He was appointed to the office of the Superintendent of Mines for the Northwest Territories in 1885 and in that year's annual report, strongly urged the federal government to develop a comprehensive irrigation system for the southern prairies. This work was to result in the Northwest Irrigation Act, passed in 1894. In 1893, Pearce established the Calgary Irrigation Company and later went on to become instrumental in the establishment of the National Parks System and to work for the Canadian Pacific Railway's Department of Natural Resources.

Pecten (railway point)
82 H/5 - Pincher Creek
21-4-30-W4
49°18′N 113°59′W
Approximately 93 km south-west of Lethbridge.

Named for the genus of shell fish which contains the scallop species that provided the basis for the Shell Oil Company logo. The station is located on a Canadian Pacific Railway spur-line which served a Shell Oil Company plant.

* Peigan (former locality)
82 H/12 - Brocket
35-8-27-W4
49°39′N 113°33′W
Approximately 52 km west of Lethbridge.

Named for the Peigan tribe of the Blackfoot confederacy, whose reserve includes this site. The word "peigan" is a corruption of the Indian name *pikuni*, which refers to people with "poorly dressed robes" or "poorly prepared hides."

Peigan Creek (creek)
72 E/11 - Maleb
4-8-8-W4
49°38′N 111°02′W
Flows west into Seven Persons Creek, approximately 50 km south-west of Medicine Hat.

For nearly two centuries the three Blackfoot tribes have been known to the white man by their separate names. They are the Pikuni or Peigan (pronounced pay-gan), the Kainah or Blood, and the Siksika or Blackfoot proper, often referred to as the Northern Blackfoot to distinguish it from the other two tribes. The three tribes were politically independent, but they spoke the same language, shared the same customs (with the exception of a few ceremonial rituals), intermarried, and made war upon common enemies. The name for this creek was made official 3 November 1911.

Peigan Indian Reserve #147
(Indian reserve)
82 H/12 - Brocket
29-7-27-W4
49°35′N 113°40′W
Approximately 65 km west of Lethbridge.

(see Peigan Creek)

Peigan Indian Reserve #147B
(Indian reserve)
82 H/12 - Brocket
11-9-30-W4
49°42′N 113°58′W
Approximately 83 km west of Lethbridge.

(see Peigan Creek)

---

*denotes rescinded name or former locality.

* Peighan (former post office)
72 E/10 - Bulls Head
27-7-5-W4
49°35′N 110°36′W
Approximately 45 km south of Medicine Hat.

This former post office was named in the earlier period after the Indian tribe although the name was later changed. (see Ranchville)

Pelican Island (island)
72 L/5 - Tilley
2-17-15-W4
50°24′N 111°58′W
Approximately 100 km north-west of Medicine Hat.

The island was named because it serves as a breeding and nesting ground for White Pelicans. It is similar to numerous other bare islands in lakes across the prairies which are used by this breed of pelican as nesting grounds.

* Pendant d'Oreille (former locality)
72 E/2 - Comrey
15-3-7-W4
49°12′N 110°52′W
Approximately 90 km south of Medicine Hat.

This locality adopted the name of a nearby coulee named by the Blackfoot Indians, possibly following a battle in which a band of Pendant d'Oreille Indians were defeated by a Cree war party. The North West Mounted Police were the first white men to continue the use of the name Pendant d'Oreille, and it was later adopted by white settlers as the locality grew. *Pendant d'Oreille* is French and means "the hanging ear" or "earring." During the 1700s, French fur trappers and traders gave this name to one of the Kallispel tribes of Eastern Washington and Idaho for the shell earrings they were known to wear. Once or twice a

year, the Pendant d'Oreille travelled northeast onto the open plains to hunt buffalo with the Flathead or Kootenai Indians.

Peters Creek (creek)
82 H/2 - Shanks Lake
24-1-23-W4
49°03′N 112°57′W
Flows east into Milk River, approximately 71 km south of Lethbridge.

The origin for the name of this creek, officially approved 12 December 1939, is unknown.

* Phidias (former locality)
82 I/15 - Cluny
8-22-22-W4
50°51′N 112°58′W
Approximately 62 km south-east of Calgary.

This former locality was named after a short-lived Canadian Pacific Railway station that existed only between 1912 and 1915, which was named after Phidias, the famous ancient Greek sculptor.

Philp Coulee (coulee)
72 E/3 - Aden
22-2-8-W4
49°08′N 111°00′W
Runs north into Milk River Valley, approximately 100 km south-west of Medicine Hat.

This feature was locally known as "Police Coulee," the same name of a similar feature located further west. The name Philp was adopted in December 1939 to avoid confusion that would result from duplication. The origin of the name is unknown.

Picture Butte (town)
82 H/15 - Picture Butte
2-11-21-W4
49°53′N 112°47′W
Approximately 20 km north of Lethbridge.

Named *anatskim-ikway* or "the beautiful hill," by the Blackfoot, or *ist-sanatshimek-ay* which translates, "that beautiful hill that can be seen from afar." A number of Indian spiritual icons in the form of signs, pictures, and laid-in patterns, all made with small stones, are located near the top of the hill. When white settlers arrived, they named their town after this hill. The butte as such no longer exists, since most of it was removed and the earth used for road and street repairs in and around this community.

Pile of Bones Creek (creek)

82 O/2 - Jumpingpound Creek
24-25-5-W5
51°08′N 114°34′W
Flows east into Jumpingpound Creek, approximately 37 km west of Calgary.

This stream was presumably named because of the severe cattle losses suffered by the Cochrane Ranche, whose cattle watered nearby on a quarter section of land set aside as a water reserve. Another source states that early bone collectors left buffalo bones at this site.

Pilling Lake (lake)

82 H/3 - Cardston
4,5-2-25-W4
49°05′N 113°17′W
Approximately 75 km south-west of Lethbridge.

Named for R.E. Pilling who owned the land circa 1919 around this lake and applied for the water rights to it.

Pincher (hamlet)

82 H/12 - Brocket
1-7-30-W4
49°32′N 113°56′W
Approximately 84 km west of Lethbridge.

(see Pincher Creek)

Pincher Creek (creek)

82 H/12 - Brocket
17-7-28-W4
49°33′N 113°46′W
Flows north-east into Oldman River, approximately 71 km west of Lethbridge.

There appear to be several versions of the origin of the name, which was used by surveyors as early as 1880. In all of them, a pair of pincers (later corrupted to pincher) used for reshodding horses and bulls, was lost along the creek near where the present Pincher Creek is located. There exist two competing explanations for the name. One basic story line revolves around an early prospecting party that lost a pair of pincers while camping beside the creek; there are three versions of this story: 1) A group of former employees of the American Fur Company went on a prospecting expedition in 1867. This group was comprised of John Wren, Charles Thomas and several other people. They left the pincers behind when they left a temporary camp beside the creek. After realizing that fact at their next camp, "young Kipp," Joseph (1847-1913), son of whisky trader James Kipp, was sent back to the campsite. He found the pincers and brought them to the new camp. 2) A prospecting group, composed of George Houk (Rouk?), Mart Holloway, John Nelson, William or Thomas Lee, Bill Olin, and others, lost the pincers, which were later found by the North West Mounted Police when they built a post on the creek in 1875. The pincers were described as being "rusty and old" when found. 3) The pincers were never found. One of the sources of this story states that Leonard Harnois lost the pincers around 1870.

A second basic story line is that a group of prospectors from Montana were attacked by Indians and several white men went missing. A search was made for the missing men but the only remains found were their horses, found in the possession of Indians, and a pair of pincers known to belong to one of the missing men which was found in their last campsite.

The First Nations peoples had a name for this creek, *unuk-spitzee* or "Little Highwood." Pincher Creek is a tributary of the Highwood River. They both flow across level plains and the trees along both are visible for a great distance. The name is a combination of *unuk* (little), *spi* (high) and *mistsis* (wood or bluff). Dr. G.M. Dawson noted the use of the name when he accompanied Henry Youle Hind across Canada in 1857 and 1858. Hugh Dempsey notes that the Blackfoot term for the community of Pincher Creek is *spitsi* (tall trees) in the Peigan tribe's tongue, and *umpska-spitsi* (south tall trees) in the Siksika tribe's tongue, to distinguish it from High River.

Pincher Creek (town)

82 H/5 - Pincher Creek
22-6-30-W4
49°33′N 113°46′W
Approximately 85 km west south-west of Lethbridge.

(see Pincher Creek)

Pine Coulee (coulee)

82 I/5 - Nanton
17-15-28-W4
50°15′N 113°49′W
Runs north into Nanton Creek, approximately 70 km south of Calgary.

The descriptive name for this coulee is derived from the large stands of pine trees that once grew along the banks of the feature. This coulee has the distinction of being the scene of the first raid and arrest of American whisky traders by the North West Mounted Police. In October 1874, NWMP Inspector Crozier, with ten men led by scout Jerry Potts, arrested William Bond and Harry Taylor, who had a well-built trading post in Pine Coulee.

Pine Creek (creek)

82 I/4 - Claresholm
27-13-28-W4
50°07′N 113°45′W
Flows south-east into Willow Creek,
approximately 81 km north-west of
Lethbridge.

This creek runs through Pine Coulee. (see
Pine Coulee)

Pine Creek (creek)

82 I/13 - Dalemead
4-22-29-W4
50°51′N 113°58′W
Flows east into Bow River, approximately 6
km south of Calgary.

The descriptive name was mistakenly
applied to this creek, referring to the many
spruce stands along the creek. It is likely
that all coniferous trees were considered
pine trees by those who named this feature.

Pine Ridge (ridge)

82 H/4 - Waterton Lakes
15-3-29-W4
49°13′N 113°49′W
Approximately 85 km west south-west of
Lethbridge.

This low ridge of 1627 m (5,388 feet) likely
has a descriptive name.

Pinepound Creek (creek)

82 H/6 - Raley
5-5-23-W4
49°22′N 113°04′W
Flows north into St. Mary River, approximately 40 km south south-west of
Lethbridge.

Named because it was the site of a buffalo
pound, made from "pine" trees. The name

may be a misnomer, however, as there are
few pine trees along the St. Mary River
Valley; the majority of the trees are fir. It is
possible, however, that people confused the
two species and assumed that the fir were
pines. The source also states that the name
could predate the arrival of whisky traders
in the area. The name was made official 8
July 1954.

Piney Ridge (ridge)

82 H/3 - Cardston
6-2-26-W4
49°06′N 113°28′W
Approximately 80 km south-west of
Lethbridge.

The name for this ridge is likely descriptive,
as this feature is one of the very few
wooded areas in this vicinity.

* Pinhorn (former locality)

72 E/3 - Aden
18-1-8-W4
49°02′N 111°03′W
Approximately 115 km south-west of
Medicine Hat.

This former locality was named for G.C.
Pinhorn, North West Mounted Police
veterinarian and the first veterinary
inspector appointed to represent the
Department of Agriculture in this region
during the early 1900s. Pinhorn was a
quarantine station for cattle entering
Alberta from the United States. One of
G.C. Pinhorn's main responsibilities was to
check all livestock entering the country at
this point. A post office was established in
Pinhorn in 1 January 1914 but was tempo-
rarily closed between 30 May 1917 and 1
July 1926. It then closed permanently 25
February 1948.

Pirmez Creek (creek)

82 O/1 - Calgary
17-24-3-W5
51°03′N 114°24′W

Flows north-east into Elbow River,
approximately 23 km west of Calgary.

(see Pirmez Creek)

Pirmez Creek (locality)

82 O/1 - Calgary
18-24-3-W5
51°02′N 114°24′W
Approximately 25 km west of Calgary.

This locality and the nearby creek were
named after Count Raoul Pirmez, a native
of Belgium. He arrived in Alberta in 1903
and until 1911 he and Baron Roels acquired
2,400 acres of land in the vicinity and built
up the Belgian Horse Ranch where they
bred Belgian horses, a breed of draft horse.
Pirmez later became Belgian Consul and
was prominent in financial affairs in
Calgary where Belgian funds were concen-
trated in western Canada.

Pivot (locality)

72 L/8 - Hilda
11-17-1-W4
50°25′N 110°02′W
Approximately 60 km north-east of
Medicine Hat.

This locality received its descriptive name
because it served as a turnaround point for
the railway. Trains also took on coal and
water here and a railroad station was
established in 1924, and remained in
operation until at least 1976. Prior to the
1940s, a grain elevator was located here.

Piyami (locality)

82 H/15 - Picture Butte
30-10-21-W4
49°51′N 112°50′W
Approximately 13 km north of Lethbridge.

(see Piyami Coulee)

Piyami Coulee (coulee)
82 H/15 - Picture Butte
10-21-W4
49°50'N 112°48'W
Runs south-east into Oldman River, approximately 13 km north of Lethbridge.

This area was called *piyami-pawaghkway* by the Blackfoot, translating as "far out coulee," and the name may be descriptive, referring to how far this coulee stretches out and away from the Oldman River Valley.

Plover Lake (lake)
72 M/6 - Plover Lake
18-29-10,11-W4
51°29'N 111°23'W
Approximately 93 km east of Drumheller.

The precise origin of the name is unknown; however, it may be named after a type of bird. Plovers are gregarious, medium-sized wading birds common to lake regions in Alberta.

Police Creek (creek)
72 E/4 - Coutts
35-1-13-W4
49°06'N 111°38'W
Flows north into Milk River, approximately 105 km south-east of Lethbridge.

This name is derived from the North West Mounted Police post that was established in 1875 at the confluence of this creek and the Milk River. The post was established by the police to help put a stop to the illicit whisky trade.

Police Outpost Provincial Park
(provincial park)
82 H/3 - Cardston
6-1-26-W4
49°00'N 113°28'W
Approximately 90 km south south-west of Lethbridge.

A North West Mounted Police outpost was located within the boundaries of the park. Approximately half of Outpost Lake is situated in the 146.26 hectare (361.44 acre) park. The Provincial Park was established by Order-in-council 68/73 in 1973.

Police Point (point)
72 L/2 - Medicine Hat
32-12-5-W4
50 °03'N 110°39'W
Located within the city limits of Medicine Hat.

This was the location of a North West Mounted Police post and barracks from 1883 to 1893.

Pollockville (hamlet)
72 M/4 - Pollockville
3-25-12-W4
51°06'N 111°35'W
Approximately 87 km south-east of Drumheller.

Named for Robert Pollock who homesteaded here in 1909 and opened a general store and post office in the fall of 1910. The Canadian National Railway reached Pollockville in 1919 and it grew rapidly as a result but has since diminished in population.

Porcupine Hills (hill)
82 G/16 - Maycroft
10,11-1-W5
49°55'N 114°00'W
Approximately 90 km west north-west of Lethbridge.

The name for these hills describe the shape of one of the hills whose outline resembles that of a porcupine. The Blackfoot name, *ky-es-kaghp-ogh-suy-iss*, means porcupine. The name was not officially approved until 7 August 1954; however, it has been in use since at least 1865.

Porter's Hill (hill)
72 L/2 - Medicine Hat
NE-28-12-5-W4
50°01'45"N 110°37'25"W
Immediately east of Medicine Hat.

Named for the man who first homesteaded on this feature from 1883 to 1900. The three Porter brothers came from Orangeville, Ontario, following and working on the Canadian Pacific Railway. They established a ranch near the hill, but moved to a site on Stony Creek which offered better protection for their stock. Dick, Jim and Bob, along with their father, Samuel, also operated a freight and water hauling business in Medicine Hat.

Pothole Creek (creek)
82 H/10 - Lethbridge
18-7-21-W4
49°34'N 112°50'W
Flows north-west into St. Mary River, approximately 10 km south of Lethbridge.

Originally named by the First Nations peoples because they thought the creek resembled a pot or kettle hole in the banks along the valley of the St. Mary River.

Potts Lake (lake)
82 O/2 - Jumpingpound Creek
31-25-5-W5
51°11'N 114°41'W
Approximately 45 km west of Calgary.

The Potts family were early homesteaders of the district who arrived from Scotland and this lake is named for them. James Potts emigrated to Canada from Scotland, settling in Cobourg, Ontario, where he married Jessie Johnston. Here they raised a family of six children and came west in 1884, with a herd of cattle, where they settled for many years.

Prairie Blood Creek (creek)

82 H/10 - Lethbridge
26-7-22-W4
49°33'N 112°56'W
Flows north-east into St. Mary River, approximately 10 km south of Lethbridge.

Named because it flows through the Blood Indian Reserve #148. The Indian name for this feature is translated as "Many Ghost River." The name was officially approved 12 December 1939.

Priddis (hamlet)

82 J/16 - Priddis
22-22-3-W5
50°53'N 114°20'W
Approximately 28 km south-west of Calgary.

Charles Priddis hailed from Paris, Ontario, and came west with a survey crew, looking after their horses. In 1884 his party had a winter camp south of Calgary at the confluence of the two branches of Fish Creek, a point later to become known as the "Forks." In 1886 Charles Priddis returned here to homestead and with the passage of time others came to settle in the district. When a meeting was held to decide a name, the unanimous choice was Priddis. The first school was held in his cabin and he donated land for the first schoolhouse. The post office opened 1 June 1894.

Priddis Creek (creek)

82 J/16 - Priddis
22-22-3-W5
50°53'N 114°20'W
Flows east into Fish Creek, approximately 14 km west south-west of Calgary.

This creek takes its name for its proximity to the hamlet of Priddis. (see Priddis)

Prince Island (island)

82 O/1 - Calgary
21-24-1-W5
51°03'N 114°04'W

Within the city limits of Calgary, in the Bow River.

The name for this island comes from Peter A. Prince (1835-1925), manager of operations for the Eau Claire and Bow River Lumber Company from 1886 to 1916. This company was a well-known and esteemed logging company during the time of its operation. I.K. Kerr was president for many years. Prince had been brought from Eau Claire, Wisconsin, to build the mill in Calgary. He retired on the same day as his son, John E. Prince, who was over sixty. Mr. Charles E. Carr succeeded Peter Prince as manager.

Princess (locality)

72 L/12 - Brooks
11-20-12-W4
50°41'N 111°34'W
Approximately 93 km north-west of Medicine Hat.

The adjoining station to this Canadian Pacific Railway station is called Patricia. Both stations were named in 1914 for Princess Patricia of Connaught. (see Patricia)

Prospy (post office)

72 E/6 - Foremost
3-8-9-W4
49°45'N 111°08'W
Approximately 56 km south-west of Medicine Hat.

The precise origin for the name of this feature is unknown.

Pulteney (locality)

82 I/4 - Claresholm
15-13-27-W4
50°05'N 113°36'W
Approximately 70 km north-west of Lethbridge.

A Canadian Pacific Railway station was established here circa 1917. The precise origin for the name of this feature is unknown.

Purple Springs (hamlet)

72 E/13   Grassy Lake
18-10-14-W4
49°49'N 111°54'W
Approximately 67 km east of Lethbridge.

This locality took its name from a nearby coulee in which a good spring existed, and where a multitude of purple flowers (American narrow leaved vetch) grew. Apparently, at one time, people gave directions stating that one's destination was "by or near a purple spring."

Quail Coulee (coulee)

82 I/13 - Granum
36-12-30-W4
49°59'40"N 113°57'35"W
South trending coulee into Trout Creek, approximately 90 km north-west of Lethbridge.

This coulee was named after William H. Quail who ranched near its head before the turn of the century. Quail Creek runs through this coulee.

Quail Creek (creek)

82 H/13 - Granum
13-12-30-W4
49°59'40"N 113°57'30"W
Flows south into Trout Creek, approximately 88 km north-west of Lethbridge.

The name was officially approved 5 December 1984. The creek runs through Quail Coulee. (see Quail Coulee)

Queenstown (hamlet)

82 I/10 - Queenstown
26-19-22-W4
50°38'N 112°56'W

Approximately 85 km south-east of Calgary.

Named in 1888 by Captain Dawson, who was surveying for the Canadian Government. The following year, he formed the Canadian Pacific Colonization Company with English capital. Advertisements for colonists to take up land in Queenstown were effective. The settlement was named after Queenstown (now Cobh) Ireland, Dawson's native city in Ireland and first appears on a map in 1925. The post office opened 1 January 1908 and operated until 30 June 1970.

Radnor (locality)

82 O/2 - Jumpingpound Creek
18-26-5-W5
51°13′N 114°42′W
Approximately 48 km north-west of Calgary.

A Canadian Pacific Railway station was established here in 1884 and was named after Wilma, daughter of the 5th Earl of Radnor and wife of the 2nd Earl of Lathom. She was awarded the C.B.E. in 1920.

Radnor Plateau (plateau)

82 O/2 - Jumpingpound Creek
26-5-W5
51°12′N 114°39′W
Approximately 42 km north-west of Calgary.

(see Radnor)

Rainier (hamlet)

82 I/8 - Scandia
26-16-16-W4
50°22′N 112°05′W
Approximately 90 km north-east of Lethbridge.

The post office here opened in 1921 under this name and the community was founded circa 1906 by Americans. It was named after a town in Washington state which, in turn, was named by Captain George Vancouver in 1792 after Rear Admiral Peter Rainier (1741-1808).

* Rainy Hills (former post office)

72 L/11 - Jenner
31-19-10-W4
50°39′N 111°25′W
Approximately 80 km north-west of Medicine Hat.

This post office operated from 1 December 1912 through 1 November 1916. The place was known as *sotaw cheimequan* by the Blackfoot and centred around a legend of "The Old Man," who, apparently, was caught in the rain in the general vicinity. It is now known as Denhart.

Raley (locality)

82 H/6 - Raley
16-4-24-W4
49°17′N 113°11′W
Approximately 51 km south south-west of Lethbridge.

The name for the locality was made official 8 July 1954, and was named for C. Raley, a prominent resident of Lethbridge.

Ralston (hamlet)

72 L/3 - Suffield
10-15-9-W4
50°15′N 111°10′W
Approximately 40 km north-west of Medicine Hat.

The name was suggested by Mr. G. W. Dunn, Administrative Deputy for the Chairman, Defence Research Board, Ottawa. A post office was established in 1949 and was named after the late Col. J.L. Ralston, who was Minister of National Defence during the war years between 1940

and 1944. This post office is approximately 3.2 km from Suffield Experimental Station. Ralston was an able minister and administrator but found himself at odds with Prime Minister W.L. Mackenzie King and resigned in 1944 over the conscription issue.

Ramsay Coulee (creek)

72 E/4 - Coutts
22-1-12-W4
49°03′N 111°32′W
Flows north-east into Deer Creek, approximately 110 km south-east of Lethbridge.

Named for Tom Ramsay (1858-1942) who settled his family on a homestead in the vicinity of this coulee. As a community-minded individual, Mr. Ramsay built the schoolhouse for his township.

Ranche Creek (creek)

82 O/7 - Wildcat Hills
25-26-6-W5
51°15′N 114°42′W
Flows south into Spencer Creek, approximately 45 km north-west of Calgary.

The precise origin for the name of this feature is unknown.

Ranche Hill (hill)

82 O/7 - Wildcat Hills
1-27-6-W5
51°18′N 114°43′W
Approximately 55 km west north-west of Calgary.

This hill is likely named for its proximity to Ranche Creek.

Ranchville (post office)

72 E/10 - Bulls Head
27-7-5-W4
49°35′N 110°36′W
Approximately 45 km south of Medicine Hat.

Known as "Peighan" until 1913, the post office name was changed to Ranchville because of its proximity to the large number of ranches established in the area since the late 1800s. The Ranchville post office was closed in July 1963. (see Peighan)

Rapid Narrows (narrows)

72 L/8 - Hilda
7-17-3-W4
50°25'N 110°24'W
Approximately 45 km north-east of Medicine Hat, on the South Saskatchewan River.

The name is descriptive of the narrowing of the river channel at this point. The river bed drops, resulting in a stretch of rapids which were troublesome to the freighting operations that operated between Medicine Hat and Saskatoon. At one time, the federal government was looking at the possibility of constructing a dam at these narrows.

Raspberry Creek (creek)

82 J/1 - Langford Creek
14-13-2-W5
50°05'N 114°10'W
Flows north into South Willow Creek, approximately 95 km south of Calgary.

The name for this creek was derived from an early settler family in Happy Valley known as the Rosburys. They came from Montana to settle, and eventually opened their own store in their cabin. The pronunciation and spelling of the name "Rosbury" was adjusted "western fashion" some time after the family left the area in 1913 or 1914. The name Raspberry Creek became the well-established local name.

Rattlesnake Lake (lake)

72 E/15 - Seven Persons
11-12-8-W4
50°00'N 110°58'W
Approximately 20 km south-west of Medicine Hat.

The precise origin for the name of this feature is unknown; however, presumably the large number of rattlesnakes in the area were provided with direct access to the South Saskatchewan River from this lake.

Raymond (town)

82 H/7 - Raymond
8,17-6-20-W4
49°27'N 112°39'W
Approximately 25 km south of Lethbridge.

This town was named in 1902 by Jesse W. Knight for his eldest son Raymond. In 1901, Jesse Knight, a prominent Mormon southern Alberta rancher originally from Utah, contracted with the North Western Coal and Navigation Company, Limited (see Galt Island) for 10,522 hectares (26,000 acres) of land to grow sugar beet and build Canada's first sugar factory. A townsite was selected and the majority of land was donated by Knight. The gift carried the provision that no liquor outlet could ever be established in the town or the land would revert to the Knight family and its heirs. Mainly because of the sugar beet factory, the town attracted 1,500 people within two years. Raymond Knight is considered by many to be the father of the "Stampede" or rodeo: in around 1900, Raymond hopped aboard a bucking horse, and helped introduce a new sport to North America.

Raymond Hill (hill)

82 P/7 - Drumheller
W-15-28-19-W4
51°23'48"N 112°36'40"W
Approximately 10 km south-east of Drumheller.

This hill, 60 m in altitude, was officially named 6 March 1986, for Andrew Raymond, a local rancher who homesteaded on SW 21-28-19-W4 on the north side of the hill. Mr. Raymond was a partner in a large grazing lease in the area.

Raymond Reservoir (reservoir)

82 H/7 - Raymond
29-5-20-W4
49°25'N 112°40'W
Approximately 31 km south of Lethbridge.

(see Raymond)

Read Creek (creek)

72 E/9 - Elkwater Lake
34-6-3-W4
49°30'N 110°20'W
Flows south into Lodge Creek, approximately 60 km south-east of Medicine Hat.

Named for John Read, also known as "baldy" or "Old John Read." Read was a rather eccentric, wealthy rancher who came to Canada from the United States, and eventually settled in the Cypress Hills region buying into the large L.A. Ranch south of Thelma. Read was known for paying his hands top money and then winning it back at the poker table several days after payday. In 1917, he bought the Royal Hotel in Medicine Hat in partnership with R.J. Rice. Read sold out his ranching interests in 1925 and moved to Medicine Hat. By 1927 he was sole proprietor of the Royal Hotel and was still playing poker with his employees. Read sold the hotel in 1938.

Red Creek (creek)

72 E/4 - Coutts
9-35-1-15-W4
49°04'50"N 111°54'10"W
Flows north-east into Milk River, approximately 93 km south-east of Lethbridge.

The origin of this name is uncertain. One resident of the area suggests that the name is descriptive, referring to the red sandstone found along its banks. Another account suggests that the creek was named for an early settler, Red Olson. Olson lived in a shack on the international border and worked as a sheep herder.

Red Deer Lake (lake)

72 L/8 - Hilda
30-15,16-3-W4
50°17′N 110°23′W
Approximately 35 km north-east of
Medicine Hat.

The precise origin for the name of this
feature is unknown.

Red Deer River (river)

72 L/16 - Bindloss
24-23-1-W4
50°58′N 110°00′W
Flows south-east across the Alberta-
Saskatchewan boundary, approximately 110
km north north-west of Medicine Hat.

The name is a translation of the Indian
name, *was-ka-sioo* in Cree, meaning "Elk
River," and *pa-chi-ci* in Stoney (Tyrrell).
The river received its name due to the
numerous elk in the area of early days,
mistaken by the Scottish factors for the red
deer of their homeland.

Red Rock Coulee Provincial Park

(provincial park)
72 E/10 - Bulls Head
15-8-7-W4
49°40′N 111°02′W
Approximately 45 km south of Medicine
Hat.

Named after the nearby Red Rock Coulee.
(see Red Rock Coulee)

■ **Red Rock Coulee** (coulee)

72 E/11 - Maleb
28-8-8-W4
49°40′N 111°02′W
Runs west into Seven Persons Creek,
approximately 45 km south-west of
Medicine Hat.

The descriptive name is taken from the
huge boulders that are covered with red
lichens, found in this area and along the
coulee.

Red Rock Coulee (natural area)

72 E/10 - Bulls Head
8-7-W4
49°40′N 111°02′W
Approximately 45 km south of Medicine
Hat.

A natural area is a parcel of land set aside to
protect sensitive or scenic features from
disturbance and to ensure their availability
in a natural state for use by the public for
recreation, education or any other purpose.
The name Red Rock Coulee is taken from
the nearby coulee. (see Red Rock Coulee)

Redcliff (town)

72 L/2 - Medicine Hat
8-13-6-W4
50°05′N 110°47′W
Approximately 10 km north-west of
Medicine Hat.

The name for this town refers to the red
cliffs on the South Saskatchewan River. The
word had become a commonplace name
long before the town was thought of, and it
was appropriate that the town be called
Redcliff after the outcropping of the red
shale overlooking the river just south and
east of the present townsite.

Redland (hamlet)

82 P/6 - Carbon
10-27-22-W4
51°18′N 113°00′W
Approximately 30 km south-west of
Drumheller.

The name for this community describes the
colour of the soil found in the area. The
Canadian Northern Railway established a
station here in 1914, as a compromise to
both the Gilbert Brothers (land agents for
Rosebud) and C.A. Nolan, Kenny, Dafoe
and Van Toll (pulling for a station at
Redland), even though the two stations
would be located 4 km apart, since most
stations were located at least 16 km apart.

A post office operated from 18 December
1914 through 4 June 1969.

Reed Lake (lake)

82 H/2 - Shanks Lake
31-2-21-W4
49°11′N 112°49′W
Approximately 55 km south of Lethbridge.

The name is descriptive and refers to the
great abundance of reeds growing in and
around the lake.

Reeder Coulee (coulee)

82 H/3 - Cardston
2-26-W4
49°07′N 113°23′W
Runs north into Lee Creek, approximately
73 km south-west of Lethbridge.

The precise origin for the name of this
feature is unknown.

■ **Reesor Lake** (lake)

72 E/9 - Elkwater Lake
20-8-1-W4
49°40′N 110°07′W
Approximately 52 km south-east of
Medicine Hat.

The Reesor family are Canadians who have
settled on both sides of this lake since 1804.
David William Reesor came to the Graburn
area to settle in 1900 and returned east for
his young family in 1902. His wife was a
Moffat whose mother was a sister of one of
the Fathers of Confederation, William
McDougall. David William Reesor was one
of the early Canadian Senators and his
picture hangs in the Senate Gallery today.
D.W. Ressor died in 1928, followed by his
wife some years later. The original Reesor
ranch house still stands not far from Twin
Lakes. It has been continuously occupied
by descendents of D.W. Reesor. The
present occupants are the fourth generation
to live there and are the seventh generation
of Reesors in Canada. This lake was

officially named for the Reesor family
6 November 1958.

* **Reid Hill** (former locality)

82 I/6 - Vulcan
36-16-23-W4
50°24'N 113°02'W
Approximately 70 km north of Lethbridge.

The post office which operated from
15 June 1906 through 15 May 1937 was
named after its first postmaster, Mr. Orick
A. Reid.

* **Reliance** (former locality)

82 II/16 - Taber
3-10-16-W4
49°47'N 112°05'W
Approximately 50 km east of Lethbridge.

Named after the Reliance Coal Company
that began mining operations in 1901. By
1908 the coal seam had become too thin to
mine profitably, and the town soon died as
a result.

Reserve Hill (hill)

82 O/7 - Wildcat Hills
35-27-6-W5
51°21'N 114°44'W
Approximately 60 km north-west of
Calgary, on the Stoney Indian Reserve.

This feature is likely named for its location
on the Stoney Indian Reserve.

Retlaw (locality)

82 I/1 - Vauxhall
9-13-17-W4
50°04'N 112°16'W
Approximately 55 km north-east of
Lethbridge.

This locality was named in 1913, for Walter
R. Baker, Secretary of the Canadian Pacific
Railway, when the rails reached this point.
Baker was the Earl of Dufferin's (then the
Governor-General of Canada) private
secretary from 1874 until 1878, and later
served as the assistant to the General
Manager of the C.P.R. Retlaw is "Walter"
spelled backwards. The post office was in
operation here from 1 September 1913
through 4 July 1960.

Rhodes Creek (creek)

82 O/7 - Wildcat Hills
15-27-5-W5
51°18'N 114°37'W
Flows east into Grand Valley Creek,
approximately 57 km north-west of
Calgary.

The precise origin for the name of this
feature, officially applied 11 June 1930, is
unknown.

* **Riverbow** (former locality)

82 I/8 - Scandia
19-15-16-W4
50°17'N 112°11'W
Approximately 92 km north-east of
Lethbridge.

The descriptive name for the post office
which operated from 15 October 1909
through 31 October 1937 referred to its
location at one of the many bends in the
Bow River.

* **Robertson** (former station)

82 O/1 - Calgary
4-25-2-W5
51°06'N 114°13'W
Within the city limits of Calgary.

A Canadian Pacific Railway station was
established here around 1917 and was
named after Private James Peter Robertson,
V.C. (1899-1917) of the 17th Battalion,
Canadian Infantry. He was a locomotive
engineer and was killed in World War I in
November 1917. His platoon was held up
by a machine gun and uncut wire, and
when he reached the machine gun, he killed
four of the crew and turned the gun on the
remainder.

* **Robinson** (former locality)

72 E/16 - Irvine
34-9-3-W4
49°47'N 110°19'W
Approximately 30 km south of Medicine
Hat.

This former locality was named for Dr.
John Lyle Robinson (1890-1953), Social
Credit Member of the Legislative Assembly
for Medicine Hat for eighteen years. Born
in Belfast, Ireland, Robinson came to
Canada in 1913 and graduated from the
Palmer School of Chiropractics in Daven-
port, Iowa, in 1929. He was first elected to
the provincial assembly in 1935 as a Social
Credit member, and was re-elected in 1940,
1944 and 1948. Premier Manning, Premier
of Alberta from 1943 to 1968, appointed
Robinson to the cabinet in May 1948 as
Minister of Industries and Labour.
Robinson died in office.

Robinson Creek (creek)

82 O/7 - Wildcat Hills
5-27-6-W5
51°17'N 114°49'W
Flows south-east into Ghost River,
approximately 50 km north-west of
Calgary.

This creek was named after Tom Robinson,
an early settler who lived on its banks. He
was born in Nova Scotia, making his way
west to Fort Edmonton is his youth. In
1882, he worked for the Cochrane Ranche.
He later settled on the SE1/4 8-27-6-W5,
north of the Ghost River and then filed on
a homestead 2.4 km north of this quarter
but failed to prove it up. The Stoney
Indians have been known to call it *chaba
wastan*, translating to "Spruce Creek."

Rock Lake (lake)

72 L/12 - Brooks
11-20-15-W5
50°41′N 111°58′W
Approximately 117 km north-west of
Medicine Hat.

The name for this lake is likely descriptive.

Rock Springs (spring)

82 P/3 - Strathmore
8-31-25-22-W4
51°10′15″N 113°03′15″W
Approximately 40 km south-west of
Drumheller.

Named for the small natural spring in the
sandstone face of this coulee. It was
originally known as "Rock Corral" since
ranchers used the natural enclosure as a
corral during round-up. The current name
is well established among local residents
and was officially approved 6 March 1986.

Rocky Coulee (creek)

82 H/14 - Monarch
29-10-24-W4
49°51′N 113°14′W
Flows south into Oldman River, approximately 30 km north-west of Lethbridge.

The name for this creek is likely descriptive.

Rocky View (locality)

82 P/4 - Dalroy
2-26-29-W4
51°11′N 113°56′W
Approximately 15 km north north-east of
Calgary.

Rocky View is a siding on a spur line of the
Canadian Pacific Railway. It was originally
installed in 1961, to service the new Petro
Gas Processing Plant, north of Calgary.
Since 1982, however, it has also served the

Turbo Refinery. "McDonald" was the
name originally proposed for the siding,
possibly for its proximity to McDonald
Lake. This name was duplicated in Manitoba, however, and the descriptive name
Rocky View was chosen instead. The siding
is located in the Municipal District of
Rocky View, and the Rocky Mountains
may be easily seen from this vantage point.

Rockyford (village)

82 P/3 - Strathmore
22-26-23-W4
51°14′N 113°08′W
Approximately 42 km south-west of
Drumheller.

Rockyford was named by the First Nations
peoples because the main channel of the
Serviceberry Creek was too narrow and
deep to cross: the Indians used the rocky
ford to cross on their way to Gleichen.
Later, the ranchers used the name, and in
1908, the surveyors used it for surveying
the right of way to Calgary. This ford was
0.4 km south of the present townsite.
Rockyford was officially named by a Mr.
Beaumont, chief surveyor of the Canadian
Northern Railway, in 1914. A post office
opened 1 August 1914.

Rogers Coulee (coulee)

72 E/7 - Manyberries
11-6-7-W4
49°27′N 110°51′W
Flows west into Fourways Creek, approximately 67 km south of Medicine Hat.

The precise origin for the name of this
feature is unknown.

Rolling Hills (hamlet)

72 L/4 - Hays
6-15-13-W4
50°13′N 111°46′W
Approximately 75 km west north-west of
Medicine Hat.

The name is descriptive of the area around
this hamlet.

Rolling Hills Lake (lake)

72 L/5 - Tilley
16-14,15-W4
50°22′N 111°55′W
Approximately 80 km west north-west of
Medicine Hat.

This lake is likely named for its proximity
to the hamlet of Rolling Hills. (see Rolling
Hills)

Rolph Creek (creek)

82 H/3 - Cardston
29-2-24-W4
49°10′N 113°11′W
Flows north into St. Mary River, approximately 64 km south-west of Lethbridge.

Named for the Rolph family, who were the
first white settlers in the district. The
Rolphs lived next to this creek for several
years. It is now locally known as "Willow
Creek," which is likely a descriptive name.

* Ronalane (former locality)

72 L/4 - Hays
9-13-12-W4
50°04′N 111°35′W
Approximately 65 km west of Medicine
Hat.

A Canadian Pacific Railway station was
established here in 1914 and was named
after Major-General Sir Ronald B. Lane
who served in the Zulu War of 1879, the
Egyptian War of 1882 and the Boer War of
1899. He was Lieutenant-Governor and
Secretary at Chelsea Royal Hospital from
1905 to 1909.

Rose Lynn (hamlet)

72 M/5 - Sunnynook
30-28-12-W4
51°25′N 111°41′W
Approximately 70 km east of Drumheller.

The descriptive name refers to the original location on which the post office was located. The ridge was covered with wild rose bushes but the name was later changed. (see Forcina)

* Rosebeg (former locality)
72 E/15 - Seven Persons
10-10-6-W4
49°49′N 110°44′W
Approximately 20 km south of Medicine Hat.

A post office was established here in 1911 but was closed 30 September 1940. The precise origin of this name is unknown.

Rosebud (hamlet)
82 P/7 - Drumheller
18-27-21-W4
51°18′N 112°57′W
Approximately 25 km south-west of Drumheller.

The post office here was called "Grierson" until 1896, but the Blackfoot name persisted. The earliest mention of this district is from High Eagle, "the Wandering Spirit of the Plains," who was born ca. 1840. He recalled how the Blackfoot often came to the "River of Many Roses" to fish, hunt, and gather berries. (see Rosebud River)

Rosebud River (river)
82 P/7 - Drumheller
5-28-28-19-W4
51°25′N 112°38′W
Flows north into Red Deer River, approximately 95 km north-east of Calgary.

The Cree Indian word for many features in this area is *mis sas ka too mina*, which translates to "serviceberry creek." The Stoney Indians call it *mi-thaga-waptan*

(Tyrrell). The Blackfoot refer to the area as *akokiniskway*, translating, "many rose-buds." Rosebud is a popular name in the area: the Rosebud School was the first in the area and the Rosebury Inn was once the Rosebud Hotel.

Rosedale (hamlet)
82 P/7 - Drumheller
28-28-19-W4
51°25′N 112°38′W
Approximately 7 km south-east of Drumheller.

John Dart was one of the first residents in Rosedale when he arrived on the north side of the Red Deer River in 1909. He bought a piece of land around this time, but sold it to Frank Moodie in 1916. Moodie had discovered there was coal under the land and named his new mine Rosedale Mine, and later the mine camp was subsequently given the name. The Canadian Pacific Railway line came through circa 1911 and Mr. W.R. Fulton built the first store at this time. The post office was built some time afterwards; it was opened on 17 April 1913, and operated until 12 March 1940. The name is derived from the many roses which grow abundantly in the area, and the fact that the Rosebud River joins the Red Deer River at this point.

Rosedale Station (post office)
82 P/7 - Drumheller
29-28-19-W4
51°25′N 112°38′W
Approximately 7 km south-east of Drumheller.

The post office opened 1 March 1921. (see Rosedale)

* Roseglen (former locality)
72 L/8 - Hilda
34-15-3-W4
50°18′N 110°21′W
Approximately 50 km north-east of Medicine Hat.

The name is now used both by the area in which this school house was located and by a Hutterian Brethren colony. The logical explanation for its origin would seem to have some connection with the wild roses that grow in the region.

Rosemary (village)
82 I/16 - Bassano
1-21-16-W4
50°46′N 112°05′W
Approximately 148 km south-east of Calgary.

This Canadian Pacific Railway village was named in 1914 for Rosemary Millicent, daughter of the 4th Duke of Sutherland. The Duke owned an extensive expanse of farmland in the Brooks area. In 1919, Millicent (1893-1930) married the Earl of Dudley. She died in an airplane accident in 1930.

Ross Coulee (coulee)
72 L/2 - Medicine Hat
28-12-5-W4
50°01′50″N 110°38′10″W
A north-south trending coulee running into the South Saskatchewan River Valley, within the city limits of Medicine Hat.

The name comes from the fact that Ross Creek flows in this coulee. (see Ross Creek)

Ross Creek (creek)
72 L/2 - Medicine Hat
33-12-5-W4
50°02′N 110°38′W
Flows north through Ross Coulee into South Saskatchewan River, located within the city limits of Medicine Hat.

This creek was named after Roderick Ross, a Métis trader who resided on the creek in 1875.

Ross Depression (hollow)

72 L/10 - Easy Coulee
18,19-4-W4
50°35′N 110°33′W
Approximately 55 km north of Medicine Hat.

The precise origin for the name of this feature is unknown.

Ross Lake (lake)

82 H/2 - Shanks Lake
30-2-22-W4
49°09′N 112°56′W
Approximately 60 km south of Lethbridge.

Named for Walter Ross (1854-ca.1935) who, from 1895 until 1935, ran a large ranch located on the shores of this lake. Ross was the eldest of ten children, and came to Alberta from his native Quebec in 1894 following the death of his wife.

Rouleau Lake (lake)

82 H/5 - Pincher Creek
27-5-28-W4
49°25′N 113°42′W
Approximately 69 km south-west of Lethbridge.

Named for Achilles "Archie" Rouleau, who settled in the area after he took his discharge from the North West Mounted Police in 1885. Originally from Quebec, he joined the NWMP and was given regimental number 497. He served as a scout at either the post on the Waterton River or at Fort Macleod. He farmed and operated a livery stable.

* Royal (former locality)

72 E/15 - Seven Persons
16-12-5-W4
49°59′N 110°40′W
Approximately 2 km south of Medicine Hat.

The precise origin for the name of this feature is unknown. (see Roytal)

Roytal (locality)

72 E/15 - Seven Persons
16-12-5-W4
49°59′N 110°40′W
Approximately 2 km south of Medicine Hat.

There is no record of a name change from Royal to Roytal; however, both these localities have the same location. The precise origin for the name of either feature is unknown.

Rush Lake (lake)

72 E/10 - Bulls Head
29-8-5-W4
49°41′N 110°39′W
Approximately 40 km south of Medicine Hat.

The precise origin for the name of this feature is unknown.

Rush Lake (lake)

82 H/3 - Cardston
SE-10-3-24-W4
49°11′50″N 113°08′30″W
Approximately 59 km south-west of Lethbridge.

The name is descriptive and refers to the abundance of rushes growing in and along the shores of this lake. The name was made official for landmark and navigational purposes.

Rush Lake (locality)

82 H/3 - Cardston
10-3-24-W4
49°12′N 113°09′W
Approximately 58 km south-west of Lethbridge.

This locality takes its name from the nearby lake. (see Rush Lake)

Rutherford Lake (lake)

72 L/1 - Many Island Lake
32-13-2-W4
50°08′00″N 110°13′00″W
35 km east north-east of Medicine Hat.

The lake was named for Bob Rutherford, son of William Rutherford a sheep farmer who came to Thompkins, Saskatchewan to herd sheep for the 76 Ranch. Bob established a homestead near the lake. It was a large operation and he eventually sold out.

S

* Sage Creek (former locality)
72 E/1 - Cripple Creek
4-1-2-W4
49°00'N 110°13'W
Approximately 122 km south south-east of Medicine Hat.

Originally named after the sage brush. The name was changed in 1926. (see Wildhorse)

St. George Island (island)
82 O/1 - Calgary
14-24-1-W5
51°03'N 114°02'W
Within the city limits of Calgary, in the Bow River.

The precise origin for the name of this feature is unknown.

St. Kilda (post office)
72 E/4 - Coutts
2-1-12-W4
49°00'N 111°31'W
Approximately 113 km south-east of Lethbridge.

Donald McDougall, one of the district's earliest settlers, suggested the name after the island of St. Kilda in Scotland. St. Kilda was McDougall's birthplace and home prior to immigrating to Canada.

St. Mary Dam (dam)
82 H/6 - Raley
12-5-24-W4
49°22'N 113°07'W
Approximately 40 km south south-west of Lethbridge.

(see St. Mary River)

St. Mary Reservoir (reservoir)
82 H/6 - Raley
20-4-24-W4
49°18'N 113°11'W

Approximately 47 km south south-west of Lethbridge.

The name was officially approved 8 July 1954. (see St. Mary River)

St. Mary River (river)
82 H/6   Raley
11-8-22-W4
49°37'N 112°52'W
Flows north-east into Oldman River, immediately south of Lethbridge.

The name for this river is derived from its source, the St. Mary Lakes, which are located in Glacier National Park, in northern Montana. These lakes were named by Father Pierre Jean de Smet (1801-1873) while on his way to a conference with some members of the Blackfoot Indians. While encamped near the lower lake, de Smet erected a large wooden cross on the shore of the lake, and gave it the name St. Mary Lakes in honour of the saint. The Blackfoot name for this feature is *pa-toxiapis-kun* which translates to "banks damming the river." Sometime after 1830, the Stevens Expedition named the lakes "Chief Mountain Lakes," but the name did not garner local usage.

St. Patrick Island (island)
82 O/1 - Calgary
14-24-1-W5
51°03'N 114°02'W
Within the city limits of Calgary, in the Bow River.

The precise origin for the name of this feature is unknown.

Salter Creek (creek)
82 O/7 - Wildcat Hills
30-28-6-W5
51°25'N 114°50'W
Flows north into Little Red Deer River, approximately 68 km north-west of Calgary.

This creek and the nearby lake are known by the natives as "Rabbit Creek" and "Rabbit Lake." (see Salter Lake)

Salter Lake (lake)
82 O/7 - Wildcat Hills
30-27-6-W5
51°20'N 114°49'W
Approximately 64 km north-west of Calgary.

This lake was named by G.M. Dawson in 1884, after his Métis packer of Scottish and Indian background. The name was officially adopted 8 December 1943.

Sam Lake (lake)
72 L/1 - Many Island Lake
6-14-2-W4
50°08'N 110°17'W
Approximately 35 km east north-east of Medicine Hat.

The precise origin for the name of this feature is unknown.

* Sampsonton (former locality)
82 O/8 - Crossfield
1-29-3-W5
51°28'N 114°17'W
Approximately 50 km north north-west of Calgary.

A post office operated here from 1 October 1906 through 1 May 1931 and was named after its first postmaster, Arthur Sampson. The name and location were changed to Madden in 1931. (see Madden)

San Francisco Lake (lake)

82 I/9 - Cassils
11-19-16-W4
50°35'N 112°08'W
Approximately 111 km north-east of
Lethbridge.

This man-made lake was constructed in
1942, from funds donated by the Pacific
Rod and Gun Club based in San Francisco,
California. A number of the members of
the club travelled to the Brooks area to
hunt in the fall and, in association with
Ducks Unlimited, they convinced the
Eastern Irrigation District to flood some
200 acres to create a bird sanctuary. The
money donated towards the project by the
club was raised from trap and skeet
shooting competitions.

Sandy Point (point)

72 L/9 - Sandy Point
34-20-1-W4
50°43'N 110°03'W
At the north bank of the South Saskatchewan River, approximately 90 km north
north-east of Medicine Hat.

The precise origin for the name of this
feature is unknown but it is likely descriptive.

Sarcee Junction (railway point)

82 P/4 - Dalroy
23-1-W5
51°00'N 114°00'W
Within the city limits of Calgary.

The name for this station, established in
1959, was selected as the Indians who were
well-established in this area at the time of
naming belonged to the Sarcee Tribe. The
Sarcee Indians are a break-away from the
Beaver Indians of the Peace River area, and
are members of the Athapascan linguistic
stock.

*denotes rescinded name or former locality.

Scabby Butte (butte)

82 H/15 - Picture Butte
3-19-11-22-W4
49°55'00"N 112°59'30"W
Approximately 27 km north north-west of
Lethbridge.

The term is probably descriptive. The rare
bedrock exposure is evidently not a
beautiful site and a garbage dump located
over the edge reflects attitudes the local
residents have towards the feature. The
feature was named by Dawson in 1884.

Scandia (hamlet)

82 I/8 - Scandia
19-15-15-W4
50°17'N 112°02'W
Approximately 83 km north-east of
Lethbridge.

One source suggests that this area was
originally settled by Scandinavians and
thus, was named Scandia. Another source
indicates that the hamlet was named for
Scandia, Minnesota, by settlers from that
region. As a large number of Scandinavians
settled in Minnesota, the town in this state
was probably derived from their cultural
heritage. The post office opened 1 January
1924.

Scandia Draw (bay)

72 L/5 - Tilley
27-16-15-W4
50°23'N 111°58'W
Approximately 100 km west north-west of
Medicine Hat.

This feature probably derives its name from
the fact that this narrow, three km long bay
on the south-west corner of Lake Newell
feeds an irrigation canal that flows south to
the hamlet of Scandia. (see Scandia)

Scholten Hill (hill)

72 L/2 - Medicine Hat
9,10-29-12-5-W4
50°01'40"N 110°39'00"W

Within the city limits of Medicine Hat,
north of the Stampede Grounds.

This hill was named for Dirk Scholten, one-
time general manager of the Medicine Hat
Exhibition and Stampede. He was instrumental in developing the fair into a first-
class small rodeo.

Schuler (hamlet)

72 L/8 - Hilda
9-16-1-W4
50°20'N 110°06'W
Approximately 55 km north-east of
Medicine Hat.

This hamlet was named after the post office
which moved to the site when the railroad
built a station there in 1923. The post office
was established on 15 December 1910
under the name. Norman Banks (Tim)
Schuler came to the district, possibly from
Russia, in the spring of 1910. In the autumn
of that year, he assumed the position of
postmaster and, needing a name for the post
office, he named it after himself. Schuler's
sister, Evelyn came to the community in
1916 and later was very active in the
community, replacing Tim at the post
office. She also helped him with the
operation of a General Store acquired
earlier, and a blacksmith shop acquired in
1919.

Schuler Lake (lake)

72 L/8 - Hilda
7-10-16-1-W4
50°20'00"N 110°06'00"W
Approximately 55 km east north-east of
Medicine Hat, immediately south of
Schuler.

(see Schuler)

* Scope (former station)

72 L/4 - Hays
17-13-14-W4
50°05'N 111°52'W

Approximately 78 km west of Medicine Hat.

The precise origin for the name of this former Canadian Pacific Railway station is unknown.

Scots Lake (lake)

72 L/5 - Tilley
20-16-12-W4
50°21′N 111°37′W
Approximately 75 km north-west of Medicine Hat.

John Scot settled on a farm on the north-west shore of this lake which carries his name. Scot originally came to Canada from Scotland in 1914 and settled on the shores of this lake in 1928, remaining for eleven years until he went to work at the Mayland Ranch.

Scotts Coulee (creek)

82 H/5 - Pincher Creek
35-5-27-W4
49°26′N 113°32′W
Flows south-east into Waterton River, approximately 58 km south-west of Lethbridge.

This creek is possibly named for Thomas Herron Scott (1866-1949). Born in Ontario, he came west with the white troops suppressing the Riel Rebellion. Lured by the reports of his cousin attached to the North West Mounted Police, John Herron, he continued on to Medicine Hat where he helped build a ferry across the river. He then moved on to Fort Macleod where he helped build the Macleod Hotel. After a stint ranching and horse-racing in Pincher Creek, he became a foreman of a crew constructing the Crowsnest Pass line for the Canadian Pacific Railway. In 1899, he went off to fight with the Canadian Mounted Rifles in the Boer War. Returning in 1901, he became a construction contractor finding jobs across the West. In 1904, he

settled in Pincher Creek and married Gertrude Mabel McCrea (1881-1952). He took up land on a hill in the Pincher Creek area, although the couple's name is not registered in the early rural directories.

Seiu Creek (creek)

82 P/1 - Finnegan
7-25-25-18-W4
51°09′N 112°23′W
Flows south-east into Seiu Lake, approximately 36 km south-east of Drumheller.

This stream takes its name from the lake into which it flows. (see Seiu Lake)

Seiu Lake (lake)

82 P/1 - Finnegan
23-25-18-W4
51°08′N 112°24′W
Approximately 36 km south-east of Drumheller.

The precise origin for the name of this feature is unknown.

Serviceberry Creek (creek)

82 P/6 - Carbon
10-27-22-W4
51°18′N 113°01′W
Flows north-east into Rosebud River, approximately 28 km south west of Drumheller.

This creek was first surveyed in 1883, and had three different names marked on the survey maps at different points. It was variously referred to as "Crowfoot Creek," "Prickly Pear Creek," and finally, Serviceberry Creek. The name was picked before 1900 due to the abundance of saskatoon berries growing along its banks. The saskatoon, or serviceberry is a popular berry which grows wild throughout the prairies, the fruit of which was used by the Indians for food while the wood provided material for their arrow shafts. The Cree equivalent for this name is *mis sas ka too mina*.

Seven Persons (hamlet)

72 E/15 - Seven Persons
4-11-7-W4
49°52′N 110°54′W
Approximately 20 km south-west of Medicine Hat.

There appear to be two or three possible explanations and variations of the origin of this name. An American-owned company built a railway line, connecting Minneapolis to Spokane, via Lethbridge and the Crowsnest Pass. It was the construction crew of this railway, working in the vicinity, who named this section after discovering seven unmarked graves in the area. It was not known if these were the graves of white men or Indians and the crew decided that this area would be called Seven Persons. It became the name of the hamlet and of the surrounding area.

Another story posits that a band of Blackfoot Indians came upon the bodies of seven men. Although dead for some time, the bodies showed no signs of decay, and their hair had been removed yet they had not been scalped. The band of Blackfoot watched the bodies for five days, yet no changes occurred, prompting them to believe that they had been struck dead by the Great Spirit. The Blackfoot leader, Yellow Calf Shirt, ordered his men to build a large pile of stones around the bodies. The same band of Indians visited the site the following spring, yet no trace of the seven persons could be found.

A third story, and the one most widely accepted claims that a Blood Indian War Party, led by Chief Calf-Shirt, was travelling through the area, encountered and did battle with a band of Cree Indians near a creek. Seven Cree were killed and their medicine pipes were taken. The site, area and creek was called *ki-tsuki-s-tapi*, which is Blackfoot for "seven persons."

The actual hamlet of Seven Persons took its name from the creek near where this battle took place. Its beginnings in the 1880s were humble. Little more than a railway siding of the narrow gauge railway, built by the North Western Coal and Navigation Company to supply the Canadian Pacific Railway at Dunmore with coal from "The Coal Banks," now known as Lethbridge.

Seven Persons Coulee (coulee)

72 E/11 - Maleb
8-8-W4
49°35'00"N 111°04'00"W
Runs north into Seven Persons Creek, approximately 55 km south-west of Medicine Hat.

(see Seven Persons)

Seven Persons Creek (creek)

72 L/2 - Shanks Lake
29-12-5-W4
50°02'N 110°39'W
Flows north-east into Ross Creek, within the city limits of Medicine Hat.

(see Seven Persons)

Seven Persons Lake (lake)

72 E/15 - Seven Persons
29-10-7-W4
49°51'N 110°54'W
Approximately 23 km south-west of Medicine Hat.

(see Seven Persons)

Severn Creek (creek)

82 P/7 - Drumheller
7-27-21-W4
51°18'N 112°56'W
Flows north into Rosebud River, approximately 25 km south-west of Drumheller.

The name for this creek was officially approved 6 December 1956. Its precise origin is unknown but it was once known locally as "Rosebud Creek."

Sexton Creek (creek)

72 E/9 - Elkwater Lake
20-7-3-W4
49°34'N 110°22'W
Flows south-west into Lodge Creek, approximately 50 km south-east of Medicine Hat.

This creek was named for Larry Sexton who settled in the Thelma area around the turn of the century, establishing a ranch on the east side of the coulee in 1905. There is some disagreement over who Sexton was, and where he came from. Some say he was an English remittance man, while others say he was a settler from the United States.

Shanks Creek (creek)

82 H/2 - Shanks Lake
18-2-20-W4
49°08'N 112°40'W
Flows north-east into Shanks Lake, drains it, continues to flow north-east into North Milk River, approximately 60 km south of Lethbridge.

(see Shanks Lake)

Shanks Lake (lake)

82 H/2 - Shanks Lake
26-1-27-W4
49°04'N 112°43'W
Approximately 65 km south of Lethbridge.

This feature was named after Thomas Shanks (1869-1926) who was Director General of Surveys for the Dominion Land Survey from 1914 to 1924.

Shannon Coulee (coulee)

82 O/1 - Calgary
6-24-2-W5
51°01'N 114°16'W
Runs north into Lott Creek, approximately 20 km south-west of Calgary.

The precise origin for the name of this feature, located within the Sarcee Indian Reserve #145, is unknown.

Sharp Hill, The (hill)

82 P/4 - Dalroy
16-26-29-W4
51°15'N 113°59'W
Approximately 18 km north of Calgary.

The name for this hill is descriptive. The local natives called the range of hills the equivalent to "Buttes Hills," dating back to the 1850s, and the name is still used today.

Sharples (locality)

82 P/6 - Carbon
17-29-22-W4
51°28'N 113°04'W
Approximately 23 km west of Drumheller.

Sharples was located on a Canadian Pacific Railway branch line from Acme to Drumheller. This siding was named after John Sharples, a railway foreman in Saskatoon, who won the Distinguished Conduct Medal in World War I. There were never any formal businesses located in Sharples, and it was merely used as a grain delivery point.

Sharrow (locality)

72 L/16 - Bindloss
35-22-2-W4
50°55'N 110°11'W
Approximately 100 km north north-west of Medicine Hat.

This locality is named after the title of a story written by Baroness Bon Hutton, who was born in the United States, but lived the better part of her life in London, England.

Shaughnessy (hamlet)

82 H/15 - Picture Butte
30-10-21-W4
49°51'N 112°50'W
Approximately 18 km north of Lethbridge.

Named for Thomas George, Lord Shaughnessy (1853-1923), an American-born shareholder in the Canadian Pacific Railway who was its president from 1898 to 1918. Shaughnessy was also the president of the Cadillac Coal Company, which operated a coal mine on what is now the townsite.

Sheep River (river)

82 I/12 - High River
32-20-28-W4
50°44′N 113°51′W
Flows east into Highwood River, approximately 29 km south south-east of Calgary.

The name for this river is descriptive. The David Thompson map of 1814 lists the name for this river as *itou-kai-you*, and the Arrowsmith map of 1859 has the name of the river as *itukaiup*, or "sheep" because the river at this point near the Highwood, was a favourite haunt of Rocky Mountain Bighorn Sheep. Both native names translate to a close estimation of Sheep River.

Sheerness (hamlet)

72 M/5 - Sunnynook
18-29-12-W4
51°29′N 111°41′W
Approximately 71 km east of Drumheller.

Named after Sheerness, a seaport in Kent, England. A post office was established 1 May 1910 and closed 2 April 1970. A primary reason for its survival for many years was due to the abundance of coal in close proximity.

Shepard (hamlet)

82 I/13 - Dalemead
18-23-28-W4
50°57′N 113°55′W
Approximately 1 km east of Calgary.

A station was built here by the Canadian Pacific Railway in 1884. The post office opened for four months in 1903, and then reopened 1 January 1905, operating until 8

March 1966. It was named after one of the partners of Shepard and Langdon, railway contractors. Langdon became a neighbouring station.

Sherburne Lake (lake)

72 E/13 - Grassy Lake
20-9-13-W4
49°46′N 111°46′W
Approximately 75 km east of Lethbridge.

This lake was named for Charles W. Sherburne and family (four daughters, seven sons) who, in 1906, were the first to travel on the Canadian Pacific Railway into the Taber area with the intention of homesteading. Charles and six of his sons took up homesteads, the father and two sons on the south shore of the lake, the other four on the north side of the lake. The Sherburnes resided in the area for several years contributing to the growth and development of the community. The school house, built in 1910 was named for them, as was the school district. A new community centre, built in the early 1950s on the site of the old Sherburne School currently bears their name. Charles' youngest daughter and her family still resided on the old homestead, at least in the 1950s. Located only eight km south of the village of Grassy Lake, a number of longtime local residents suggested that Sherburne Lake is commonly known as "Grassy Lake."

Shouldice (hamlet)

82 I/10 - Queenstown
22-20-22-W4
50°43′N 112°59′W
Approximately 78 km south-east of Calgary.

This hamlet was named for James Shouldice, original owner of the land on which the present community is situated. James, his wife, Margaret, and their children, first came from Ontario to the Namaka district in 1901. He originally

leased 13,000 acres, later purchasing 1,700 acres in the Namaka area from the Calgary Land and Ranch Company. In 1911 he purchased the land where Shouldice now stands and a year later, bought the original Critchley Ranch of 480 acres near Calgary's Bowness Park, 50 acres of which is the present-day Shouldice Park. Shouldice farmed and ranched until his death in 1925.

Sibbald (hamlet)

72 M/8 - Sibbald
13-28-2-W4
51°23′N 110°09′W
Approximately 177 km east of Drumheller.

This hamlet may be named for either John Sibbald, a prominent railway construction engineer, or Frank Sibbald, an early rancher and son of Andrew Sibbald who had arrived in the Morley district in 1875.

Silver Lake (lake)

82 I/5 - Nanton
32-17-28-W4
50°24′N 113°48′W
Approximately 62 km south of Calgary.

Since nearby Connemara was once known as "Silver City" and remembered as such by some local residents, this lake was likely named for its proximity to this "Silver City." Some people refer to the lake as "Connemara Slough." (see Connemara)

Silver Springs (locality)

82 O/1 - Calgary
SE1/4-1-25-2-W5
51°06′N 114°09′W
Within the north-west city limits of Calgary.

The descriptive name for this locality refers to the underground springs that sparkle like silver. H.H. Horne, a resident of Calgary, thought the name appropriate.

Simons Valley (locality)
82 O/1 - Calgary
3-26-2-W5
51°11′N 114°12′W
Approximately 25 km north-west of
Calgary.

The post office which operated here from 1
April 1907 through 27 February 1926 was
named after its first postmaster, W.E.
Simons.

Skiff (hamlet)
72 E/5 - Legend
26-6-14-W4
49°30′N 111°47′W
Approximately 80 km south-east of
Lethbridge.

Some local residents explain the origin of
this name through a story that describes
high water levels in the slough south-west
of this town. This required people living in
the area to use a small boat, or skiff, to
cross it. Perhaps a former seaman chose the
name. Many of the names for the streets are
taken from parts of a small boat or skiff; for
example, Bow Avenue, Stern Avenue,
Rudder Street, and Tiller Street. It therefore
seems appropriate to have applied this
nautical name to the entire community. The
post office was opened 15 October 1918.

Slick-up Lake (lake)
82 I/10 - Queenstown
21-18-21-W4
50°32′40″N 112°50′10″W
Approximately 98 km north of Lethbridge.

Mrs. Brown was known as the oldest
woman settler in the county in 1928. She
and her husband and family came to the
area in 1889 from Scotland. Mr. and Mrs.
Brown entertained the cowboys in the old-
fashioned style, and this lake, south-east of

_____
*denotes rescinded name or former locality.

Milo, received its name from the fact that it
was there that the boys used to stop and
"slick-up" for the parties. The Brown
household was known for the great
hospitality of its mistress, and people
gathered from near and far to partake of the
festivities. The "Circle Cowboys" named
the lake where they used to shave and
"slick-up" their appearance in general
because they knew the Browns were sure to
put on a dance when the round-up arrived
near the Queenstown ranch. The Browns
always had wonderful home-cooked
meals—and five lovely daughters.

Smith Coulee (coulee)
72 E/3 - Aden
3-11-W4
49°08′N 111°18′W
Runs north into Milk River, approximately
103 km south-west of Medicine Hat.

The precise origin for the name of this
feature is unknown.

Snake Creek (creek)
82 I/7 - McGregor Lake
36-17-22-W4
50°29′N 112°53′W
Flows east into McGregor Lake, approximately 77 km south-east of Calgary.

The name is likely descriptive. The
Blackfoot called the creek *ak-ustsik-
siniskway*, translating to "place of many
snakes." Prior to the creation of McGregor
Lake, the lake and valley were locally
known as "Snake Lake" and "Snake
Valley."

* Social Plains (former locality)
72 L/9 - Middle Sand Hills
28-20-2-W4
50°44′N 110°11′W
Approximately 77 km north-east of
Medicine Hat.

This name was chosen by residents to
express the sociable character of the area's
settlers. Originally the name was applied to
the school district and was later assumed by
the post office that operated from 1 April
1915 through 23 July 1929.

South Drywood Creek (creek)
82 H/5 - Pincher Creek
16-4-30-W4
49°18′N 113°58′W
Flows north-east into Drywood Creek,
approximately 93 km south-west of
Lethbridge.

(see Drywood Creek)

South Easy Coulee (coulee)
72 L/10 - Easy Coulee
18-6,7-W4
50°35′N 110°52′W
Approximately 60 km north of Medicine
Hat.

Named for its proximity to Easy Coulee.
(see Easy Coulee)

South Manyberries Creek (creek)
72 E/7 - Manyberries
11-5-6-W4
49°22′N 110°43′W
Flows west into Manyberries Creek,
approximately 72 km south of Medicine
Hat.

Named as a tributary to Manyberries
Creek. (see Manyberries Creek)

South Saskatchewan River (river)
72 L/16 - Bindloss
25-22-1-W4
50°53′N 110°00′W
Flows north-east across the Alberta-
Saskatchewan boundary, approximately
105 km north-east of Medicine Hat.

This river is the confluence of the Oldman
and Bow rivers, and flows north-east into

Saskatchewan to meet with the North Saskatchewan River, and eventually flows east to the Hudson Bay. It is named from the Cree Indian word *kis-is-ska-tche-wan*, meaning "swift current." David Thompson mistakenly denoted this river as the Bow River on his 1814 map.

Southesk (locality)
82 I/9 - Cassils
33-19-16-W4
50°39′N 112°10′W
Approximately 117 km north-east of Lethbridge.

This locality was named for its proximity to Southesk Lake, Mount Southesk, Southesk River and Southesk Cairn, all named after James Carnegie, 9th Earl of Southesk (1827-1905). The Earldom of Southesk had been forfeited by the 5th Earl due to his participation in the rebellion of 1745 when the Catholic Young Pretender, "Bonnie Prince Charlie," received the support of some of the Highland Chiefs, Southesk among them, in his attempt to put his father, James III on the throne of the U.K. James III was referred to as the "Old Pretender." In the spring of 1859, the 9th Earl left England for Canada to help his ailing health. A literate person, he read Shakespeare as he hunted and travelled across the northwest. After extensive exploration of the Rockies and foothills area, his party returned to Fort Edmonton 12 October. Here he wrote *Saskatchewan and the Rocky Mountains* (1875), describing his travels along the Saskatchewan River and in the Canadian Rockies.

Spencer Creek (creek)
82 O/2 - Jumpingpound Creek
17-26-5-W5
51°13′N 114°40′W

Flows south into Bow River, approximately 48 km west north-west of Calgary.

(see Spencer Hills)

Spencer Hills (hill)
82 O/7 - Wildcat Hills
25-26-6-W5
51°15′N 114°44′W
Approximately 53 km west north-west of Calgary.

The name for the hills was first approved 11 June 1930, and a note on the file states that they take their name from the creek. J.W. Spencer began as an assistant to Robert Bell in 1874 and left the Geological Survey in 1890: the index to the Geological Survey of Canada reports from 1885 to 1906 contain a number of references to his work, although his entry is followed by one for J.R. Spencer as well as John Spencer and Miles Spencer of the Hudson's Bay Company. Apparently, a Mr. Spencer came to the area with the McDougalls in 1873, and was subsequently afflicted with snow blindness; however, it is not clear from which Spencer the creek takes its name. Both Spencer Hills and Spencer Creek were named by Mr. A.H. Whitcher, who was the Secretary of the Geographic Board of Canada in 1897. The names appear first on Palliser's map of 1865, although the area was surveyed in 1884 by Fawcett.

Spring Coulee (hamlet)
82 H/6 - Raley
28-4-23-W4
49°20′N 113°03′W
Approximately 45 km south-west of Lethbridge.

A post office was opened here 1 May 1902 and took its name from the nearby coulee which contained numerous springs. The original site centred on a large spring in a coulee. The original coulee is now known as "Pinepound Creek."

Spring Creek (creek)
82 P/1 - Finnegan
18-25-15-W4
51°08′N 112°06′W
Flows north into Red Deer River, approximately 55 km south-east of Drumheller.

The precise origin for the name of this feature is unknown.

Spring Hill (hill)
82 I/16 - Bassano
21-17-W4
50°46′N 112°16′W
Approximately 135 km south-east of Calgary.

The name reflects the spring located on this hill.

Spring Hill Canal (canal)
82 I/9 - Cassils
16-8-20-16-W4
50°41′N 112°11′W
Runs east-west across the Trans-Canada highway to Lathom, approximately 120 km north-east of Lethbridge.

Named for its proximity to Spring Hill. (see Spring Hill)

* Spring Point (former locality)
82 H/12 - Brocket
10-9-29-W4
49°43′N 113°51′W
Approximately 76 km west of Lethbridge.

A post office was opened here 1 September 1904 with the descriptive name that refers to the large number of springs found in the area. The post office closed 28 February 1950.

Springbank Creek (creek)
82 O/1 - Calgary
11-24-3-W5
51°02′N 114°19′W

---

*denotes rescinded name or former locality.

Flows south-east into Elbow River, approximately 18 km west of Calgary.

The descriptive name for this creek was first applied to the municipal district in 1918. It was first given as a school name circa 1887-89 because of the numerous springs breaking out in the sides of lesser coulees all over the district. Most of the early settlers located near the springs.

Springhill Creek (creek)

82 I/5 - Nanton
7-16-28-W4
50°20′N 113°51′W
Flows north-east into Nanton Creek, approximately 68 km south of Calgary.

The precise origin for the name of this feature is unknown, but it may be descriptive.

* Springridge (former locality)

82 H/5 - Pincher Creek
12-6-28-W4
49°27′N 113°39′W
Approximately 64 km west south-west of Lethbridge.

The descriptive name for the post office which was opened 1 September 1909 and closed 30 July 1946 was chosen because it was located on a ridge with many springs.

Spruce Coulee Reservoir (reservoir)

72 E/9 - Elkwater Lake
26-8-2-W4
49°41′N 110°11′W
Approximately 50 km south-west of Medicine Hat.

This is a descriptive name and refers to the large stand of spruce trees that grows along the shores of the reservoir. The Prairie

Farm Rehabilitation Administration built a dam in Spruce Coulee in the 1950s.

Spy Hill (hill)

82 O/1 - Calgary
24,25-25-3-W5
51°09′N 114°17′W
Approximately 18 km north-west of Calgary.

The descriptive name for this hill refers to its height, making it an excellent place for the early natives to place a scout. According to tradition, this spot was used for signalling purposes. Apparently, there are three other places in the district unofficially called Spy Hill, one opposite the Nose, one between Coalbanks and Rocky Coulee and one north of the Red Deer River.

Stafford Lake (lake)

72 L/12 - Brooks
4-19-14-W4
50°35′N 111°53′W
Approximately 105 km north-west of Medicine Hat.

This lake is likely named after Norman Stafford, an early homesteader to this area. The Stafford family had eight children, and they all came to the district in 1911. Norman Stafford was described by old timers of the area as a good sport, a helpful neighbour, and a leader in the "Sheep Wars" of 1919. The new irrigation district attracted many settlers like the Staffords who moved to Duchess in 1924.

Stafford Reservoir (reservoir)

82 H/9 - Chin Coulee
6-9-18-W4
From 49°44′25″N 112°21′20″W
to 49°41′00″N 112°21′20″W
Approximately 27 km east of Lethbridge.

This reservoir was named for William Stafford, who was a mine superintendent for the North Western Coal and Naviga-

tion Company and a prominent citizen of early Lethbridge. The natural elongated depression was originally known as "Stafford Channel." This was later changed to Stafford Reservoir when the area was flooded to form the reservoir.

Stand Off (hamlet)

82 H/6 - Raley
21-6-25-W4
49°28′N 113°19′W
Approximately 43 km south-west of Lethbridge.

The name of this hamlet is derived from an incident that involved a confrontation between American authorities and whisky traders. In 1871, a group of whisky traders, Joe Kipp and Charlie Thomas or John Wren, "Dutch" Fred Wachter, W. McLean, Mr. Juneau, and John "Liver-Eating" Johnson, among others, were trailed into Canada by a United States marshall. Their possession of whisky was against a U.S. law forbidding it in the Indian territory of northern Montana. When Marshall Herd of Jarding overtook them, where the Benton Trail crossed the Milk River, the traders successfully argued that they were in Canada and therefore, the Marshall was out of his jurisdiction, and had no authority. When the traders arrived at their destination (the junction of the Belly and Waterton rivers) they named the fort they built "Fort Stand Off" in honour of the fact that they had successfully repelled the law. The name has survived through history because the North West Mounted Police established a post on "Dutch" Fred Wachter's land under that name in 1882.

Standard (village)

82 P/2 - Hussar
3-25-22-W4
51°07′N 112°59′W
Approximately 43 km south south-west of Drumheller.

---

*denotes rescinded name or former locality.

Standard was originally a Danish settlement that began in 1909. The Canadian Pacific Railway reserved 8498.7 hectares (21,000 acres) of land for this purpose, and in 1910, the first settlers began to arrive, from Iowa, North Dakota, and some directly from Denmark. The first was likely Jens Rasmussen, who arrived in the spring of 1910 from Elk Horn, Iowa. The settlement was first named "Dana," or "Danaview," by Mr. Rasmussen; however, there was already a stop by that name on the C.P.R. line in Saskatchewan. The name Standard was therefore suggested, possibly after the flag of Denmark, which was the oldest of the European Standards, dating back to the thirteenth century.

Starlight (locality)

82 J/16 - Priddis
23-2-W5
50°58'N 114°10'W
Approximately 15 km west south-west of Calgary.

This village is located within the Sarcee Indian Reserve. Its precise origin is not known but may be descriptive.

Stavely (town)

82 I/4 - Claresholm
8-14-27-W4
50°10'N 113°38'W
Approximately 78 km north-west of Lethbridge.

This town was named after Alexander Staveley Hill, Q.C., M.P., Judge Advocate of the Fleet, who was the first chairman, owner and founder of the Oxley Ranching Company. This English-owned company leased a vast tract of land in this area between 1880 and 1900. Established in 1882, Hill named the ranch after his residence, Oxley Manor, Wolverhampton, England. The town of Stavely was also originally named "Oxley," but was changed in honour of Hill. When the settlement

became a town in 1912, the second "e" was dropped from official records of the community.

Steveville (locality)

72 L/13 - Wardlow
4-22-12-W4
50°50'N 111°37'W
Approximately 108 km north-west of Medicine Hat.

Formerly the name of the Canadian National Railway station, this locality was named for Stephen (Steve) Hall (d. 1937), one-time postmaster. He and his wife came from Ontario between 1908 and 1909, and homesteaded on the site of the future locality. They operated a store, post office and ferry as well as a stopping place that became noted for its excellent service to all travellers to and from Brooks.

Stewart (railway point)

82 H/10 - Lethbridge
13-8-21-W4
49°39'N 112°44'W
Approximately 5 km south-east of Lethbridge.

This railway point was named for the Honourable Charles Stewart (1868-1946), Liberal Premier of Alberta from 1917 through 1921. Originally a farmer in the Killam area, Stewart was first elected to represent the riding of Sedgewick in the Legislative Assembly in 1909 where he represented the riding until 1922. Stewart held several cabinet positions until the defeat of the Liberals by the United Farmers of Alberta in the 1921 election. He resigned from provincial politics in 1922 to pursue a career in federal politics which lasted until 1935. He was elected to the House of Commons for Argenteuil, Quebec in a by-election in 1922. In 1925, he was elected to represent Edmonton West and was re-elected in 1926 and 1930 although he was defeated in the 1935

election. In 1936 Stewart was appointed chairman of the International Joint Commission.

Stewart Depression (hollow)

72 L/10 - Easy Coulee
18-7,8-W4
50°32'N 110°57'W
Approximately 55 km north-west of Medicine Hat.

The precise origin for the name of this feature is unknown.

Stirling (village)

82 H/7 - Raymond
29-6-19-W4
49°30'N 112°31'W
Approximately 30 km south-east of Lethbridge.

This village was incorporated in 1901 and was named for John A. Stirling, Managing Director of Trusts, Executors and Securities Corporation based in London, England. This company had large holdings in the Alberta Railway and Coal Company and built a narrow gauge line from Lethbridge to Great Falls, Montana. When the Canadian Pacific Railway bought the Alberta Railway and Irrigation Company rail line, Stirling was made the junction point for branch lines to Cardston and Foremost. However, the lack of space in the townsite caused by a nearby coulee forced the actual junction to be made a mile north in what later became known as Maybutt.

Stirling Lake (lake)

82 H/10 - Lethbridge
31-6-19-W4
From 49°31'02"N 112°32'20"W
to 49°32'03"N 112°34'35"W
Approximately 28 km south-east of Lethbridge.

(see Stirling)

Stobart (locality)

82 I/14 - Gleichen
28-22-23-W4
50°54′N 113°08′W
Approximately 55 km east of Calgary.

This locality was named by the Canadian Pacific Railway in 1906 after F.W. Stobart and Company who were early Winnipeg traders and merchants. (see Bartstow)

Stobart Lake (lake)

82 I/14 - Gleichen
31-22-23-W4
50°55′N 113°11′W
Approximately 51 km east of Calgary.

(see Stobart)

Stone Plain (plain)

82 J/16 - Priddis
23-23-2-W5
50°59′N 114°11′W
Approximately 3 km west of Calgary, within Camp Sarcee Military Reserve.

The precise origin for the name of this feature is unknown but it is likely descriptive.

Stonepile Hill (hill)

72 M/5 - Sunnynook
22-27-12-W4
51°19′N 111°36′W
Approximately 85 km east of Drumheller.

The name for this hill is likely descriptive.

Stoppington (locality)

72 M/6 - Plover Lake
4-29-10-W4
51°27′N 111°21′W
Approximately 94 km east of Drumheller.

_____
*denotes rescinded name or former locality.

The post office was named 1 February 1910 after Louisa E. Stopp, the original postmistress. The post office closed 31 March 1931.

Stornham (station)

72 E/15 - Seven Persons
35-10-8-W4
49°52′N 110°59′W
Approximately 25 km south-west of Medicine Hat.

This Canadian Pacific Railway station was named after Stornham Castle, England.

Stornham Coulee (creek)

72 E/15 - Seven Persons
29-10-7-W4
49°51′N 110°55′W
Approximately 25 km south-west of Medicine Hat.

(see Stornham)

* **Stowe** (former locality)

82 H/12 - Brocket
31-8-26-W4
49°41′N 113°30′W
Approximately 49 km west of Lethbridge.

This former Canadian Pacific Railway station which was established in the early 1900s was possibly named for Harriet Beecher Stowe, the author of *Uncle Tom's Cabin* . This 1850s novel, which presented the evils of a slave-based economy, has been described as the book that started the American Civil War.

Strangmuir (locality)

82 I/14 - Gleichen
23-22-25-W4
50°53′N 113°22′W
Approximately 50 km east south-east of Calgary.

Named for the residence of Major-General Thomas Bland Strange (1831-1925), best known in Canada for his involvement in

putting down the 1885 North West Rebellion. Strange commanded the Alberta Field Force and was in command during the engagement at Frenchman's Butte. Major-General Strange's residence, the Mansion Strangmuir, was located on the Military Colonization Company Ranch, the first corporate farm in the area west of the Blackfoot Indian Reserve #146. Strange founded the ranch and sat on its Board of Directors from 1881 to 1887. The name Strangmuir is a combination of the Major-General's name and the word "muir," which is the Scottish word for moor. The prairies of southern Alberta, believed to be useful only as rangeland for horses and cattle, possibly reminded Strange of the moors of northern England and southern Scotland. Strange returned to England in 1889, and lived there until his death.

Another source regarding the origin of the name suggests that the Major-General's son, Alex W. Strange, sent for a wife from England, namely a Miss Muir. Before she was able to take the trip, however, she died of consumption. A conjunction of the two names emerged. Alex W. Strange was the first postmaster of Strangmuir, which was established 1 November 1889.

Strathmore (town)

82 P/3 - Strathmore
14-24-25-W4
51°03′N 113°23′W
Approximately 45 km east of Calgary.

This Canadian Pacific Railway station was established in 1884 and was named after Claude Bowes-Lyon, 13th Earl of Strathmore (1824-1904). His descendent became Governor-General of Canada in 1941 on the death of John Buchan, Lord Tweedsmuir. Earl Bowes-Lyon was the grandfather of Queen Elizabeth (b. 1902), the mother of Queen Elizabeth II.

Strawberry Lake (lake)
82 H/5 - Pincher Creek
5-4-27-W4
49°16′N 113°36′W
Approximately 73 km south-west of
Lethbridge.

The precise origin for the name of this lake
is unknown.

Suds Lake (lake)
82 H/8 - Warner
N-27-5-18-W4
49°25′N 112°20′W
Approximately 42 km south-east of
Lethbridge.

The precise origin for the name of this
feature is unknown. The name was officially approved 12 December 1939.

Suffield (hamlet)
72 L/3 - Suffield
34-14-9-W4
50°12′N 111°10′W
Approximately 35 km north-west of
Medicine Hat.

Named after Charles Harbord, 5th Baron
Suffield (1830-1914). He married Cecelia
Annetta, sister of Edward, 1st Lord
Revelstoke, who assisted in financing the
Canadian Pacific Railway, in 1854. This site
is home to the Defence Research Board,
which cost millions of dollars and is in
operation at Suffield for studies of biologi-
cal warfare. A large area of land is in the
protected area, which is also used as a
military training ground.

Suiste Creek (creek)
72 E/8 - Thelma Creek
3-6-3-W4
49°27′N 110°19′W
Flows east into Lodge Creek, approximately 68 km south-east of Medicine Hat.

Named after Al Suiste, a round-up cook
from Montana who lived in the area until
1912, when he moved back to the United
States. Suiste was best known for the great
variety of pies that he baked for the
cowhands. One longtime resident of the
area referred to this feature as "Greasewood
Coulee," describing the bushes that grow
along the banks of the feature. Often
confused with sage bushes, the leaves of
these plants have a greasy feel to them.

Summerview (locality)
82 H/12 - Brocket
21-7-29-W4
49°35′N 113°53′W
Approximately 80 km west of Lethbridge.

The descriptive name was chosen for the
post office, established 1 April 1904,
because this locale enjoys warm southern
exposure at the southern end of the
Porcupine Hills. The post office was closed
11 July 1933.

Sundial Butte (butte)
82 I/2 - Travers
13-21-W4
50°07′N 112°45′W
Approximately 45 km north of Lethbridge.

The name for this butte is descriptive and
refers to a cairn, made from rocks, and what
appear to be the remains of a primitive
sundial, also made from rocks, located on
top of this hill. Circles and lines radiate
from the cairn in all directions. In
Blackfoot, this feature is known as *onoka-
katzi*, and is regarded with much reverence
by the natives of this area.

Sunnydale (locality)
72 M/2 - Cappon
36-25-5-W4
51°11′N 110°35′W
Approximately 132 km north of Medicine
Hat.

The original post office which opened in
1911 was descriptively named due to its
location at a protected position in the
valley. The post office has been closed since
29 September 1962. It was formerly known
as "Kenamul."

Sunnynook (hamlet)
72 M/5 - Sunnynook
8-27-12-W4
51°17′N 111°40′W
Approximately 75 km east south-east of
Drumheller.

The name is descriptive of the long sunny
days of Alberta summers, and was adopted
by the Canadian National Railway at the
request of the local residents. The post
office opened here 1 April 1911.

Swanson Creek (creek)
82 O/7 - Wildcat Hills
18-28-5-W5
51°24′N 114°41′W
Flows north into Dogpound Creek,
approximately 55 km north-west of
Calgary.

Named after Paul H. Swanson, born 27
January 1892, at Morril, Nebraska, who
came to Alberta 1 March 1911. He was in
the Canadian Expeditionary Force for 42
months but he resided in the Cochrane
district after 1919.

Swanson Hills (hill)
82 O/7 - Wildcat Hills
28-5-W5
51°22′N 114°42′W
Approximately 55 km north-west of
Calgary.

(see Swanson Creek)

* **Sweet Valley** (former post office)

82 I/2 - Travers
27-15-19-4
50°15′N 112°33′W
Approximately 65 km north-east of
Lethbridge.

The name for this post office described the
surrounding area. The name was later
changed to Travers. (see Travers)

Taber (town)

82 H/16 - Taber
5-10-16-W4
49°47′N 112°08′W
Approximately 48 km east of Lethbridge.

There are many histories which offer the beginnings of the town bearing the name Taber. One of these is that the first part of the word "tabernacle" was used out of consideration for Mormon settlers in the vicinity, and the next Canadian Pacific Railway station was named Elcan ("nacle" spelled backwards). The second origin says the townsite plan was named after Mount Tabor, near the Sea of Galilee. And the third origin has it that the name came from a visiting Senator Tabor of Colorado whose spelling was changed when the town was incorporated in 1907. The final version relates that the town was named after a C.P.R. official.

Taber Lake (lake)

82 H/16 - Taber
10-10-16-W4
49°48′N 112°05′W
Approximately 53 km east of Lethbridge.

(see Taber)

Taber Provincial Park (provincial park)

82 H/16 - Taber
7-10-16-W4
49°49′N 112°10′W
Approximately 48 km east of Lethbridge.

This provincial park was established by Order-in-council, 111/73, and contains 50.73 hectares (125.35 acres). (see Taber)

Table Butte (butte)

82 I/4 - Claresholm
NE-8-14-28-W4
50°09′44″N 113°46′40″W

Approximately 85 km north-west of Lethbridge.

The name is descriptive of the butte's flat-topped appearance, apparently the result of glacial action which scoured the butte. It formed one wing of a well-used buffalo jump at Boneyard Coulee.

Tanner Butte (butte)

82 G/9 - Blairmore
34-8-1-W5
49°41′25″N 114°03′00″W
Approximately 87 km west of Lethbridge.

This feature was named after Sam Tanner who came from Utah in 1902 with about 300 head of cattle. He took out a homestead and designed the school which was named after him. He returned to the United States circa 1913 because the open range was beginning to be homesteaded.

* Tapscott (former post office)

82 P/5 - Irricana
32-29-25-4
51°30′N 113°30′W
Approximately 65 km north-east of Calgary.

(see Acme)

Taylor (railway point)

82 P/7 - Drumheller
33-27-20-W4
51°21′N 112°46′W
Approximately 14 km south of Drumheller.

Mr. J.E. Taylor, after whom this former railway station which now serves as a siding was named, was an early farmer who owned a large amount of land in the area. He built a large granary on top of a steep hill, with a large pipe running down to a boxcar sitting on the railway tracks below.

T~U~V

Taylorville (locality)

82 H/3 - Cardston
15-1-24-W4
49°02′N 113°06′W
Approximately 75 km south-west of Lethbridge.

This one-time village, established in 1900 was named for James H. Taylor, one of three brothers, two of whom were among the first settlers in the area. He later became the first postmaster.

Tempest (locality)

82 H/10 - Lethbridge
21-9-19-W4
49°45′N 112°32′W
Approximately 19 km east of Lethbridge.

The post office here was established 16 April 1913 and was named after Marie Tempest, an English opera singer. The post office closed 13 November 1916.

Tennessee Creek (creek)

82 H/12 - Brocket
25-7-30-W4
49°35′N 113°57′W
Flows south into Oldman River, approximately 87 km west of Lethbridge.

This feature was named after a settler nicknamed "Tennessee" who built a house in the vicinity of the creek in 1876.

* Tennion (former locality)

82 H/15 - Picture Butte
31-11-19-W4
49°58′N 112°35′W
Approximately 30 km north-east of Lethbridge.

---

*denotes rescinded name or former locality.

The precise origin of the name of this former Canadian Pacific Railway station is unknown.

* Terrace (former railway point)
72 L/4 - Hays
29-13-12-W4
50°07′N 111°36′W
Approximately 65 km west of Medicine Hat.

(see Cecil)

Thelma (post office)
72 E/9 - Elkwater Lake
20-7-2-W4
49°34′N 110°15′W
Approximately 55 km south-east of Medicine Hat.

A post office was established here in 1911. The precise origin for the name of this feature is unknown.

Thelma Creek (creek)
72 E/8 - Thelma
22-6-3-W4
49°29′N 110°20′W
Flows south into Lodge Creek, approximately 66 km south-east of Medicine Hat.

The precise origin for the name of this feature is unknown.

Thigh Hills (hill)
82 I/6 - Vulcan
24-16-24-W4
50°21′N 113°11′W
Approximately 75 km north north-west of Lethbridge.

The name is a translation of the descriptive native name *motuksina*, which in Blackfoot means "thigh flesh" or *ohsokinascu* meaning "man's thigh," from the shape of the hill.

Third Lake (lake)
82 I/13 - Dalemead
4-21-27-W4
50°45′N 113°41′W
Approximately 33 km south south-east of Calgary.

The name for this feature is descriptive since the lake is the third and largest in a chain of lakes southeast of the confluence of the Highwood and Bow rivers. The chain begins with Blizzard Lake.

Thirty Mile Coulee (creek)
72 E/15 - Seven Persons
1-10-8-W4
49°48′N 110°57′W
Approximately 33 km south-west of Medicine Hat.

Probably a descriptive name, as it is located approximately 48 km (30 miles) above the mouth of Seven Persons Creek.

Thumb Hill (hill)
82 P/8 - Dorothy
SE-10-28-17-W4
51°22′40″N 112°18′30″W
Approximately 40 km south-east of Drumheller.

The hill is "thumb" of the Hand Hills, while the fingers are the Verdant Valley Hill, Mother's Mountain, McDonald Ridge, and Don Benedict Ridge. It may have been named by the ranching Kelly brothers before 1905, when the Thumb Hill Ranch was established by W.M. Parslow and John Hamilton.

Tide Lake (lake)
72 L/11 - Jenner
29-18,19-10-W4
50°33′N 111°20′W
Approximately 73 km north-west of Medicine Hat.

During the early part of the century, this lake was intermittent, with the water drying up in some years and appearing in others. The name is probably descriptive, likening the action of the lake to the ebb and flow of tides.

Tillebrook-Trans-Canada Provincial Park
(provincial park)
72 L/12 - Brooks
18-14-W4
50°31′N 111°46′W
Approximately 95 km north-east of Medicine Hat.

The community of Tilley was named after Sir Samuel L. Tilley, Federal Minister of Finance, and the town of Brooks was named after N.E. Brooks, Divisional Engineer for Canadian Pacific Railway. This park is located between the two communities so the name acknowledges both. The Trans-Canada Highway borders the park on the north-east, and this name is also incorporated. The 139.15 hectare (343.83 acres) park was established by Order-in-council 969/77.

Tilley (village)
72 L/5 - Tilley
19-17-12-W4
50°27′N 111°39′W
Approximately 83 km north-west of Medicine Hat.

A Canadian Pacific Railway station was established here in 1894 and grew and the resulting village was named after Sir Samuel Leonard Tilley (1818-1896), one of the first Fathers of Confederation. He entered politics in 1850 and left provincial politics in 1867. Sir Samuel then went on to serve as Minister of Customs and as Minister of Finance, and finally served as Lieutenant-Governor of New Brunswick. Another source suggests that the village was not named after Sir Samuel, but rather after his brother, Sir Malcolm Tilley, who was a

C.P.R. Director. This source suggests that it was common practice for the C.P.R. to name its towns and sidings after directors and various employees of the company.

Tilley Slough (marsh)

72 L/6 - Alderson
29-17,18-12-W4
50°28'N 111°37'W
Approximately 80 km north-west of Medicine Hat.

(see Tilley)

* **Tilley Station** (former post office)

72 L/5 - Tilley
19-17-12-W4
50°27'N 111°39'W
Approximately 80 km north-west of Medicine Hat.

The Canadian Pacific Railway station was established here in 1884. The post office operated from 1 October 1910 through 30 September 1918 under this name until it was changed to simply Tilley. (see Tilley)

Timber Coulee (coulee)

82 J/1 - Langford Creek
22-14-1-W5
50°11'N 114°04'W
An east-west trending coulee running south into Willow Creek, approximately 85 km south of Calgary.

The precise origin for the name of this feature is unknown but the name may be descriptive of the treed area around the coulee.

Timber Creek (creek)

72 E/7 - Manyberries
28-5-6-W4
49°25'N 110°47'W

Flows south-west into Irrigation Creek, approximately 68 km south of Medicine Hat.

A number of sawmills were supplied by a large stand of timber in the vicinity of this creek during the early part of this century. The name is, therefore, likely descriptive.

Timber Creek (creek)

82 J/1 - Langford Creek
35-14-3-W5
50°13'N 114°18'W
Flows south into Willow Creek, approximately 85 km south of Calgary.

This creek runs through Timber Coulee. (see Timber Coulee)

Timko Lake (Bantry Reservoir)

(lake and reservoir)
72 L/5 - Tilley
33-17-13-W4
50°28'N 111°44'W
Approximately 88 km north-west of Medicine Hat.

Named for the two brothers, Andrew and George Timko, who came to Canada from Slovakia and eventually settled in the Eastern Irrigation District in the spring of 1929. The brothers farmed adjoining quarter sections two km south of this feature.

Togo Lake (lake)

72 M/6 - Plover Lake
6-29-8-W4
51°28'N 111°08'W
Approximately 108 km east of Drumheller.

The precise origin for the name of this feature is unknown.

Tongue Creek (creek)

82 I/12 - High River
30-19-28-W4
50°38'N 113°51'W
Approximately 40 km south of Calgary.

There are several competing possibilities for the origin of the name of this creek. Blackfoot legend states that Old Man (see Oldman River) hunted a band of elk, killing all but one doe. He hung the tongues on a pole so they could dry. He then ran a race with a wolf who fooled him into leaving his camp, and the rest of the wolves ate all of his meat while a mouse ran up the pole and ate the tongues. This camp along the creek became known to the Blackfoot as *matsin-awastam*, translating to "tongue." Another version was that an Indian hunter killed a buffalo but could not carry it away himself. So the hunter then cut the tongue and put it on a pole to mark the spot so others could come and take the remaining carcass. A third possible origin is that a great number of wagon tongues were broken at that point in the Macleod Trail before the bridge was built.

Tothill (locality)

72 E/9 - Elkwater Lake
23-9-4-W4
49°44'N 110°27'W
Approximately 30 km south-east of Medicine Hat.

Named after Alfred Tothill, the first postmaster, when this post office was established 1 January 1924. It closed 30 October 1959.

Tough Creek (creek)

82 H/4 - Waterton Lakes
1-27-W4
49°05'N 113°31'W
Flows north-east into Lee Creek, approximately 83 km south south-west of Lethbridge.

The precise origin of the name is unknown but it is likely descriptive.

* **Towes** (former locality)

82 I/15 - Cluny
21-20-W4
50°48'N 112°46'W

Approximately 110 km east south-east of Calgary.

A former Canadian Pacific Railway station from 1912 to 1915, the precise origin for the name of this feature is unknown.

Towers Creek (creek)

82 O/2 - Jumpingpound Creek
20-25-4-W5
51°09′N 114°31′W
Flows north into Bighill Creek, approximately 35 km west north-west of Calgary.

This creek was named after the Towers Family, Francis and Elizabeth Glover, the first homesteaders in the area. Francis was born in Birmingham, England and Elizabeth was from Guernsey, in the Channel Islands off the coast of France. Francis was employed by the Canadian Pacific Railway building the main line.

Towers Ridge (ridge)

82 O/1 - Calgary
25-4-W5
51°06′N 114°28′W
Approximately 25 km west of Calgary.

(see Towers Creek)

Trail Coulee (coulee)

82 J/1 - Langford Creek
12-1-W5
50°02′N 114°03′W
Runs south-west into Trout Creek, approximately 96 km west north-west of Lethbridge.

The precise origin for the name of this feature is unknown.

Traung Lake (lake)

72 M/5 - Sunnynook
28-14-W4
51°23′N 111°53′W
Approximately 57 km east of Drumheller.

The precise origin for the name of this feature is unknown.

Travers (hamlet)

82 I/2 - Travers
9-15-19-W4
50°15′N 112°33′W
Approximately 60 km north of Lethbridge.

The precise origin for the name of this feature is unknown. The post office that opened 1 February 1915 was previously known as "Sweet Valley."

Travers Reservoir (reservoir)

82 I/2 - Travers
31-14,15-21,22-W4
50°12′N 112°51′W
Approximately 55 km north of Lethbridge.

(see Travers)

Trefoil (locality)

82 P/1 - Finnegan
26-16-W4
51°12′N 112°11′W
Approximately 143 km east north-east of Calgary.

This locality was named after the plant of the genus trifolium, having triple or trifoliate leaves. It is also another word for clover.

Trivett Ridge (ridge)

82 H/4 - Waterton Lakes
7-1-28-W4
49°01′30″N 113°43′35″W
Approximately 85 km south-west of Lethbridge.

This ridge was named by the Government of Alberta and the Canadian Permanent Committee on Geographical Names to commemorate the 100th anniversary of the arrival of the Reverend Samuel Trivett, Anglican Missionary, at the Blood Indian Reserve #148.

Trout Creek (creek)

82 H/13 - Granum
5-12-27-W4
49°58′N 113°40′W
Flows east into Willow Creek, approximately 67 km north-west of Lethbridge.

The name for this stream was officially approved in May 1938 and is likely descriptive.

Trout Creek Ridge (ridge)

82 J/1 - Langford Creek
13-1-W5
50°05′N 114°05′W
Approximately 100 km south of Calgary.

The precise origin for the name of this feature is unknown.

Tudor (locality)

82 P/3 - Strathmore
33-25-23-W4
51°10′N 113°09′W
Approximately 65 km east north-east of Calgary.

The name for this post office which operated from 1 February 1912 through 30 June 1944 commemorates the Royal House of Tudor in England. This house included the English sovereigns from Henry VII to Elizabeth I.

Turin (hamlet)

82 H/15 - Picture Butte
4-12-19-W4
49°58′N 112°31′W
Approximately 35 km north-east of Lethbridge.

This hamlet was named in 1910 after an imported Percheron stallion owned by a syndicate of farmers in the district. The post office opened 1 November 1910.

Turnbull Creek (creek)

82 O/7 - Wildcat Hills
17-29-6-W5
51°28'N 114°48'W
Flows south into Grease Creek, approximately 68 km north-west of Calgary.

This creek was named after one of the original settlers in the district who owned a sawmill on the creek.

Turner (railway point)

82 O/1 - Calgary
23-1-W5
50°59'N 114°05'W
Within the city limits of Calgary.

(see Turner Valley)

Turner Valley (town)

82 J/9 - Turner Valley
12-20-3-W5
50°40'N 114°17'W
Approximately 40 km south south-west of Calgary.

This town was named after Robert and James Turner, early settlers who homesteaded in the north end of the valley in 1886. They had come from Scotland and had settled on the north fork of Sheep Creek at the head of the long valley now named for them. There is a railway point to the north also named for them.

Turner Valley (valley)

82 J/9 - Turner Valley
23-20-3-W5
50°43'N 114°19'W
Approximately 40 km south south-west of Calgary.

(see Turner Valley)

Twelve Mile Coulee (coulee)

72 L/4 - Hays
2-14,15-12,13-W4
50°08'N 111°40'W
Runs south into Bow River, approximately 65 km west north-west of Medicine Hat.

(see Twelve Mile Creek)

Twelve Mile Creek (creek)

72 L/4 - Hays
13-15-13-W4
50°12'N 111°37'W
Flows south into Bow River, approximately 68 km west north-west of Medicine Hat.

This creek was named by the Military Colonization Company, circa 1885-86, because the creek was 19.3 km (12 miles) down river from their headquarters.

Twin Butte (hamlet)

82 H/5 - Pincher Creek
4-4-29-W4
49°16'N 113°51'W
Approximately 90 km south-west of Lethbridge.

The name refers to two prominent hills located in close proximity to each other and was suggested by H.C. Glasgow and A.E. Wyckoff at a 28 January 1904 meeting held at Wesley Shannon's home for the purpose of organizing a school district. A post office was established near here 1 June 1905 and later moved to its present location.

Twin Lakes (lake)

82 P/4 - Dalroy
10-26-28-W4
51°12'N 113°50'W
Approximately 23 km north-east of Calgary.

This is actually one lake bisected by a highway that crosses it.

Twin Peaks (peak)

72 L/7 - Watching Hill
32-16-5-W4
50°23'N 110°39'W
Approximately 35 km north of Medicine Hat.

The name is likely descriptive, as the feature has two peaks.

* **Twin River** (former locality)

82 H/2 - Shanks Lake
10-1-20-W4
49°02'N 112°36'W
Approximately 70 km south-east of Lethbridge.

This former locality was originally called Hacke post office until 1921. William Hacke came from North Dakota with his family to homestead in 1912, and was the first postmaster. Annie Robinson gave the new post office a descriptive name in 1922, after the north and south branches of the Milk River between which it is located. The rivers are very similar in shape, and flow together, therefore the local people felt the name to be an appropriately descriptive one.

Two Bar Lake (lake)

82 P/7 - Drumheller
2-27-19-W4
51°17'N 112°34'W
Approximately 107 km east north-east of Calgary.

Possibly named after a ranch although the precise origin is unknown. According to a 1922 sectional map the name should read Two Bar, but has also appeared as "Twobar."

Two Guns (locality)

82 J/16 - Priddis
23-2-W5
50°57'N 114°10'W

---

*denotes rescinded name or former locality.

Approximately 10 km south-west of Calgary.

This feature is a village located on the Sarcee Indian Reserve. The origin for the name is unknown.

Tyler's Hill (hill)

72 M/1 - Acadia Valley
1,2-24-1-W4
51°00′30″N 110°01′40″W
Approximately 118 km north of Medicine Hat.

This hill was named after George Tyler, an early settler in the Empress area. He was known to have owned the land on which the hill was located prior to 1919. Mr. Tyler died in 1982.

Tyrrell Lake (lake)

82 H/8 - Warner
19-5-17-W4
49°23′N 112°16′W
Approximately 49 km south-east of Lethbridge.

This lake was named for J.B. Tyrrell, assistant to Dr. G.M. Dawson of the Geological Survey, who participated in the surveys of the Rocky Mountains in 1883. The name was officially approved 12 December 1939.

Ueland Reservoir (reservoir)

82 I/10 - Queenstown
10-19-21-W4
50°36′N 112°50′W
Approximately 95 km south-east of Calgary.

The origin for the name of this reservoir is unknown.

Vale (settlement)

72 L/1 - Many Island Lake
6-15-3-W4
50°13′N 110°24′W
Approximately 30 km north-east of Medicine Hat.

The post office was established in 1913, although this settlement is also a municipal district established in 1913, and named after Vale, Oregon. The postmaster, John Evers, was from this American city. The settlement name was rescinded in 1974 and then reinstated in 1977.

Van Cleeve Coulee (coulee)

72 E/4 - Coutts
1-13-W4
49°05′N 111°39′W
Approximately 100 km south-east of Lethbridge.

The local name for this feature is "Rocky Coulee" because of the hoodoos located in it. The official name was taken from an early homesteader and horse rancher, Claude Van Cleeve (1882-1964) who came to Alberta from Missouri in 1919 and settled in Taber.

* Van Dyne (former locality)

72 M/1 - Acadia Valley
12-24-3-W4
51°02′N 110°18′W
Approximately 185 km east south-east of Drumheller.

A post office opened here in 1912 and closed in 1930. The precise origin of the name is unknown.

Vaughn Meadows (meadow)

82 H/3 - Cardston
3,10-1-24-W4
49°01′N 113°08′W
Approximately 78 km south-west of Lethbridge.

Named for William Vaughn and family who came to this area in 1889 from the United States, through Immigration Gap. Apparently, William was so taken with the beauty of the meadow of waist-high flowers with the mountains in the background that he and his family decided to stay and settle.

Vauxhall (town)

82 I/1 - Vauxhall
10-31-16-W4
50°04′N 112°07′W
Approximately 68 km north-east of Lethbridge.

This town was named for a district of the city of London, England. The town started as a camp of the Canada Land and Irrigation Company, and eventually expanded. Vauxhall was apparently given its name in an effort to attract overseas capital.

* Verdant Valley (former locality)

82 P/7 - Drumheller
6-29-18-W4
51°27′N 112°31′W
Approximately 115 km north north-east of Calgary.

A post office was established here 1 March 1910 and closed 19 January 1945. The locality was named by Mr. Clark, a homesteader from Ireland, because the name is descriptive of a green valley. *Vert* is the French word for the colour green.

Verdigris Coulee (coulee)

82 H/8 - Warner
9-4-16-W4
49°18′N 112°03′W
Runs north-south between Westin and Verdigris lakes, approximately 62 km south-east of Lethbridge.

Named for a green crystalline substance found along the banks of the coulee. This could perhaps be produced naturally by

---

acid interacting with copper in the soil. The name was officially approved 12 December 1939.

Verdigris Lake (lake)

82 H/1 - Milk River
25-3,4-15,16-W4
49°14′N 112°00′W
Approximately 73 km south-east of Lethbridge.

This feature's name comes from a green crystalline substance found along the banks of the lake. (see Verdigris Coulee)

Verger (locality)

72 L/13 - Wardlow
34-22-15-W4
50°56′N 112°00′W
Approximately 132 km north-west of Medicine Hat.

Named after the church official who serves as sacristan, caretaker, usher and general attendant. This was a railway station north of Brooks.

Vulcan (town)

82 I/6 - Vulcan
5-15-24-W4
50°24′N 113°15′W
Approximately 85 km south south-east of Calgary.

The post office was established here 1 October 1910, and the town was named after the Roman god of fire and metal-working. The streets of this town were once named after mythological beings and heavenly bodies such as Apollo, Juno, Jupiter, Venus, and Neptune, but the names were later changed to numbers.

Wager Coulee (coulee)

82 J/1 - Langford Coulee
12-1-W5
50°01′N 114°02′W
Runs south-east into Trout Creek, approximately 95 km west north-west of Lethbridge.

Named after a homesteader, Weger, who lived in the area circa 1909. The name was misspelled when it became official.

Waiparous Creek (creek)

82 O/7 - Wildcat Hills
6-27-6-W5
51°17′N 114°50′W
Flows south-east into Ghost River, approximately 62 km north-west of Calgary.

The name is a corruption of the Stoney Indian name meaning "Crow (Indian) scalp."

Walsh (hamlet)

72 E/16 - Irvine
35-11-1-W4
49°57′N 110°03′W
Approximately 45 km east of Medicine Hat.

This hamlet was named for North West Mounted Police Superintendent James Morrow Walsh, who in 1875, established Fort Walsh in the Cypress Hills, just east of the Alberta-Saskatchewan boundary. A major at this time, Walsh was dispatched to this area because it was considered extremely volatile due to the arrival of some 5,000 Sioux Indians led by Chief Sitting Bull. The Indians had fled north across the "Medicine Line" (the Canada-U.S. border) following the Battle of Little Big Horn where General Custer and his cavalry were killed. The Sioux returned to the United States in 1881 and Walsh quit the force in 1883. With the onset of the Klondike Gold Rush, James Walsh returned to service in

1897 as the first Superintendent and Commissioner of the Yukon Territory.

Ward Creek (creek)

82 J/1 - Langford Creek
14-13-2-W5
50°05′N 114°10′W
Flows north into South Willow Creek, approximately 100 km south of Calgary.

The creek was named after Alfred Ward, from Virginia, who came to the Happy Valley area in April of 1907. He remained in the area for about three years and then returned to Rochester, Minnesota.

Wardlow (hamlet)

72 L/13 - Wardlow
25-22-12-W4
50°54′N 111°33′W
Approximately 115 km north-west of Medicine Hat.

The two possibilities for the origin of the name Wardlow are as follows:
the first story posits that it was named after a daughter of J.R. Sutherland, through whose ranch the railway runs. The second has it that the locality was centred around a Canadian National Railway station on the Cessford-Steveville line. This station was named Wardlow when it was established in the fall of 1920.

Warner (village)

82 H/8 - Warner
10-4-17-W4
49°17′N 112°12′W
Approximately 60 km south-east of Lethbridge.

This village was named in 1906 for A.L. Warner, a land agent from the United States who, with his partner, O.W. Kerr, signed an agreement in 1906 to work in conjunction with the Alberta Railway and Irrigation Company, a successor to the North Western Coal and Navigation Company, to

settle people on the land adjacent to the railway. This village was originally named "Brunton."

Watching Hill (hill)

72 L/7 - Watching Hill
17-5-W4
50°28′N 110°38′W
Approximately 45 km north of Medicine Hat, within the Canadian Forces Base Suffield area.

The precise origin for the name of this hill is unknown but is likely descriptive of its viewpoint.

Waterton Reservoir (reservoir)

82 H/5 - Pincher Creek
4-28-W4
49°18′N 113°41′W
Approximately 75 km south-west of Lethbridge.

This reservoir, officially named 30 July 1970, takes its name from the lakes. The chain of lakes lying in the main valley of Waterton Lakes National Park consists of four bodies of water connected by a river. Named by Thomas Blakiston of the Palliser Expedition, the lakes commemorate Charles Waterton (1782-1865), a famous English naturalist. He was widely known for his research into the sources of Indian poisons and ornithological work. He expended a large part of his fortune creating a sanctuary for birds.

Waterton River (river)

82 H/11 - Fort Macleod
1-7-25-W4
49°32′N 113°16′W

Flows north-east into Belly River, approximately 36 km south-west of Lethbridge.

This river is named for its source, the Waterton Lakes. (see Waterton Reservoir)

Watkins Slough (marsh)

72 L/1 - Many Island Lake
13-4-W4
50°07'N 110°27'W
Approximately 15 km north-east of Medicine Hat.

This feature was named after the applicant for the water rights, a Mr. Watkins.

Wayne (hamlet)

82 P/7 - Drumheller
7-28-19-W4
51°23'N 112°39'W
Approximately 10 km south-east of Drumheller.

This was a Canadian National Railway station in 1914, while the hamlet was formerly known as "Rosedeer." The precise origin is unknown.

Webber Creek (creek)

82 G/16 - Maycroft
2-10-1-W5
49°48'N 114°02'W
Flows north-west into Heath Creek, approximately 90 km west of Lethbridge.

Two of the first settlers were Mr. and Mrs. Tom Webber. Mr. Webber raised longhorn cattle on what was called the George Celland place. The little stream that flows into Heath Creek was called Webber Creek.

* **Websdale** (former post office)

72 L/11 - Jenner
33-20-9-W4
50°45'N 111°11'W

Approximately 88 km north-west of Medicine Hat.

The post office was named after the first postmaster, A. Websdale. The name was changed to Jenner in 1913. (see Jenner)

Welling (hamlet)

82 H/7 - Raymond
17-6-21-W4
49°28'N 112°47'W
Approximately 24 km south of Lethbridge.

This name was apparently suggested by Elder Taylor at a community meeting held just prior to February 1904 to decide upon a name for the Mormon church then being built. The group unanimously agreed upon the name after Horace Welling who had come to the area in 1902 to farm. Welling was an early pioneer to the area and was involved in the purchase of the locality's first threshing machine, powered by twelve horses.

West Arrowwood Creek (creek)

82 I/14 - Gleichen
9-21-23-W4
50°46'N 113°08'W
Flows north-east into Bow River, approximately 70 km south-east of Calgary.

This creek was named as a tributary to Arrowwood Creek which in turn is a translation of an Indian name. Presumably the Indians obtained wood for arrows on the banks of this stream. (see Arrowwood)

West Carseland (railway point)

82 I/13 - Dalemead
8-22-26-W4
50°51'N 113°34'W
Approximately 37 km south-east of Calgary.

This railway point was named for its proximity to and direction from Carseland. (see Carseland)

West Nose Creek (creek)

82 O/1 - Calgary
14-25-1-W5
51°08'N 114°02'W
Flows south-east into Nose Creek, within the city limits of Calgary.

This feature was named as a tributary to Nose Creek.

(see Nose Creek)

Western Monarch (hamlet)

82 P/8 - Dorothy
21-27-18-W4
51°20'N 112°28'W
Approximately 30 km south-east of Drumheller.

The precise origin for the name of this feature is unknown.

Weston Lake (lake)

82 H/8 - Warner
35-4-17-W4
49°20'N 112°10'W
Approximately 60 km south-east of Lethbridge.

This lake was named for T.C. Weston, who worked for the Geological Survey of Canada. The name was made official 12 December 1939.

* **Wheat Centre** (former locality)

82 I/8 - Scandia
4-16-18-W4
50°19'N 112°25'W
Approximately 100 km north north-east of Lethbridge.

A post office was established here 1 May 1910, and at that time, it had every promise of becoming a wheat centre. The post office closed 30 November 1947.

---

*denotes rescinded name or former locality.

Whey Lake (lake)
82 P/7 - Drumheller
9-27-19-W4
51°18'N 112°37'W
Approximately 20 km south-east of Drumheller.

This lake is very shallow, is saline, and contains many soapholes which give it a milky appearance. It covers about 50 acres, and is dry most of the year; however, the lake bottom is very flat, and when there is a heavy rain, or during spring runoff, the lake can fill completely.

Whiskey Creek (creek)
82 J/9 - Turner Valley
7-19-16-3-W5
50°31'50"N 114°23'40"W
Flows south into Sullivan Creek, approximately 17 km south-west of Turner Valley.

The creek drains Whiskey Ridge where Shorty McLaughlin is reported to have had his still.

Whiskey Gap (locality)
82 H/3 - Cardston
16-1-23-W4
49°02'N 113°02'W
Approximately 73 km south-west of Lethbridge.

Named by American whiskey traders who took advantage of this natural gap in the Milk River Ridge to smuggle liquor to Fort Whoop-Up from Montana during the 1870s and 1880s. The flow of whiskey slowly dwindled over the years with the arrival of the Mounted Police in 1874 although it boomed once again when Alberta imposed prohibition in 1916: this lasted until 1924 when prohibition was lifted. The liquor flow reversed when the United States banned recreational consumption of alcoholic beverages from 1921 through 1931. The name of this locality was changed to "Fareham" for a short time,

through the influence of a local temperance supporter. Local inhabitants were not pleased with the change, and through protestations, finally had the name changed back to the original Whiskey Gap.

White Elk (locality)
82 J/16 - Priddis
23-2-W5
50°58'N 114°11'W
Within the Sarcee Indian Reserve, immediately south-west of Calgary.

The precise origin for the name of this locality is unknown.

White Horse Lake (lake)
72 L/9 - Middle Sand Hills
4-20-4-W4
50°39'50"N 110°29'15"W
Approximately 70 km north north-east of Medicine Hat, within Canadian Forces Base Suffield.

The precise origin for the name of this feature is unknown.

White Rock Coulee (coulee)
72 L/8 - Hilda
18-17-3-W4
Runs west into South Saskatchewan River, approximately 15 km north of Medicine Hat.

The precise origin for the name of this feature is unknown.

Whitla (locality)
72 E/14 - Bow Island
5-11-8-W4
49°52'N 111°03'W
Approximately 33 km south-west of Medicine Hat.

This locality was named for R.J. Whitla, a well-known Winnipeg wholesale merchant who did extensive business with prairie merchants.

Whitla Coulee (creek)
72 E/14 - Bow Island
3-10-8-W4
49°48'N 111°00'W
Flows south-east into Thirty Mile Coulee, approximately 35 km south-west of Medicine Hat.

(see Whitla)

Whitney (locality)
82 H/15 - Picture Butte
18-10-22-W4
49°50'N 112°58'W
Approximately 15 km north-west of Lethbridge.

This locality was probably named for Albert J. Whitney, a pioneer cattleman who arrived in southern Alberta from Ontario in 1881. He acquired a ranch near what would later become Whitney siding.

Wild Horse (port of entry)
72 E/1 - Cripple Creek
4-1-2-W4
49°00'N 110°13'W
Approximately 115 south south-east of Medicine Hat, on the Canada-U.S. border.

This locality was named after "Wild Horse Lake," now Grassy Lake, which, in turn, was named by the Indians for the large herds of wild horses found in the region (see Grassy Lake). A post office operated here from 1 February 1926 through 27 June 1968. It was previously known as "Sage Creek."

Wild Turnip Hill (hill)
82 H/11 - Fort Macleod
18-8-24-W4
49°38'N 113°06'W
Approximately 25 km west of Lethbridge, in the Blood Indian Reserve #148.

The descriptive name for this feature is taken after the Indian bread or prairie turnip (*Psoralea esculenta*), known to the Blackfoot as *mas-etomo*, that grows in abundance on this hill. This edible root was frequently used by the Indians and early explorers as an easily transportable food-stuff.

Wildcat (locality)

82 O/2 - Jumpingpound Creek
16-26-5-W5
51°13′N 114°39′W
Approximately 47 km north-west of Calgary.

Named due to its proximity to the Wildcat Hills. (see Wildcat Hills)

Wildcat Hills (hills)

82 O/7 - Wildcat Hills
26,27-5-W5
51°18′N 114°39′W
Approximately 50 km north-west of Calgary.

The Wildcat Hills were named by Wilhelmina Bell-Irving in 1885, because there were wildcats and wolves in the hills and ridges. The name was officially approved in 1939.

Williams Coulee (coulee)

82 I/5 - Nanton
15,16-16-29-W4
From 50°20′20″N 113°53′00″W
to 50°21′08″N 113°57′30″W
Approximately 75 km south south-east of Calgary.

This feature was named for Orin Cravath Williams and his wife Emma. They arrived in Alberta from Kansas in 1901 to homestead near the coulee.

Willingdon Hill (hill)

82 O/1 - Calgary
24-2-W5
51°02′N 114°12′W

Within the south-west portion of the city of Calgary.

This hill is 1198 m in altitude, and was named in honour of Freeman Freeman-Thomas, Marquis of Willingdon. He was educated at Eton and Cambridge, and spent some time in Australia. He sat in the British House of Commons as a Liberal Member from 1900 to 1910, served as Governor of Bombay from 1910 to 1913, and of Madras from 1919 until 1924. He was Governor-General of Canada from 1926 to 1931. From 1931 through 1936, he served as Viceroy of India after which time he returned to England.

Willow Creek (creek)

82 H/14 - Monarch
12-29-9-25-W4
49°46′N 113°22′W
Flows south-east into Oldman River, approximately 40 km west north-west of Lethbridge.

The name is descriptive of the willow trees on the banks of this creek, and within the general vicinity. The Blackfoot name for this feature is *stiapiskan* which translates to "ghost hound."

Willow Creek (creek)

82 P/7 - Drumheller
7-28-18-W4
51°23′N 112°32′W
Flows south-west into Red Deer River, approximately 13 km south-east of Drumheller.

The descriptive name is taken after the willow trees found on its banks.

Willow Creek (locality)

82 P/7 - Drumheller
12-28-19-W4
51°23′N 112°32′W
Approximately 14 km south-east of Drumheller.

This locality was named for its proximity to Willow Creek. (see Willow Creek) A post office operated here from 1 November 1929 through 17 February 1947.

Willow Creek Provincial Park

(provincial park)
82 I/4 - Claresholm
28-13-28-W4
50°07′N 113°46′W
Approximately 100 km south south-east of Calgary.

This 108.69 hectare (268.6 acre) provincial park was created by Order-in-council 851/76 and is named for its location on the creek whose banks are lined with willow trees. (see Willow Creek)

Willow Island (island)

82 I/14 - Gleichen
34,35-21-25-W4
50°49′N 113°23′W
Approximately 52 km east south-east of Calgary.

The precise origin for the name of this feature is unknown but it is likely descriptive.

Wilson (locality)

82 H/10 - Lethbridge
33-7-20-W4
49°36′N 112°39′W
Approximately 13 km south-east of Lethbridge.

This locality was named for Ernest Henry Wilson (1872-1965), an early pioneer of Lethbridge and comptroller of the Alberta Railway and Irrigation Company until the line was absorbed by the Canadian Pacific Railway. Originally from London, England, Wilson also worked for the Hudson's Bay Company for twelve years in Victoria as a land agent, after working for the A.R. & I.C.

Wilson Coulee (coulee)

82 J/16 - Priddis
21-1-W5
50°45′N 114°01′W
Runs north-east into an unnamed lake,
approximately 20 km south south-east of
Calgary.

This coulee was named for one of the
earliest families who settled in the area.

Winchell Coulee (coulee)

82 O/7 - Wildcat Hills
29-5-W5
51°27′N 114°36′W
Runs north into Stony Creek, approximately 65 km north north-west of Calgary.

This coulee was named after Frank
Winchell, born in 1869 in Trimball,
Wisconsin. He came to the area in 1903.

Winnifred (locality)

72 E/14 - Bow Island
17-11-9-W4
49°54′N 111°12′W
Approximately 40 km south-west of
Medicine Hat.

This once-booming settlement is now a
ghost town, and was previously known as
"Whistle Stop Mile 31." The name
Winnifred was taken from the daughter of
R.J. Whitla (see Whitla), one of the charter
members of the Turkey Track Railroad.
Winnifred's boom years began in 1913 and
lasted only until 1916. By 1960, most
businesses and people had moved away. All
there is left of Winnifred now are the grain
elevators and those who run them.

Wintering Hills (hills)

82 P/2 - Hussar
26-19-W4
51°13′N 112°34′W
Approximately 27 km south of Drumheller.

These hills are located at the south end of
the confluence of the Red Deer and
Rosebud rivers. The spot was selected as
winter quarters by natives of mixed blood
background because of the water, timber
and winter grazing resources found here.
The Blackfoot term for the hills is *kikichep*,
translating to "braced up" hills.

* **Wisdom** (former locality)

72 E/10 - Bulls Head
31-8-5-W4
49°42′N 110°41′W
Approximately 35 km south of Medicine
Hat.

This name expressed the opinion of early
homesteaders in the district who thought
they were wise to settle in this part of the
province. The post office was opened in
June 1913 and closed in March 1960.

Wolf (locality)

82 J/16 - Priddis
23-2-W5
50°57′N 111°10′W
Within the Sarcee Indian Reserve, immediately west south-west of Calgary.

The precise origin for the name of this
locality is unknown.

Wolf Coulee (coulee)

72 L/11 - Jenner
20-11-W4
50°45′N 111°26′W
Approximately 97 km north-west of
Medicine Hat.

This coulee is likely named after the
mammal.

Wolf Island (island)

72 E/13 - Grassy Lake
20-11-14-W4
49°53′N 111°53′W
Approximately 75 km east of Lethbridge.

This island was named for the frequent
sighting of wolves by pioneers of the area.
One story claims that some local cowboys
cornered a wolf in a coulee but it escaped
by swimming across the Oldman River to
this island. Another tale suggests that cattle
put on the island for grazing purposes were
attacked by wolves who, in turn, were shot
by settlers. A third story posits that local
residents named the feature because of the
continuous howling at night, by wolves,
distinguishable from the higher pitched
howl of the coyotes.

Wolf Lake (lake)

82 P/1 - Finnegan
24-17-W4
51°02′N 112°19′W
Approximately 58 km south south-east of
Drumheller.

The precise origin for the name of this
feature is unknown.

Woltan Coulee (creek)

72 E/10 - Bulls Head
14-7-7-W4
49°34′N 110°50′W
Approximately 50 km south-west of
Medicine Hat.

This creek was named for Mr. P. Woltanski,
an early settler in the district who applied
for the water rights for this feature.

Woodhouse (locality)

82 H/13 - Granum
30-11-26-W4
49°57′N 113°32′W
Approximately 57 km north-west of
Lethbridge.

The post office was opened 1 December
1916 and was closed 30 April 1969. A
Canadian Pacific Railway station established here in 1909 was named after W.E.
Woodhouse of Calgary, one-time Superintendent of Motive Power of the Canadian
Pacific Railway.

___

*denotes rescinded name or former locality.

Woodpecker Island (island)

82 H/16 - Taber
18-10-16-W4
49°49′N 112°10′W
Approximately 48 km east north-east of Lethbridge.

This island, located in Oldman River, is called *akka-kima-toskway*, by the Blackfoot which translates to "many woodpeckers," this term is likely descriptive, and likely refers to the one-time abundance of woodpeckers in the vicinity.

Woolchester (locality)

72 E/15 - Seven Persons
12-10-5-W4
49°49′N 110°34′W
Approximately 20 km south of Medicine Hat.

This general area was known for its sheep ranching and Woolchester became its focal point. The post office was established 1 May 1900 and was closed 15 July 1963.

Woolf Coulee (coulee)

82 I/2 - Travers
31-14-21,22-W4
50°12′N 112°52′W
Approximately 60 km north of Lethbridge.

The name is possibly misspelled, but in years gone by the area was a haven for wolves. As the story goes, a settler in the area killed a wolf with the throw of his axe, and from then on the coulee was named Woolf.

Woolford (hamlet)

82 H/3 - Cardston
4-3-24-W4
49°11′N 113°08′W
Approximately 60 km south-west of Lethbridge.

This hamlet was named for Thomas Henry Woolford (1856-1944) who first came to the United States from his home in England in 1873. He married Hannah Priscilla Thompson in 1878 and they had eight children before moving to the Cardston area in 1899. Woolford was a renowned farmer, civic worker and humanitarian. Two years after his arrival, Woolford and his family moved to take up residence on the Latter Day Saints Church farm. Later, he and his family moved on to flat land where this settlement was established, near a ford on the St. Mary River. This ford was locally known as "Woolford Ford." Thomas Woolford moved back to Utah in 1911 where he remained the rest of his life. A post office was established 1 January 1912 and closed 15 May 1958.

Woolford Provincial Park

(provincial park)
82 H/3 - Cardston
5-3-24-W4
49°11′N 113°11′W
Approximately 63 km south south-west of Lethbridge.

This provincial park was established by Order-in-council 2047/67 and contains 35 hectares (86.51 acres) that runs along a bend in the St. Mary River. (see Woolford)

Wrentham (hamlet)

82 H/9 - Chin Coulee
36-6-17-W4
49°32′N 112°10′W
Approximately 50 km east south-east of Lethbridge.

It is generally accepted that this hamlet was named by the Canadian Pacific Railway in 1913 after the village of Wrentham in the English county of Suffolk. Some local inhabitants, however, disagree and have their own story. The original homesteaders were very poor and few had good clothes to wear. When they travelled to the town of Lethbridge, people rented suitable clothing for the trip, from a lady who had the first store in the community. In time, the community became locally known as the place where one could "Rent 'em."

Writing Creek (creek)

82 O/8 - Crossfield
25-27-1-W5
51°20′N 114°01′W
Flows south-east through McPherson Coulee into Nose Creek, approximately 32 km north of Calgary.

Writing Creek is the name used locally for this creek. It is so called because of the Indian pictographs on the walls of the coulee near its headwaters. The name has been used since 1872 when Colonel P. Robertson-Ross, C.O. and Adjutant General of the Militia of Canada related his report, "… travelled over bare plains until 12:30 when we halted for breakfast in 'Writing Creek.' We had a splendid view of the Rockies this day. Started again at 3:00 p.m. and camped for the night at 5:45 about ten miles further on in the valley of 'canyon,' Writing Creek."

Writing-on-Stone Provincial Park

(provincial park)
72 E/4 - Coutts
35-1-13-W4
49°05′N 111°38′W
Approximately 110 km south-east of Lethbridge.

Writing-on-Stone is a literal translation of the Cree word *masinasin*. The name refers to the petroglyphs or rock carvings of men, horses, bows, shields, spears and animals located along the sandstone banks of the Milk River Valley. The carvings and paintings, from a variety of time periods, were first recorded in 1850 by James Doty. Doty was working for the American government and attempting to conclude a treaty with the Blackfoot. With the arrival of the North West Mounted Police, a post was established at the confluence of Police

Creek and the Milk River, to put an end to the illicit whiskey trade. In May 1957, the area was designated a provincial park. The park is small, covering only about 325 hectares (803 acres). (see Masinasin)

Writing-on-Stone, 1897

Wynder Coulee (coulee)

82 H/3 - Cardston
12-2-27-W4
49°06'N 113°29'W
Runs north into Lee Creek, approximately 78 km south-west of Lethbridge.

The origin for the name of this coulee is unknown.

Wyndham-Carseland Provincial Park

(provincial park)
82 I/14 - Gleichen
31,32-21-25-W4
Approximately 50 km south-east of Calgary.

This 178.19 hectare (440.3 acres) provincial park was established in 1979 by Order-in-council 856/79. It was named for its proximity to the town of Carseland (see Carseland) and in honour of the family of Caroline Elizabeth and Lieutenant-Colonel Alfred E. Wyndham (1837-1914). This family has a long history of ranching in this region and they operated a ferry at this crossing. Colonel Wyndham led the 12th Battalion of the York Rangers during the 1885 North West Rebellion under General Strange. Impressed with the north west, Mr. and Mrs. Wyndham, formerly of Ontario, took up a homestead. Their eldest son, Alex, also took up homesteading nearby. The name for the park is a combination of the two names.

Yarrow Creek (creek)

82 H/5 - Pincher Creek
15-4-29-W4
49°18'N 113°49'W
Flows north-east into Drywood Creek, approximately 83 km south-west of Lethbridge.

The yarrow weed (*Achillea millefolium*) grows abundantly along the river flats. This long-stemmed, flat-topped cluster of white or pink flowers has carrot-like feathery leaves and a strong smell. Old timers used the dried weed to make a bitter, remedial tea. The scientific name for the plant honours Achilles, who is said to have made an ointment from the juice of the yarrow to heal his soldiers' wounds. The name for this creek may take its name from the weed. The name may also be derived from the Yarrow parish, Selkirkshire, Scotland, or the Yarrow River in Lancashire, England.

Yellow Lake (lake)

72 E/12 - Skiff
13-9-12-W4
49°44'N 111°30'W
Approximately 68 km south-west of Medicine Hat.

The name is possibly descriptive of the prevailing colour of the prairie surrounding the lake. The shape of the lake itself has been altered by the irrigation development.

BIBLIOGRAPHY

A Brief History of Cardston: The Temple City. Cardston Golden Jubilee Souvenir Programme, 1887-1937. Cardston Jubilee Committee, Cardston, Alberta, 1937.

Acadia Valley Community Club. *Times to Remember: Acadia Valley, Alberta*. Acadia Valley, Alberta: Acadia Valley Community Club, 1981.

Acme and District Historical Society. *Acme Memories*. Acme, Alberta: Acme and District Historical Society, 1979.

Alberta Farmer and Calgary Weekly Herald. "Early History of Carmangay." 1 May 1929.

Alberta Women's Institute. *Memories of Early Walsh and Graburn*. Walsh, Alberta: Alberta Women's Institute (Walsh Branch), 1980.

Albertan, The
"Many Others are Following the Example of the English Landlord," from the *Aberdeen Free Press* (Scotland) reprinted in *The Albertan*, 13 June, 1912.
"Town Boomed Till 1913, But Then Slumped." 10 April 1937.
"Pioneer Dies at Bow Island," 8 March 1940.
"Charles Stewart Dies in Ottawa After Illness," 7 December 1946.
"90th Birthday Marked by Cardston Pioneers," 2 September 1948.
"Founder of Nobleford Dies in Lethbridge," 6 July 1957.
"Art Webster Compiled Fine Story of Stavely," 8 June 1962.
Whitney, Frank (Obit.) 6 March 1970.
"Around Alberta," regular feature column by K. Wood, 13 January 1973.

Arrowwood-Mossleigh Historical Society. *Furrows of Time: A History of Arrowwood, Shouldice, Mossleigh and Farrow, 1883-1982*. Mossleigh, Alberta: Arrowwood-Mossleigh Historical Society, 1982.

Baker, Edna. *Prairie Place Names*. 1978.

Ball, Norman. *Building Canada: A History of Public Works*. Toronto, Ontario: University of Toronto Press, 1988.

Balla, Joe. "Writing-On-Stone: A Public Park." in *Farm and Ranch Review*, May, 1957.

Barnwell Relief Society. *Barnwell History*. Ann Arbor, Michigan: Edwards Bros., 1952.

Barons History Book Club. *Wheat Heart of the West: A History of Barons and District*. Barons, Alberta: Barons History Committee, 1972.

Bassano History Book Club. *Best in the West by a Damsite, 1900-1940*. Bassano, Alberta: Bassano History Book Club, 1974.

Beal, R.F., J.E. Foster and Louise Zuk. "The Métis Hivernement Settlement at Buffalo Lake, 1872-1877." Unpublished Historical Report, Alberta Culture and Multiculturalism, 1987.

Beatty, C.B. *The Landscapes of Southern Alberta: A Regional Geomorphology*. Lethbridge, Alberta: The University of Lethbridge Productions Services, 1975.

Beiseker Historical Society. *Beiseker's Golden Heritage*. Beiseker, Alberta: Beiseker Historical Society, 1977.

Berton, Pierre. *Klondike: The Life and Death of the Last Great Gold Rush*. Toronto, Ontario: McLelland and Stewart, 1959.

Bethlehem Lutheran Church. *The History of Dalum*. Drumheller, Alberta: Bethlehem Lutheran Church, 1968.

Bindloss Pioneer Committee. *Golden Memories, 1912-1963*. Bindloss, Alberta: Bindloss Pioneer Committee, 1963.

Blumell, James E., ed. *This is Our Land: A Centennial History*. New Cessford High School English 10 and 20 Classes, 1967.

Board of Trade: Okotoks. *Okotoks: The Eldorado of Southern Alberta*. Calgary, Alberta: Okotoks Board of Trade, 1908.

Book Committees of Sundial, Enchant and Retlaw, The. *Drybelt Pioneers of Sundial, Enchant and Retlaw*. Lethbridge, Alberta: Southern Printing Company Limited, 1967.

Brado, Edward. "General Strange." *Western People* (a supplement to the *Western Producer*, No. 219). Saskatoon, Saskatchewan: Western Producer Publications, 12 January 1984.

Brooks Bulletin, The
   "Rolling Hills Area 25 Years Old," 30 July 1964.
   "Charles Sherwood Noble… His Thrilling Career," 22 September 1966.
   "Rolling Hills Settled 40 Years Ago," 8 August 1979.

Bow Island Lion's Club (Book Committee). *Silver Sage: Bow Island, 1900 to 1920.* Bow Island, Alberta: compiled by Jack Thomas. Bow Island Lion's Club, 1972.

Brink, Jack. *Dog Days in Southern Alberta.* Occasional Paper 28, Alberta Culture and Multiculturalism, n.d.

Brown, Donald Edward. "History of the Cochrane Area," Unpublished M.A. thesis, Edmonton, Alberta: University of Alberta, 1951.

Burchill, C.S. *The Development of Irrigation in Alberta: An Historical Survey.* Lethbridge, Alberta: Dominion Economics Division, University of Alberta, Sir Alexander Galt Museum, 1949.

Burdett History Book Committee. *Burdett Prairie Trails: A History of Burdett and Area.* Lethbridge, Alberta: Ronalds Western Printing Ltd., 1978.

Butterwick, Alice (editor-in-chief). *Shortgrass Country: A History of Foremost and Nemiskam.* Foremost, Alberta: Foremost Historical Society, 1975.

Calgary Herald, The
   "Soldier, Diplomat, Statesman and Author," 15 April 1914.
   "One of Alberta's New Towns—Milo—Four Years After Its Inception," 8 December 1928.
   "Judge Cawley, Ex-Premier North West Territories and Calgary Herald Editor, Dies," 1934.
   "Nanton Founded and Rich Land with Favourable Climate," 10 May 1935.
   "Drumheller Becomes Modern: Swift Growth of District Founded on Rich Minerals and Expanding Agriculture," 22 June 1935.
   "John Herron, Member of Original NWMP Dies At Pincher Creek," 20 August 1936.
   "What's In A Name: Lomond," 7 January 1937.
   "What's In A Name: Hussar," 23 January 1937.
   "What's In A Name: Pincher Creek," 6 March 1937.
   "Old Man River Origin," (Letter to the Editor), W.A. Fraser, 11 March 1937.

"Settler's Donated Community Name," 1 October 1937.
"Pioneer Cattleman, A.J. Whitney, Dies," 3 October 1938.
"Stirring Career Comes to An End," 5 April 1940.
"A Prairie Community Vanishes Away As War Takes Over," Betty Crook, 2 August 1941.
"Agriculture Alberta: High River Will Honour the Late George Land," Fred Kennedy, 14 June 1951.
"Tales of the Old Town: Calgary, 1875-1950," Leishman McNeill, 1951.
"Ardenode: Picture of Garden Beauty," Ken Liddell's Furrow's and Foothills (column) 15 August 1953.
"Mountie Once Kicked Sitting Bull In the Pants," 6 August 1954.
"Furrow's and Foothills" (column) Ken Liddell, 26 February 1955.
"Pincher Creek Rates as Modern Cowtown," 31 August 1955.
"Stavely Survived Big Fire of 1924," 31 August 1955.
"Granum Once Called Leavings," 13 September 1955.
"Jovial Lawyer was 'Paddy' Nolan," Shelagh Nolan, 3 September 1955.
"Pearce Called Czar of the West," 3 September 1955.
"John Furman Pioneered in Macleod," 23 March 1956.
"Town Fare—Acme," Ray Guay, 26 April 1956.
"Hair of a Dog Is No More In Whistle Stop Whiskey Gap," 14 June 1956.
"Furrow's and Foothills" (column) Ken Liddell, 22 June 1956.
"Furrow's and Foothills" (column) Ken Liddell, 23 June 1956.
"Belly River," in "Furrow's and Foothills" (column) Ken Liddell, 31 October 1956.
"George Murray, Alberta's Biggest Rancher, 270,000 Acres, 6,200 Cattle and 7,000 Sheep: Whitla Homesteader of 1910 Bought First Ranch in 1927," Tony Primrose, 8 December 1956.
"Life of Early Ranchers Tinged by Varied Hazards," 22 April 1957.
"Many Attend Rites for Magrath Mayor," 20 January 1958.
"Furrow's and Foothills" (column) Ken Liddell, 18 June 1960.
"Stirling," in "Furrow's and Foothills" (column) Ken Liddell, 30 July 1960.
"Furrow's and Foothills" (column) Ken Liddell, 6 May 1961.
"Pincher Creek: Progress Seen," 5 January 1964.
"Baron's History Found in Fields," A.H Sloan, 15 July 1964.
"Looking Back: Siren Song of the Promoter Ended Up As A Ghost Town," Jack Peach, 22 November 1980.
"Nobleford Founder Honoured," Grant McEwan, 14 June 1982.
"Origin of River's Name," J.N. Wallace (Letter to the Editor) (no date given).

Campbell, Alice A. *Milk River Country*. Lethbridge, Alberta: Lethbridge Herald, 1959.

Canada, Geographic Board of. *Place-Names of Alberta*. Ottawa, Ontario: Department of the Interior, 1928.

Canadian Encyclopedia, The: Vols. 1-4. Edmonton, Alberta: Hurtig Publishers Ltd., 1988.

Canadian Who's Who, The: Vol. V, 1949-51. Toronto, Ontario: Trans-Canada Press, 1952.

Cardston and District Historical Society. *Chief Mountain Country: A History of Cardston and District*. Cardston, Alberta: Cardston and District Historical Society, 1978-1987.

Carmangay and District History Book Committee, The. *Bridging the Years: Carmangay and District*. Carmangay, Alberta: The Carmangay and District History Book Committee, 1968.

Carseland and Cheadle Historical Book Committee. *Trails to the Bow: Carseland and Cheadle Chronicles*. Carseland and Cheadle, Alberta: Carseland and Cheadle Historical Book Committee, 1971.

Cayley Women's Institute. *Under the Chinook Arch: A History of Cayley and Surrounding Areas*. Cayley, Alberta: Cayley Women's Institute, 1967.

Centennial Committee: Drumheller East Farmers Union of Alberta. *Memories of Verdant Valley, Cassil Hill, Livingstone, Rainbow*.

Champion History Committee. *Cleverville-Champion, 1905 to 1970: A History of Champion and Area*. Champion, Alberta: Champion History Committee, 1972.

Chestermere Historical Society. *Saddles, Sleighs, and Sadirons*. Chestermere, Alberta: Chestermere Historical Society, 1971.

Church of Jesus Christ of Latter Day Saints—Lethbridge Stake Historical Committee. *A History of the Mormon Church in Canada*. Lethbridge, Alberta: Lethbridge Stake Historical Committee, 1968.

Claresholm History Book Club. *Where the Wheatlands Meet the Range*. Claresholm, Alberta: Claresholm History Book Club, 1974.

Clarke, Ian. "Irrigation and the Settlement Frontier in Southern Alberta, 1878-1935." Edmonton, Alberta: Alberta Culture and Multiculturalism, n.d.

Coaldale: The Gem of the West. The Coaldale Jubilee Committee, Coaldale, Alberta, December 1955.

Cochrane and Area Historical Society. *Big Hill Country*. Cochrane, Alberta: Cochrane and Area Historical Society, 1977.

Cormack, R.G.H. *Wild Flowers of Alberta*. Edmonton, Alberta: Department of Industry and Development, 1967.

_____. *Wild Flowers of Alberta*. Edmonton, Alberta: Hurtig Publishers, ca. 1977.

Correspondence Files of the Geographic Board of Canada, The Geographic Board of Alberta, and The Canadian Permanent Committee on Geographical Names.

Coyote Flats Historical Society. *Coyote Flats: Historical Review, 1905-1965*. Lethbridge, Alberta: Southern Printing Co., 1967.

_____. *Coyote Flats: Volume II*. Mary Sorgard (ed.). Lethbridge, Alberta: Southern Printing Co., 1976.

Crossfield Historical Committee. *Prairie Sod and Goldenrod: Crossfield and Area*. Crossfield, Alberta: Crossfield Historical Committee, 1977.

Cummins Map Company. *Cummins Rural Directory Map*. Winnipeg, Manitoba: Cummins Map Company, ca. 1919.

Cypress Hills Provincial Park: Master Plan. Government of Alberta: Recreation and Parks, Parks Division, 1981.

Dalemead Indus History Committee. *Tales From Two Townships: The Story of Dalemead, Indus and Shepard*. Dalemead, Alberta: Dalemead Indus History Committee, ca. 1967.

Del Bonita Historical Society. *Heritage of the High Country: A History of Del Bonita and Surrounding Districts*. Del Bonita, Alberta: Del Bonita Historical Society, 1981.

Delday, Eva. *Brooks: Beautiful-Bountiful*. Brooks, Alberta: E. Delday, 1975.

_____. *Brooks: Between the Red Deer and the Bow*. Brooks, Alberta: E. Delday, ca. 1975.

De Winton and District Historical Committee. *Sodbusting to Subdivision*. De Winton, Alberta: De Winton and District Historical Committee, 1978.

Dempsey, Hugh. *A History of Rocky Mountain House*. Occasional Papers in Archaeology and History 6. Ottawa, Ontario: 1963.

_____. *Indian Names for Alberta Communities*. Occasional Paper number 4. Calgary, Alberta: Glenbow Alberta Institute, 1969.

den Otter, Andy. *Irrigation in Southern Alberta 1882-1901*. Occasional Paper 5, Whoop-Up County Chapter, Historical Society of Alberta, 1975.

Dictionary of Canadian Biography: Volume 9, 1861-1870. Toronto, Ontario: The University of Toronto Press, 1976.

Dictionary of National Biography, 1912-1921, The. H.W.C. Davis and J.R.H. Weaver, eds. London, England: Oxford University Press, 1976.

Dorcas Ladies Aid, The. *Down the Trail of Memories*. Monarch, Alberta: The Dorcas Ladies Aid (Monarch Chapter), 1963.

_____. *The Eagle Calls: History of Eagle Hill*. Olds, Alberta: The Dorcas Ladies Aid (Olds Chapter), 1975.

Dragland, Margaret. *The Peigan Country*. Maleb, Alberta: M. Dragland, 1966.

Drumheller Valley Historical Association, The. *The Hills of Home*. Drumheller, Alberta: The Drumheller Valley Historical Association, 1973.

Duchess and District Historical Society. *Duchess and District Memories*. Brooks, Alberta: Duchess and District Historical Society, 1982.

Edmonton Journal, The
   "Waterton National Park in South Border Region is Land of Rare Beauty," C. Frank Steel, 22 June 1929.
   "Hand Hills Story," 12 November 1969.

Elliot, Jean, Julia Higgins, Stella Niedzwiecki, and Margaret Orr. "Hub of Three Hamlets: Community Cooperation East of Calgary," in *Communities of Calgary: From Scattered Towns to a Major City,*

Volume 2. The Century Calgary Historical Series, various authors, Century Calgary Publications, 1975.

Empress Golden Jubilee Committee. *Golden Jubilee: Empress, 1914-1964*. Empress, Alberta: Empress Golden Jubilee Committee, 1964.

Encyclopedia Canadiana: Vols. 5, 8. Toronto: Grolier, 1970.

Featherstone, Francis Pollock. "The History of Pollockville," in *This is Our Land*. New Cessford High School, James E. Blumell (ed.), 1967.

Fencelines and Furrows History Book Society. *Fencelines and Furrows* (1st ed.). Calgary, Alberta: Fencelines and Furrows History Book Society, 1969.

Forgotten Corner History Book Society Committee, The. *The Forgotten Corner: A History of the Communities of Comrey, Catchem, Hooper-Pendland, Onefour, Wildhorse*. Medicine Hat, Alberta: The Forgotten Corner History Book Committee, ca. 1981.

Fort Macleod Gazette, The
   "A Trip to the Rockies," 29 August 1884.

Fort Macleod History Book Committee. *Fort Macleod—Our Colourful Past: A History of the Town of Fort Macleod from 1874-1924*. Fort Macleod, Alberta: Fort Macleod History Book Committee, 1977.

Frontiers Unlimited. *Frontier Guide to Waterton—Land of Leisure*. Calgary, Alberta: Frontiers Unlimited, 1968.

Fryer, Harold. *Ghost Towns of Alberta*. Langley, British Columbia: Stagecoach Publishing Co., 1976.

Garner, Don. "N.W.M.P. Posts of Southern Alberta, 1874-1904: Vol. I; Maple Creek and Lethbridge." Unpublished ms., 1975.

Gazetteer of Canada: Alberta. Ottawa, Ontario: Minister of Supply and Services Canada, 1958, 1974, 1988.

Gershaw, F.W. *Saamis: The Medicine Hat*. Medicine Hat, Alberta: F.W. Gershaw, 1967.

Gleichen United Church Women. *The Gleichen Call: A History of Gleichen and Surrounding Areas, 1877-1968* (1st ed.). Gleichen, Alberta: Gleichen United Church Women, 1968.

Glenwood Historical Society. *100 Years Between the Rivers: A History of Glenwood, Hartley and Stand Off*. Cardston, Alberta: Golden Press, 1984.

Gould, Ed. *All Hell For a Basement*. Medicine Hat, Alberta: The City of Medicine Hat, 1981.

Grassy Lake and Purple Springs Historical Society, The. *Faded Trails. History of Grassy Lake and Purple Springs Area*. Grassy Lake, Alberta: The Grassy Lake and Purple Springs Historical Society, 1982.

Hand Hills Book Committee, The. *Hand Hills Heritage*. Hand Hills, Alberta: The Hand Hills Book Committee, 1968.

Hanna Herald and East Central Alberta News, The
    "Oyen Progresses...." Lillian A. Gibson, 25 August 1955.

Hays 25th Book Committee. *From Sod to Silver*. Hays, Alberta: Hays 25th Book Committee, 1977.

Hesketh Pope Lease Historical Society. *Memories—Yours and Mine: A History of Beveridge Lake, East View, Garrett, Hesketh, Humbolt, Kirby, Lenox, Marne, Webbs School Districts*. Hesketh, Alberta: Hesketh Pope Lease Historical Society, 1972.

Hester, Leo. "Cattleman's Paradise," in *Canadian Cattlemen* Vol. 17, No. 9, September 1954, pp. 10, 22-24.

Hieken, J.O. *Raymond, 1901 1967*. Lethbridge, Alberta: J.O. Hieken, 1967.

Higgonbotham, John D. *When the West Was Young*. Toronto, Ontario: Ryerson Press, 1933.

High River Pioneers and Oldtimers Association. *Leaves From the Medicine Tree: A History of the Area Influenced by the Tree, and Biographies of Pioneers and Old Timers Who Came Under its Spell Prior to 1900*. High River, Alberta: High River Pioneers and Oldtimers Association, 1960.

Hilda Town and Country Ladies Club. *Hilda's Golden Heritage*. Hilda, Alberta: Hilda Town and Country Ladies Club, 1974.

Hill Spring Cultural Society. *Hill Spring and Its People*. Hill Spring, Alberta: Hill Spring Cultural Society, 1975.

Hills of Home Historical Committee, The. *The Hills of Home*. Lethbridge, Alberta: The Hills of Home Historical Committee, 1975.

Holmgren, Eric J. *Over 2000 Place Names of Alberta* (3rd ed.). Saskatoon, Saskatchewan: Western Producer Prairie Books, 1976.

Holtslander, Dale. *School Districts of Alberta: A Listing of All Protestant Public Schools Organized in the Province of Alberta* (1st ed.). Edmonton, Alberta: D. Holtslander, 1978.

Hughes, Neil. *Post Offices of Alberta, 1876-1986*. Edmonton, Alberta: Neil Hughes, 1986.

Hussar Ladies Aid, The. *The Hussar Heritage*. Hussar, Alberta: The Hussar Ladies Aid, 1964.

Hustak, Alan. "Hot Times in Prairie Coal Town: How the Mines and Sir Alexander Galt Built Lethbridge," in *Alberta Report*, Vol. 9, No. 39, 13 September 1982, p. 51.

Hymas, Kay (ed.) *Akokiniskway, "By the River of Many Roses..." Beynon, Rosebud, Redland, 1883-1983*. Rosebud, Alberta: The Rosebud Historical Society, 1983.

Ings, Fred. *Before the Fences: Tales From the Midway Ranch*. reprinted and edited by Jim Davies, Nanton, Alberta: F. Ings, 1980.

Johnson, J.K. (ed.) *The Canadian Directory of Parliament, 1867-1967*. Ottawa, Ontario: The Public Archives of Canada, 1968.

Johnston, Alex and Andy den Otter. *Lethbridge: A Centennial History*. Lethbridge, Alberta: The City of Lethbridge and The Whoop-Up Country Chapter, Historical Society of Alberta, 1985.

Johnston, Alex and Barry R. Peat. *Lethbridge Place Names and Points of Interest*. Occasional Paper No. 14, Lethbridge, Alberta: Whoop-Up Country Chapter, Historical Society of Alberta, 1987.

Johnstone, J.A. "Place Names of Southern Alberta," in *Canadian Cattlemen* Vol. 20, No. 10, October 1957, pp. 22-25.

K.I.K. Historical Committee. *K.I.K. Country*. Keoma, Alberta: K.I.K. Historical Committee, 1974.

Kelly, Leroy Victor. *The Range Men: The Story of the Ranchers and Indians of Alberta*. Toronto, Ontario: William Briggs, 1913.

Knupp, Lillian. *Life and Legends: A History of the Town of High River.* Calgary, Alberta: Sandstone Publisher, 1982.

Langdon Women's Institute. *The Langdon Legend.* Calgary, Alberta: Langdon Women's Institute, 1965.

Layzell, Denny. "Claresholm," in *The Herald Magazine* (published weekly by the *Calgary Herald*) 15 December 1962, p. 1.

_____. "Colourful Tribe of Many Chiefs," in *The Herald Magazine*, Friday, 17 February 1967, pp. 3, 5.

Leitch, W.G. *Ducks and Men.* Winnipeg, Manitoba: Ducks Unlimited, Canada, 1978.

Lethbridge Herald, The
    "Lethbridge Loses Its Returning Mayor," 13 December 1909.
    "Writing-On-Stone Bears Tales of Incidents In Lives of People of Ancient Day," Thyrza Young Burkitt, 4 April 1936.
    "Garden City of Alberta Once Bald Prairie Traces Half Century of Growth," J.A. Spencer, 20 July 1949.
    "Milk River On Old Fort Benton Trail," 25 June 1955.
    "Cardston's Oldest Resident Given Tribute At Rites," 21 February 1956.
    "Johnny Furman; Pioneer Cowboy and Rancher, Honoured in Death," 24 March 1956.
    "Parkland Isn't On Road Maps But Southern Alberta Cattle Men Know All About Its Sales," Jim Peacock, 26 September 1956.
    "Writing-On-Stone Is Opened As Provincial Park by Honourable Holmrost," Del Koenig, 21 May 1957.
    "Brothers-In-Law Play Major Roles For Area: Organized by Sir Alexander Galt," 5 October 1957.
    "Charles A. Magrath Passes At Victoria," January 1958.
    "Community Life Fading Away: Two Empty Elevators All That's Left at Bradshaw," D'Arcy Pickard, 31 July 1963.
    "William Stafford: Coal Banks Pioneer," 31 August 1963.
    "City Pioneer Dies At Coast," 24 August 1965.
    "Originally Named Leavings: Granum Incorporated in 1910," C. Cesar, 6 July 1967.
    "Ranchers—25—Came First to Vulcan," J. Lundy Finlay, 18 July 1967.
    "Wrentham Goes Back to 1898," Leeta Whitrow, 29 July 1967.
    "Founding of Taber," J.S. Hull, 1 August 1967.
    "Leavings Stopping Place Will be Historic Site," 28 November 1967.
    "Picarello Had A Reputation: Mounties Aid Rum Runner," 30 July 1968.

    "Writing-On-Stone, A Page of History," June 1970.
    "Before They Rolled Up the Land, Grassy Lake was Sky and Grass," Katherine Macdonald, 22 July 1971.
    "Little Plume (Tom)" (Obit.) 4 November 1971.
    Ockey, Eugene Edward (Obit.) 31 May 1972.
    "Anniversary Flashback: Galt's Importance to the Area," Dave Mabel, 8 January 1985.

Liddell, Ken E. *Roamin' Empire of Southern Alberta.* Calgary, Alberta: Frontiers Unlimited, ca. 1963.

Lomond's Jubilee Book Committee. *History of Lomond and District.* Lomond, Alberta: Lomond's Jubilee Book Committee, 1966.

Lone Butte Book Club, The. *Lone Butte North: A History of Bull Pound, Earltown, Eden, Frasertown, Golden Hill, Lake Rose, Lone Butte, Normandale, Olive, Red Rose.* 2 vols. Hanna, Alberta: The Lone Butte Book Club, 1974.

Long Lance, Chief Buffalo Child. *Long Lance.* New York: Cosmopolitan Book Corporation, 1928.

Lyalta, Ardenode, Dalroy Historical Society. *Along the Fireguard Trail: A History of Lyalta-Ardenode-Dalroy Districts.* Lyalta, Ardenode, Dalroy Historical Society, 1979.

M.I.P. History Book Society. *Spurs and Shovels Along the Royal Line.* Patricia, Alberta: M.I.P. History Book Society, 1979.

MacEwan, Grant. *Pat Burns: Cattle King.* Saskatoon, Saskatchewan: Western Producer Prairie Books, 1979.

MacGregor, James G. *Blankets and Beads: A History of the Saskatchewan River.* Edmonton, Alberta: The Institute of Applied Art, Ltd., 1949.

_____. *Father Lacombe.* Edmonton, Alberta: Hurtig Publishers, 1975.

Macmillan Dictionary of Canadian Biography, The (3rd ed.). W. Stewart Wallace (ed.). Toronto, Ontario: The Macmillan Company of Canada, Ltd., 1963.

Magrath and District History Association. *Irrigation Builders.* Lethbridge, Alberta: Magrath and District History Association, 1974.

Magrath Golden Jubilee Celebrations Committee. *Magrath's Golden Jubilee Celebrating 50 Years of Irrigation: Magrath, July 24, 25, 26, 1949*. Magrath, Alberta: Magrath Golden Jubilee Celebrations Committee, 1949.

Majestic-Farrell Lake Women's Institute. *Harvest of Memories*. Majestic, Alberta: Majestic-Farrell Lake Women's Institute, 1968.

Mardon, Ernest G. *Community Names of Alberta*. Lethbridge, Alberta: University of Lethbridge, 1973.

Martin, John J. *The Rosebud Trail*. Rosebud, Alberta: John J. Martin, 1963.

_____. *The Dinosaur Valley*. Rosebud, Alberta: John J. Martin, 1969.

Masinasin Historical Society and Masinasin New Horizons Society. *From Sandstone to Settlers: Writing-On-Stone District History*. Masinasin, Alberta: Masinasin Historical Society and Masinasin New Horizons Society, 1984.

McAndrews, C.J. *Alberta's Experience in Irrigation*. Lethbridge, Alberta: Sir Alexander Galt Museum, n.d.

McCall, Ralph R. *The Acme Story, 1910 1960*. Acme, Alberta: Ralph R. McCall, 1960.

McCallum, J.F. "Cattle In Assiniboia," in *Canadian Cattlemen* Vol. 18, No. 11, November 1955, pp. 9, 28-32.

McDougall, R.A. *The Cochrane Ranche, 1881-1894: A Local History*. Edmonton: Alberta Teachers' Association. Social Studies Council, 1968.

Medicine Hat News, The
        "Irrigation Pioneer D.W. Hayes, Dies," 12 September 1958.
        "Letter to Francis Fatt, esq., Medicine Hat, from Rudyard Kipling, Sussex, England." 9 December 1910, originally published in R. Kipling's *(Medicine) Hat Trick*, reprinted in pamphlet form by the *Medicine Hat News* in 1965.
        "Pioneer Dunmore Rancher, Henry Caven is Dead," 6 June 1966.

Michael, Hope, and Hope Johnson. *Down the Years at Elkwater*. Medicine Hat, Alberta: The Medicine Hat Museum and Art Gallery, 1981.

Michael, Hope Hargrave. *Ninety Years at Elkwater Lake, Cypress Hills, Alberta: An Interesting Account of the Early Days in the Elkwater Area*. Medicine Hat, Alberta: The Medicine Hat Museum and Gallery, 1948, reprinted 1972.

Michichi History Book Committee. *A History of the People of Michichi*. Michichi, Alberta: Michichi History Book Committee, 1970.

Millarville, Kerr, Priddis and Bragg Creek Historical Society. *Our Foothills*. Calgary, Alberta: Millarville, Kerr, Priddis and Bragg Creek Historical Society, 1975.

Milo and District Historical Society. *Snake Valley: A History of Lake MacGregor and Area*. Milo, Alberta: Milo and District Historical Society, 1973.

Morgan, Henry James, ed. *The Canadian Men and Women of the Time* (2nd ed.). Toronto, Ontario: William Briggs, 1912.

Morning Albertan, The
        "How Old Man River Was Named: An Indian Tradition," 16 March 1912.

Morrow, J.W. *Early History of the Medicine Hat Country*. Medicine Hat, Alberta: Medicine Hat and District Historical Society, 1974, rev. ed.

Mudiman, Freda Smith. "Akoniskway," in *Canadian Cattlemen*, Vol. 15, No. 7, 1 July 1952, pp. 10, 11, 31, 38.

Nagle, Patrick and Bruce Moss. "Birthday in the Badlands," in *Weekend Magazine* (a weekly supplement to the *Montreal Standard*), Vol. 14, No. 33, 22 August 1964, pp. 18-22.

Namaka Community Historical Committee. *Trails to Little Corner: A Story of Namaka and Surrounding Districts*. Namaka, Alberta: Namaka Community Historical Committee, 1983.

Nanton and District Historical Society. *Mosquito Creek Round-up: Nanton-Parkland*. Nanton, Alberta: Nanton and District Historical Society, 1975.

New Dayton History Book Committee. *Memories: New Dayton and District, 1900-1978*. New Dayton, Alberta: New Dayton History Book Committee, 1979.

Nightingale History Committee. *The English Colony: Nightingale and District*. Nightingale, Alberta: Nightingale History Committee, 1979.

Nobleford, Monarch History Book Club. *Sons of Wind and Sail*. Nobleford, Alberta: Nobleford, Monarch History Book Club, 1976.

Okotoks and District Historical Society. *A Century of Memories: Okotoks and District, 1883-1983*. Okotoks, Alberta: Okotoks and District Historical Society, 1983.

Oltman, Ruth. *The Valley of Rumours: The Kananaskis*. Seebe, Alberta: Ruth Oltman, 1976.

Oyen and District Historical Society. *Many Trails Crossed Here: A History of Oyen, Alberta, and the Surrounding District*. Oyen, Alberta: Oyen and District Historical Society, 1981.

Palmer, Howard and Tamara Palmer. *Alberta: A New History*. Edmonton, Alberta: Hurtig Publishers, 1990.

Patterson, Raymond M. *Far Pastures*. Sydney, B.C.: Gray's Publishing, 1963.

Pendant D'Oreille Lutheran Church Women, The. *Prairie Footprints: A History of the Community in Southern Alberta Known as Pendant D'Oreille*. Pendant D'Oreille, Alberta: The Pendant D'Oreille Lutheran Church Women, 1970.

Pincher Creek Historical Society. *From Prairie Grass to Mountain Pass: A History of the Pioneers of Pincher Creek and District*. Pincher Creek, Alberta: Pincher Creek Historical Society, 1974.

Pincher Creek/New Horizons Local History Committee of Pincher Creek and District Historical Society. *Pincher Creek Memories* (pictorial work). Pincher Creek, Alberta: Pincher Creek Historical Society, 1975.

"Pioneer Cattleman, Friend of Prince of Wales Passes On," in *Alberta Farmer*, 1 October 1925.

Primrose, Tom. "The Fort in the Thunder Breeding Hills," in *The Cypress Hills of Alberta-Saskatchewan*, Frontier Book Series #22, Art Downs (ed.), 1969.

Rainier-Bow City History Book Club. *Settlers Along the Bow: A History of Rainier, Bow City*. Bow City, Alberta: Rainier-Bow City History Book Club, ca. 1975.

Rasporich, A.W. *The Making of the Modern West: Western Canada Since 1945*. Calgary, Alberta: University of Calgary Press, 1984.

Regina Leader Post, The
    "Walsh Credited With Preventing Epic Slaughter," Doreen Mierau, 12 July (no year).

Rockyford and District History Book Society. *Where We Crossed the Creek and Settled: Rockyford*. Rockyford, Alberta: Rockyford and District History Book Society, 1980.

Roen, Hazel B. *The Grass Roots of Dorothy, 1895-1970*. Dorothy, Alberta: Hazel Roen, 1972.

Scandia Historical Committee. *Scandia Since Seventeen*. Scandia, Alberta: Scandia Historical Committee, 1978.

Schuler History Committee. *Saga of Schuler Stalwarts*. Schuler, Alberta: Schuler History Committee, 1973.

Seven Persons Historical Society. *Seven Persons: One Hundred Sixty Acres and a Dream*. Medicine Hat, Seven Persons Historical Society, 1981.

Sheep River Historical Society. *In the Light of the Flares: History of Turner Valley Oilfields*. Sheep River, Alberta: Sheep River Historical Society, 1979.

Short Grass Historical Society. *Long Shadows: A History of Short Grass Country*. Bow Island, Alberta: Commentator Publishing Co., 1974.

Sibbald Community Club. *Sibbald Community History, 1908-1980* (rev. ed.). Sibbald, Alberta: Sibbald Community Club, 1980.

Sibbald Women's Institute, W.I.C. *Sibbald Community History, 1910-1962*. Hanna, Alberta: Sibbald Women's Institute, W.I.C., 1962.

Skiff History Book Committee. *Skiff, In the Prairie Wind*. Skiff, Alberta: Skiff History Book Committee, 1980.

Standard Historical Book Society. *From Danaview to Standard*. Standard, Alberta: Standard Historical Book Society, 1979.

Stanley, G.D. *A Roundup of Fun in the Foothills.* (privately published), 1951.

Stavely and District School Reunion Book Committee. *Stavely and District School Reunion Book, 1904-1957.* Stavely, Alberta: Stavely and District School Reunion Book Committee, 1976.

Stein, Jess (ed.) *The Random House College Dictionary.* (rev. ed.) New York, New York. Random House, Inc., 1980.

Stirling Sunset Society. *Stirling: Its Story and People, 1899-1980.* Stirling, Alberta: Stirling Sunset Society, 1981.

Strathmore Standard, The
     "The Early History of Namaka," H. Colpoys, 11 May 1939.
     "Cheadle's Early History," A. McLean, 17 October 1946.

Sunshine Women's Institute History Committee. *The History of the Border Country of Coutts.* Coutts, Alberta: Sunshine Women's Institute History Committee, 1965.

Summer Village of Chestermere Lake Book Committee. *Growing Through Time: Stories of Chestermere Lake.* Chestermere Lake, Alberta: Summer Village of Chestermere Lake Book Committee, 1981.

Surveyors' Field Notes: Abstracts From Reports on Townships West of the Fourth Meridian. Ottawa, Ontario: Ministry of the Interior.

Taber Historical Society, The. *From Tank 77 to Taber Today: A History of Taber, Its District and Its People.* Taber, Alberta: The Taber Historical Society, 1977.

"The Colonel," The Medicine Hat Museum and Monarch Broadcasting (CHAT-TV), video-tape production, January 1980.

The Goodland of Albertan Carbon District: Crop, Coal and Cattle Centre, 1895-1962. Pamphlet in Commemoration of the 67th Anniversary of Carbon, Carbon, Alberta, 1962.

The History of Cravath Corners, 1910-1926. Margaret Cravath Bell (ed.), published by *Brooks Bulletin*, Brooks, Alberta, 1963.

The Pincher Creek Oldtimers Souvenir Album. The Oldtimers Association of Pincher Creek, Pincher Creek, Alberta, 1958.

Thomas, Lewis G. (ed.) *The Prairie West to 1905.* Toronto, Ontario: Oxford University Press, 1975.

Tilley Historical Society. *Tilley: Trails and Tales.* Tilley, Alberta: Tilley Historical Society, 1980.

Tyrrell, J.B. (ed.) "David Thompson's Narrative, of His Experiences in Western America, 1784-1812." Publications of the Champlain Society, 1916.

Warner Old Timer's Association. *Warner Pioneers.* Warner, Alberta: Warner Old Timer's Association, 1962.

Webster's Biographical Dictionary. Springfield, Massachusetts: G. and C. Merriam Co., 1972.

West Lethbridge History Book Society. *The Bend: A History of West Lethbridge.* Lethbridge, Alberta. West Lethbridge History Book Society, 1982.

Whitla Community Club. *Tribute to Whitla Pioneers.* Medicine Hat, Alberta: Whitla Community Club, 1969.

Who Was Who, 1929-1940, Volume III. [A Companion to Who's Who Containing the Biographies of Those Who Died During the Period 1929-1940.] London: Adam and Charles Brook, 1941.

Who's Who in America, Vol. 16, 1930-1931. Chicago, Illinois: The A.N. Marquis Company, Inc., Chicago, 1932.

Williams, M.B. *Waterton Lakes National Park.* Ottawa, Ontario: Department of the Interior, circa 1927; Reprinted 1982.

Wilk, Stephen. *One Day's Journey.* Calgary Alberta: Alcraft Printing Ltd., 1963.

Willow Creek Historical Society. *Echoes of Willow Creek.* Willow Creek, Alberta: Willow Creek Historical Society, 1965.

Women's Institute of Cereal. *Down Cereal's Memory Trail.* 2 vols. Cereal, Alberta: Women's Institute of Cereal, 1967.

Wrentham Historical Society. *Homestead County: Wrentham and Area.* Wrentham, Alberta: Wrentham Historical Society, 1980.

Youngstown Women's Institute, W.I.C. *Youngstown and District Pioneers.* Youngstown, Alberta: Youngstown Women's Institute, W.I.C., 1962.

*P*HOTOGRAPHS

Chin Coulee

Big Rock

Eagle Butte

Cypress Hills

Etzikom Coulee

East Fort Macleod Wheatfields

Foremost

Head-Smashed-In Buffalo Jump

Maher Coulee

Lost River

Lost River

Red Rock Coulee

Manyberries Creek

Reesor Lake